LOST IN TRANSLATION

Eva Hoffman was born in Cracow, Poland, and emigrated to America at the age of thirteen. She was an editor of the *New York Times Book Review* and has written on a variety of cultural subjects. She is the recipient of the Guggenheim Fellowship, the Whiting Award and an award from the American Academy and Institute of Arts and Letters. She is currently living in London.

Also by Eva Hoffman and available in Minerva

Exit into History

Eva Hoffman

LOST IN TRANSLATION

A Life in a New Language

Minerva

A Minerva Paperback
LOST IN TRANSLATION

First published in Great Britain 1989
by William Heinemann Ltd
This Minerva edition published 1991
by Mandarin Paperbacks
an imprint of Reed Consumer Books Ltd
Michelin House, 81 Fulham Road, London sw3 6rb
and Auckland, Melbourne, Singapore and Toronto

Reprinted 1991, 1992, 1993, 1994, 1995 (twice)

Copyright © 1989 by Eva Hoffman

A CIP catalogue record for this title
is available from the British Library
ISBN 0 7493 9070 0

An excerpt from "Among School Children" by W. B. Yeats
is reprinted with permission of Macmillan Publishing Company
from *The Poems of W. B. Yeats: A New Edition*,
edited by Richard J. Finneran. Copyright 1928
by Macmillan Publishing Company, renewed 1956 by Georgie Yeats,

An excerpt from "The Love Song of J. Alfred Prufrock"
in *Collected Poems 1909 to 1962* by T. S. Eliot,
copyright 1936 by Harcourt Brace Jovanovich, Inc.
copyright © 1963, 1964 by T. S. Eliot
is reprinted by permission of the publisher

Printed and bound in Great Britain
by Cox & Wyman Ltd, Reading, Berks

*To my family, which has given me my first world,
and to my friends, who have taught me how to appreciate
the New World after all.*

ACKNOWLEDGMENTS

I wish to thank the American Council of Learned Societies for a grant that made it possible for me to begin this book.

Part I

PARADISE

It is April 1959, I'm standing at the railing of the *Batory*'s upper deck, and I feel that my life is ending. I'm looking out at the crowd that has gathered on the shore to see the ship's departure from Gdynia—a crowd that, all of a sudden, is irrevocably on the other side—and I want to break out, run back, run toward the familiar excitement, the waving hands, the exclamations. We can't be leaving all this behind—but we are. I am thirteen years old, and we are emigrating. It's a notion of such crushing, definitive finality that to me it might as well mean the end of the world.

My sister, four years younger than I, is clutching my hand wordlessly; she hardly understands where we are, or what is happening to us. My parents are highly agitated; they had just been put through a body search by the customs police, probably as the farewell gesture of anti-Jewish harassment. Still, the officials weren't clever enough, or suspicious enough, to check my sister and me—lucky for us, since we are both carrying some silverware we were not allowed to take out of Poland in large pockets sewn onto our skirts especially for this purpose, and hidden under capacious sweaters.

When the brass band on the shore strikes up the jaunty mazurka rhythms of the Polish anthem, I am pierced by a youthful sorrow so powerful that I suddenly stop crying and try to hold still against the pain. I desperately want time to stop, to hold the ship still with the force of my will. I am suffering my first, severe attack of nostalgia, or *tęsknota* —a word that adds to nostalgia the tonalities of sadness and longing. It is a feeling whose shades and degrees I'm destined to know intimately, but at this hovering moment, it comes upon me like a visitation from a whole new geography of emotions, an annunciation of how much an absence can hurt. Or a premonition of absence, because at this divide, I'm filled to the brim with what I'm about to lose—images of Cracow, which I loved as one loves a person, of the sun-baked villages where we had taken summer vacations, of the hours I spent poring over passages of music with my piano teacher, of conversations and escapades with friends. Looking ahead, I come across an enormous, cold blankness—a darkening, an erasure, of the imagination, as if a camera eye has snapped shut, or as if a heavy curtain has been pulled over the future. Of the place where we're going—Canada—I know nothing. There are vague outlines of half a continent, a sense of vast spaces and little habitation. When my parents were hiding in a branch-covered forest bunker during the war, my father had a book with him called *Canada Fragrant with Resin* which, in his horrible confinement, spoke to him of majestic wilderness, of animals roaming without being pursued, of freedom. That is partly why we are going there, rather than to Israel, where most of our Jewish friends have gone. But to me, the word "Canada" has ominous echoes of the "Sahara." No, my mind rejects the idea of being taken there, I don't want to be pried out of my childhood, my pleasures, my safety, my hopes for becoming a pianist. The *Batory* pulls away, the foghorn emits its lowing, shofar sound, but my being is engaged in a stubborn refusal to move. My parents put their hands on my shoulders consolingly; for a moment, they allow themselves to acknowledge that there's pain in this departure, much as they wanted it.

Many years later, at a stylish party in New York, I met a

woman who told me that she had had an enc...
father was a highly positioned diplomat in a...
she had lived surrounded by sumptuous elega...
servants, and the delicate advances of older men...
said, that when this part of her life came to an end,
she felt she had been exiled from paradise, and had...
for it ever since.

No wonder. But the wonder is what you can mak... a paradise
out of. I told her that I grew up in a lumpen apartment in Cracow,
squeezed into three rudimentary rooms with four other people,
surrounded by squabbles, dark political rumblings, memories of
wartime suffering, and daily struggle for existence. And yet, when
it came time to leave, I, too, felt I was being pushed out of the
happy, safe enclosures of Eden.

I am lying in bed, watching the slowly moving shadows on the
ceiling made by the gently blowing curtains, and the lights of an
occasional car moving by. I'm trying hard not to fall asleep. Being
awake is so sweet that I want to delay the loss of consciousness. I'm
snuggled under an enormous goose-feather quilt covered in hand-
embroidered silk. Across the room from me is my sister's crib.
From the next room, "the first room," I hear my parents' breathing.
The maid—one of a succession of country girls who come to work
for us—is sleeping in the kitchen. It is Cracow, 1949, I'm four years
old, and I don't know that this happiness is taking place in a country
recently destroyed by war, a place where my father has to hustle
to get us a bit more than our meager ration of meat and sugar. I
only know that I'm in my room, which to me is an everywhere, and
that the patterns on the ceiling are enough to fill me with a feeling
of sufficiency because . . . well, just because I'm conscious, because
the world exists and it flows so gently into my head. Occasionally,
a few blocks away, I hear the hum of the tramway, and I'm filled
by a sense of utter contentment. I love riding the tramway, with its
bracing but not overly fast swaying, and I love knowing, from my
bed, the street over which it is moving; I repeat to myself that I'm
in Cracow, Cracow, which to me is both home and the universe.

rrow I'll go for a walk with my mother, and I'll know how
to get from Kazimierza Wielkiego, the street where we live, to
Urzędnicza Street, where I'll visit my friend Krysia—and already
the anticipation of the walk, of retracing familiar steps on a route
that may yet hold so many surprises, fills me with pleasure.

Slowly, the sights and sounds recede, the words with which I
name them in my head become scrambled, and I observe, as long
as possible, the delicious process of falling asleep. That awareness
of subsiding into a different state is also happiness.

Each night, I dream of a tiny old woman—a wizened Baba Yaga,
half grandmother, half witch, wearing a black kerchief and sitting
shriveled and hunched on a tiny bench at the bottom of our courtyard, way, way down. She is immeasurably old and immeasurably
small, and from the bottom of the courtyard, which has become
immeasurably deep, she looks up at me through narrow slits of
wise, malicious eyes. Perhaps, though, I am her. Perhaps I have
been on the earth a long, long time and that's why I understand the
look in her eyes. Perhaps this childish disguise is just a dream.
Perhaps I am being dreamt by a Baba Yaga who has been here since
the beginning of time and I am seeing from inside her ancient frame
and I know that everything is changeless and knowable.

It's the middle of a sun-filled day, but suddenly, while she's knead-
ing some dough, or perhaps sewing up a hole in my sweater's
elbow, my mother begins to weep softly. "This is the day when she
died," she says, looking at me with pity, as if I too were included
in her sorrow. "I can't stop thinking about her."

I know who "she" is; I feel as if I've always known it. She's
my mother's younger sister, who was killed during the war. All the
other members of my mother's family died as well—her mother,
father, cousins, aunts. But it's her sister whose memory arouses my
mother's most alive pain. She was so young, eighteen or nineteen—
"She hadn't even lived yet," my mother says—and she died in such
a horrible way. The man who saw her go into the gas chamber said

that she was among those who had to dig their own graves, and that her hair turned gray the day before her death. That strikes me as a fairy tale more cruel, more magical than anything in the Brothers Grimm. Except that this is real. But is it? It doesn't have the same palpable reality as the Cracow tramway. Maybe it didn't happen after all, maybe it's only a story, and a story can be told differently, it can be changed. That man was the only witness to what happened. Perhaps he mistook someone else for my mother's sister. In my head, without telling anyone, I form the resolve that when I grow up, I'll search the world far and wide for this lost aunt. Maybe she lived and emigrated to one of those strange places I've heard about, like New York, or Venezuela. Maybe I'll find her and bring her to my mother, whose suffering will then be assuaged.

My own sister is named after this person who exists like an almost concrete shadow in our lives—Alina—and my mother often feels a strange compassion for her younger daughter, as if with the name, she had bestowed on her some of fate's terrible burden. "Sometimes my heart aches for her," she tells me, "I don't know why. I'm afraid for her." I inherit some of this fear, and look on my sister as a fragile, vulnerable creature who needs all my love and protection. But then, my mother too seems breakable to me, as if she had been snatched from death only provisionally, and might be claimed by it at any moment. The ocean of death is so enormous, and life such a tenuous continent. Everyone I know has lost some relatives during the war, and almost none of my friends have grandparents. On the tramway, I see men with limbs missing—and the thought of how difficult life must be for them terrifies me. To be an adult, I conclude, is to be close to death. Only my father, who saved my parents' lives repeatedly during the war by acts of physical strength and sheer wiliness, seems strong and sturdy enough to resist its ever-present tug.

My father is a short, powerfully built man who, of course, seems very tall to me, and who, in his youth, had a reputation for being "strong as a bull." I am later told that almost the only time he has ever been seen crying was when I was born. But then, my life was claimed from near death too; I came into the world about two months after the end of the war. While my mother was in the advanced stages of pregnancy, my parents made the trek from Lvov—which during the war was unceremoniously switched from Polish to Russian territory—to Cracow, where they were going because it was the nearest large Polish city. They made this journey on a rattling truck filled with potato sacks and other people trying as quickly as possible to cross the new borders so they could remain within their old nationality even at the cost of leaving home. So when I was born after all these travails, in the safety of a city hospital and with some prospect of a normal life resuming after the horror, I must have signified, aside from everything else, a new beginning—and my parents wanted, badly, to begin again, to live. Later, they told me how happy they were to have "all that" behind them, how happy when, on rare occasions, someone they thought was dead reappeared from somewhere or other. But how poignant that happiness must have been! My father—this is one of the few hints I have of the pain of loss he must have felt—asked if I could be named after his mother, even though in the natural course of events, a first daughter would have been named after the nearest dead maternal relative. But my parents have no lack of the dead to honor, and I am named after both my grandmothers—Ewa, Alfreda—two women of whom I have only the dimmest of impressions. There aren't even any photographs which have survived the war: the cut from the past is complete.

My parents tell me little about their prewar life in Zalosce, a small town near Lvov, as if the war erased not only the literal world in which they lived but also its relevance to their new conditions. "Well, we were just ordinary mass men," my father once tells me in reply to some question, dismissing the significance of that chunk of their lives. Only sketchy outlines of a picture emerge. Both of them came from families of respectable merchants. My father was the coddled son and the village rake, who lassoed girls on street corners and didn't finish high school just because he was a ne'er-do-well. My mother's family was the more Orthodox, and even though she was a prize pupil, she was not allowed to go to the university, which she ardently wanted to do, or to study the violin when one of her teachers offered to give her free lessons because he thought she was "musical." She was also not allowed to bare her arms or her legs, or to talk to boys on her own. I don't have a clear notion of how my parents' courtship proceeded, but I know that my mother's decision to marry my father—one of the town's bad boys—was an act of considerable rebellion. Her own history instilled in my mother a determined—and, in someone of her time, surprising—aversion to "feminine" pursuits, and throughout my childhood and youth, she is quite set on not teaching me how to cook or sew, lest such skills prevent me from turning to more interesting things.

My father, I think, in his excess of happiness, mistakes his firstborn for a son, and he tends in many ways to treat me like a little boy. He prefers to see me in "sports outfits"—meaning shorts or long pants—and with my hair cropped. Altogether, he wants me to be *sportif*—good at games and all manner of physical endeavor. So in our "first room," he teaches me how to perform "gymnastics"—acrobatic exercises, which are very popular at the time, maybe because of the general call for physical fitness that is part of the new ideology and a feature of the New Man. Outside, he tries to initiate me into as many sports as possible. Sometimes his pedagogy is less than encouraging. When I am five or so, he buys me a boy's bicycle that is too high for me, and once I learn how to keep my balance, he pushes me off, shouting "faster, faster, faster!"—till I rush headlong into a fall. He initiates me into swimming by that time-honored method of dunking me into a river and watching from a nearby bridge, till I nearly go under and come up again with my mouth full of water and a sense of injured dignity. He takes me to Cracow's outdoor skating rink and pulls me around in the freezing cold at fast speeds. One of his happier inspirations for me and my sister is buying a Hula Hoop. This happens when the Hula Hoop craze, imported straight from America, hits Cracow with symbolic force, and he gets this incredibly desirable object by cutting his way into one of the snakelike queues that are ubiquitous on Polish streets. My father is particularly ingenious at making his way into such lines, but in this case the item is so rare that some people have waited through the night for their chance to purchase it, and he is courting mob assault by his bold move. Nevertheless, he brings home an orange plastic wheel that, as far as I am concerned, is worth every risk, for it makes me extremely popular with my friends, and we spend hours learning how to twirl it around our hips, waists, and necks and holding competitions for who can do it the longest.

And then, when I am about eleven years old, my father acquires a motorcycle. Ah, the motorcycle! This pièce de résistance comes from Russia (nobody calls it the Soviet Union in ordinary speech), where my parents take their one and only trip in 1956, for the purpose of purchasing some advanced goods unavailable in postwar Poland—a fridge, a vacuum cleaner, a fur coat for my mother—and this large, ungainly machine, which is the envy of our whole neighborhood. At this point, no one we know owns a motorized vehicle of any kind, not to speak of a car. The traffic on Cracow's cobblestone roads is made up mostly of tramways and horse-drawn *dorozhkas,* although in the busiest parts of the city there are occasionally several cars in a row, which seem to tear by at enormous speeds.

Now I get to taste how such speed feels on my body, for as soon as he learns how to operate the motorcycle, my father picks me as his first companion for an outing to the country. Over my mother's worried protestations, I climb on the large seat behind him, the motor starts up with a great drumroll of noise, and then we are off, bumping over the cobblestones, moving smoothly over stretches of asphalt, and then gathering speed as we enter open country roads in the most thrilling, rhythmical momentum. We fall down twice during this first adventure—my father, as usual, is being more reckless than methodical—but somehow we get up with only a scraped knee or two, which I hardly mind. I'm certainly not afraid of a real accident—I have too much confidence in my father for that—and the truth is that I like being treated like my father's buddy, and I come back flushed with wind and triumph.

"Bramaramaszerymery, rotumotu pulimuli," I say in a storytelling voice, as if I were starting out a long tale, even though I know perfectly well that what I am making up are nonsense syllables. "What are you talking about?" my mother asks. "Everything," I say, and then start again: *"Bramarama, szerymery . . ."* I want to tell A Story, Every Story, everything all at once, not anything in particular that might be said through the words I know, and I try to roll all sounds into one, to accumulate more and more syllables, as if they might make a Möbius strip of language in which everything, everything is contained. There is a hidden rule even in this game, though—that the sounds have to resemble real syllables, that they can't disintegrate into brute noise, for then I wouldn't be talking at all. I want articulation—but articulation that says the whole world at once.

I'm playing hopscotch or riding a sort of skateboard with handlebars on the street below our building when my mother's face appears at the window, and she shouts, "Ewa, it's time to come in!" After the requisite protest, I run in; the entryway, as usual, is blocked by the Fellini-fat figure of the caretaker, her enormous breasts emerging nearly whole from her sloppy dress. I try to slide by, but she angrily mutters something about "The little Jew, she thinks she's somebody," and I run up the stairs half in fear, half laughing at this dragonlike apparition.

Our modest apartment is considered respectable by postwar Polish standards, if only because we have it all to ourselves. The kitchen is usually steamy with large pots of soup cooking on the wood stove for hours, or laundry being boiled in vats for greater whiteness; behind the kitchen, there's a tiny balcony, barely big enough to hold two people, on which we sometimes go out to exchange neighborly gossip with people peeling vegetables, beating carpets, or just standing around on adjoining balconies. Looking down, you see a paved courtyard, in which I spend many hours bouncing a ball against the wall with other kids, and a bit of a garden, where I go to smell the few violets that come up each spring and climb the apple tree, and where my sister gathers the snails that live under the boysenberry bushes, to bring them proudly into the house by the bucketful.

Aside from the kitchen, our apartment consists of the "first room," with a large mahogany chifforobe, a blue porcelain-tile stove reaching from floor to ceiling, the table on which we take our meals, and my parents' sofa bed. The "second room" serves as the bedroom for my sister and me. The bathroom has a gas stove to heat up the water, and it's quite an ado to prepare a hot bath. At the beginning of each winter, a man in peasant garb brings us a supply of coal and thin-chopped wood for the whole apartment, and sometimes I'm sent to fetch some from the basement—a dark, damp place into which I peer nervously before plunging in and filling my two buckets with the coal stacked on our pile.

The three-story building is always full of talk, visits, and melodrama. The dragon caretaker is married to a thin, forlorn man, at whom she shouts perpetually and whom one day she stabs with a knife. After that, he slumps even more sadly than before, avoids everyone, and takes to breeding chickens in the enormous attic under the roof. Their squawks and flying feathers turn the interior into a place of Bruno Schulz surrealism, and I'm drawn there as if it were inhabited by magic.

The other downstairs apartment is occupied by a shoemaker, who, in more classic style, gets drunk and beats his wife. Everyone has heard her cry behind their leathery-smelling shop, and everyone nods in commiseration when the couple is mentioned. But nobody is astonished. Husbands sometimes beat their wives. That's life.

Then there are the real neighbors—people between whose apartments there's constant movement of kids, sugar, eggs, and teatime visits. The Czajkowskis, on the second floor, are "better people," meaning that they have some prewar cachet: perhaps they had money, or education, or a prestigious profession. Pan (Mr.) Czajkowski, a gaunt, handsome man, is ill often, and from his bed he speaks intensely about what they did to "our country," as if he is trying to burn some message on my mind. Later, I realize that during the war he fought in the underground resistance. The Rumeks get the first telephone on the block, and from then on, there are often several people in their tiny foyer waiting to avail themselves of this instrument. Across the hall from us are the Twardowskis, who come to our apartment regularly to talk politics and listen to Radio Free Europe—our front door is carefully locked for these occasions—and to discuss what snippets of information can be heard through the static. I particularly like the Twardowskis' daughter, Basia, who is several years older than I and who has the prettiest long braids, which she sometimes coils around her head; she stays with me and my sister when there is no one else to mind us. She wants to study medicine, and she shows me books with horrific drawings of body parts and diseases, and I talk to her about questions that occupy me deeply, such as whether it would be worse to die yourself or to have somebody close to you die first. But then, one day when I go to her apartment to borrow something, I find Basia in the middle of being spanked: she is stretched across her father's lap—she is about sixteen at the time—and he is methodically applying a leather strap to her behind. He doesn't stop when I come in, and, not knowing what to do, I stand there through this humiliation, until Basia is allowed to walk away. After that, she does not talk to me in the old friendly way.

The building where all of this happens, at Kazimierza Wielkiego 79, is situated on the periphery of the city, in an area where urban houses give way to small rural cottages, patches of garden, and weed-covered no-man's-land. And, like the apartment in which we live, we ourselves are located somewhere on the tenuous margins of middle-class society, in an amphibian, betwixt and between position. This, actually, seems just fine with my parents. They are as aware of the nuances of class as anyone, but their pretensions are unaffected. In the melee of postwar Poland, they've done well, and they tackle their lives with great zest. My father prefers the adventurism of independent entrepreneurship—illegal though it is in his society—to the industriousness of everyday routine. Although he has a regular job at an "Import-Export" store, his real resourcefulness and cleverness are deployed in risky money-making schemes—buying forbidden dollars, or smuggling silver from East Germany. He is one of a large number of people who engage in such games—part of the constant, ongoing Game of outwitting the System of which so much Polish life consists, and which, given people's attitude toward that System, is thought to be honorable and piquantly reckless. Everyone—this is the common wisdom—is involved in an illicit activity of some kind: moonlighting, or using the factory equipment to make extra goods for private sale after hours, or going to Hungary to sell some items unavailable there—sheets or plastic combs, for example (for a while, plastic products are all the rage)—in exchange for those forbidden and invaluable dollars. How anyone can get along without such sidelines is a mystery, for the normal job wage is hardly enough to feed a family, never mind to clothe them.

So, throughout my childhood, my father vanishes for several days at a time, and reappears just as unexpectedly, bringing into the apartment the invigorating aroma of cigarettes, his capacious leather coat, and the great world. Usually, when he comes back, my mother and he fall into an earnest conversation in Yiddish—the language of money and secrets. But it's only when we are about to leave for Canada that he shows me a jigsaw puzzle he has made within our parquet floor, which opens to expose a little hiding place where, through all these years, he has kept his foreign currency.

It's pretty dangerous stuff, as we learn when one of his pals is sentenced to a camp in Siberia—but my father thrives on it, as he thrives on riding his motorcycle at top speed on Poland's bumpy roads. His illicit initiatives are also what keeps us within the bounds of the respectable middle class, which means that we go to a restaurant perhaps once a month, take long summer vacations, have a live-in maid and more than one change of clothing, and can occasionally afford to buy an imported item, like spike-heeled shoes for my mother, or a nylon blouse for me.

My mother, in a modest way, fashions herself as a lady and

leads a pleasantly bustling life. She runs her household with the help of a maid, makes new friends at the park where she takes me and my sister daily, reads her books, takes me for ice cream to one of Cracow's lovely coffeehouses, and counsels my father in his enterprises. We go to the theater, the opera, the movies—all accessible to us at popular prices—and on a constant round of visits. For a while, my parents are satisfied, pleased to be in a big urban center with its culture, its lively talk, its news from other parts of the world.

Of course, both my parents want "something better" for their children. In fact, they have great ambitions, particularly for me—the firstborn, who turns out to be clever and talented. But neither of them is very clear about how you get to those other things, whatever they may be—how much work you need to do, how much discipline is required. No matter how many accoutrements of middle-class life they'll later acquire, my parents never quite buy into the work ethic. Life has been irrational enough for them to believe in the power of the gamble—in games of luck and risk—more than in orderly progress. Anyway, there is no such thing as orderly progress in the Socialist People's Republic. It's clear enough to everybody that you don't get anywhere by trying. Working hard in your "chosen profession," when the profession is most often chosen for you, when there's no reward and no possibility of improving your conditions, and when anything may happen tomorrow, is for fools or schlemiels. The System—compounded by the Poles' perennial skepticism about all systems—produces a nation of ironists and gamblers.

But aside from responding to their immediate conditions, my parents have inherited the ancient notion—which came from centuries of hard, involuntary labor—that the ideal state of life is getting enough rest. My mother has a not-so-hidden respect for lazy women. Laziness shows a certain luxuriance of character, the eroticism of valuing your pleasure. "You know, Ormianska calls the maid from the kitchen to get her matches, which are lying ten centimeters away from her," my mother says, half in criticism, half in admiration. Such egotism is at the heart of feminine power, which consists in the ability to make others do things for you, to be pampered. My mother is not alone in this conviction—that a certain kind of selfishness is the most sexy of vices, a sort of queenliness. Later on, my mother will be amazed at how much energy I'm willing to expend in order to feed my ambition. She can't quite figure out—and who can blame her?—why I'm in such a rush, where I'm trying to get to.

In some ways, my parents will always retain something preurban in their attitudes, something that escapes the categories of the industrial world. But at the same time, the war—their second birthplace—has thrust them, in one enormous leap across the abyss, into modernity. Most of their obedient preconceptions and beliefs have been corroded away by the lye of extreme suffering, and have been replaced by a perfectly modernist nihilism. They have little respect for law, politics, ideology. They have been divested of religious faith, and the residues of both Victorian and Orthodox prudishness. They are, in a way, unshockable; they've lost the innocence of an inherited, unquestioned morality. The only thing they're left with is a deep skepticism about human motives, and a homegrown version of existentialism—a philosophy born of the War, after all—with its gamble that since everything is absurd, you might as well try to squeeze the juice out of every moment. They want happiness fervently, and they implore their children to be happy, to be happy no matter what. It turns out, in the long run, to be a terribly paradoxical recipe.

I am walking home from school slowly, playing a game in which it's forbidden to step on the cracks between the slabstone squares of the pavement. The sun is playing its game of lines and shadows. Nothing happens. There is nothing but this moment, in which I am walking toward home, walking in time. But suddenly, time pierces me with its sadness. This moment will not last. With every step I take, a sliver of time vanishes. Soon, I'll be home, and then this, this nowness will be the past, I think, and time seems to escape behind me, like an invisible current being sucked into an invisible vortex. How can this be, that this fullness, this me on the street, this moment which is perfectly abundant, will be gone? It's like that time I broke a large porcelain doll and no matter how much I wished it back to wholeness, it lay there on the floor in pieces. I can't do anything about this backward tug either. How many moments do I have in life? I hear my own breathing: with every breath, I am closer to death. I slow down my steps: I'm not home yet, but soon I will be, now I am that much closer, but not yet . . . not yet . . . not yet . . . Remember this, I command myself, as if that way I could make some of it stay. When you're grown up, you'll remember this. And you'll remember how you told yourself to remember.

I lower myself into the fast-flowing river on my back, and let myself be taken down by its tiny, foaming rapids without offering any resistance. I feel a slight, gratifying thrill of danger; it's great to be enveloped in this current, to feel its energy and movement. Then I stand up triumphantly and run to the shore to join a gathering of family and friends. There's my mother, her best friend, Pani Ruta— *Pani* means something like Madame—and several other ladies with their children. Their husbands, who can't get away from their jobs, come just for part of the summer. The women are sitting on the green riverbank, with neat patches of wheat fields just back of them, playing cards, reading, or doing nothing much. The maids, who have come with us from Cracow, are either preparing our lunch or taking their pastimes elsewhere.

There is a group of about four families, which are in the habit of taking vacations together, and for several summers in a row, we rent a few peasant houses in the small village of Biały Dunajec, in the foothills of the Tatry Mountains, where we ensconce ourselves for nine or ten weeks of unqualified leisure. Getting there is the hardest part of the enterprise, for the village is quite primitive, and we take with us not only our summer clothing but also such accessories of civilization as bassinets, soft bedding, pots and pans, and lots of books. One fine morning each summer, we get up early in the morning, take a taxi—a rare event!—to the train station, and then, with much hustle and bustle, hoist all of our possessions onto the train. Then I'm ready for my summer mood, and spend much of the trip hypnotized by the train's irregularly repetitive rhythm, staring out the window at the patches of farmland, the rows of birches that give me such a sense of calm and order, the golden haystacks baked by the sun, and the peasants unbending from their work to wave at the passing-by train.

The houses we rent in Biały Dunajec are owned by *górale*, a tribe of mountain people who speak a somewhat different dialect of Polish from us, and who are known for their fierce habits—many of the men carry small, graceful axes stuck into their belts, and sometimes, after weddings or other festivities, we hear of fights in which these instruments are used in pretty violent ways. But we are city folks, and such news reaches us only through the village grapevine. The house we stay in is clean and bare, with unsanded wooden floors and sharp straw sticking out of the mattresses, with oil-lit lamps and rough wooden tables. The rooms have a good, strong smell of raw wood and hay and clear mountain air, and outside there's a small, casually planted garden, which seems to contain all of life's dappled variety: many-colored pansies, sweet pea flowers climbing up the house's wall, dill giving off its tangy smell, and hard, bright radishes, which we occasionally pick to have with our rye bread for breakfast.

In the mornings, I go inside the barns, where I can watch the peasant women, dressed in long, broad skirts, milk their cows or churn butter in small wooden barrels. They rarely talk to me or to each other, but I like to sit near them, following their hard, patient movements. Or I stand by as they do their wash in the cold stream, and I watch the linen turn dazzling white in the clear water. Later in the day, I go roaming through the nearby forests and fields with Marek, inventing games or discovering new parts of the territory. Marek is Pani Ruta's son, and we have known each other since babyhood, running races in the park, visiting each other's houses, and practicing our piano lessons together. He's my best friend, I suppose, except there's a twist here—I'm in love with him. I can't stay away from him, even though sometimes he plays boyishly mean pranks on me: he drops an enormous tome on my head when I pass in front of his window, and once, he tries to stuff me into a hole in the forest, which turns out to have been left there by the Germans, and might still have some mines in it.

For a while, his spirits get so wild that my mother forbids me to see him or play with him: but it's no use—I run to his house at every opportunity. We talk to each other ceaselessly, and in games with other kids, we're a team. Sometimes, in the evenings, we climb up through the forest to an open, flower-filled meadow, and we join a group of barefoot peasant children who are baking potatoes in an outdoor fire; the burned skin of the potatoes tastes delicious in the night air, and afterward, we make our way down using the gnarled tree roots as steps on the dark path. Or, on sunny days, we stand under a waterfall, getting our clothes soaked through, and I feel both the wildness of my own spirits and the safety of being with Marek. In spite of these risky games we play with each other, I have a deep belief that his greater physical strength is there to protect me.

When the hay-gathering season comes, Marek and I join the entire village and go off on rattling horse-drawn carts to the fields dotted with low, fat haystacks. We spend as much time burrowing into these straw igloos as using our pitchforks, but the peasants work hard, until the middle of the day, when some women come from the village bringing potatoes and sausage and sour milk. Then the work resumes until sundown, when we climb on the carts again, now filled with tall mountains of hay—so tall that they almost reach to the top of the barn where they get stored for the winter. After the hay is unpacked, Marek and I play around in the barn attic, which smells warmly of horses and fresh straw.

Often, while the adults are engaged in their card games or in their conversations, I lie down under the apple tree in the garden and look upward at the moving clouds, and it is enough. I like being alone sometimes, and having thoughts that are no thoughts, green thoughts against the blue sky. And I like meandering on the narrow paths through the fragrant fields after sunset, when the stars begin to come out and the horizon fills out into a great bowl and the silence hums just for me, creating a great silence inside me.

On Sundays, the noises of village life stop, but at midmorning, the church bells start pealing, and a grave procession moves slowly down the main, unpaved village road. The peasants all wear shoes on these occasions, and are dressed in their festive Sunday clothes— the women have elaborately embroidered camisoles over their white blouses, and the men's heads are covered by black hats with stiff broad brims, pierced by an aslant feather. They all walk together in a slow, common rhythm, singing sweet, naïve melodies about Jesus and Mary.

And at night, as I fall asleep, I sometimes hear the peasants coming back from fields and meadows, singing fierce, pure, modal songs that sound like no other music I've heard—and then I am filled by *tęsknota,* though I don't know for what.

I'm in my bassinet, placed on our living-room table, and I'm being washed by Ciocia Bronia's rough, large hands. They feel good, those hands, and I like the way she folds me into a towel as if I were a small, pliant animal. Then she dries my hair and molds it into waves, so that I'll look "as pretty as a flower."

Ciocia means "Auntie," but I know that she's not a real relative, and that in our house she has an ambiguous status. She's a social inferior—that much is clear to me—but she also occupies a special, untouchable place in my parents' affections. After all, during the war she helped save them from near starvation; perhaps she helped save their lives.

My parents met Ciocia Bronia in a house where they came to be hidden in the last year of the war, after their forest bunker was discovered by some Ukrainians. Despite the assurances of these chance passersby that their secret was safe, my parents knew that it was time to move on. Too many Ukrainians were on the Germans' side. My parents' hunch turned out to be right; such hunches had to be right in their situation. A few days later, the area was intensively searched by the local gestapo; but by that time, my mother and father had found someone who was willing to shelter them. My mother offers a strange picture of the peasant who was effectively their savior—stingy, nearly mute, a hunchback. His two strapping sons belonged to the Banderowcy—a Fascist group of pro-German partisans. And yet, this glum, seemingly harsh man started showing signs of affection and attachment to my parents, and found it hard, when the time came, to part with them. "You never know what can come out of a person," my mother says musingly as she talks about him, and sometimes tears come to her eyes.

For one whole year, my parents were sequestered in this man's attic, where they mostly sat on a clump of hay—cold, lice covered, often hungry. It was here that my father once saw the Germans approaching, presumably for a house search—and without thinking twice, decided to jump out of the back window. He tried to pull my mother after him—but she refused. "I didn't care anymore whether I lived or died," she told me. "By that time, it just didn't matter. But your father, he wanted to live so much. That's what saved us." In this particular instance, the Germans were diverted.

It was in this house, also, that my parents came to know Ciocia Bronia. She was ostensibly a servant, working downstairs for the relatively rich peasant; but one day, she revealed to my parents the tainted secret—she too was Jewish. She had come from far enough so that nobody in this village knew it, and she looked enough like a Pole—large boned and broad faced—that she could easily pass.

From then on, whenever she could, she brought my parents some extra bread or soup. The Ukrainian never caught on to the fact that he was harboring yet another Jew in his house.

After the war was over, my parents and Ciocia Bronia, all of them left without any family, cleaved to each other. After spending some months in Lvov, they made their journey to Cracow together. They all had a hunch—yet another one of their hunches—that they'd rather be in Poland than in the new Russia.

So now, Ciocia Bronia lives with us, the first of a series of women—after her, they are all simply maids—to inhabit the narrow bed in our narrow kitchen. She's my parents' only link with the prewar past—and with the prewar hierarchy of the shtetl. Yes, almost a relative, except my mother comes from a family of solid merchants and she aspires to being a "better" person, while Bronia will forever remain a poor Jew, nearly a peasant. My mother reads a lot, and sometimes, while I am pretending to sleep in the "second room," I hear my parents and their friends discussing a new book or film into the late hours of the night. I don't know where Bronia is during those talks, probably really sleeping in the kitchen, rather than just faking it like me. Bronia doesn't read or go to the movies. My mother follows the latest fashions in popular journals, and sometimes even—the excitement, when this happens, is great—in the pages of American magazines that somehow find their way into her circle of friends. We pore over the clothes shown in those magazines—we make no distinctions between advertisements and other pictures—with the closest attention, analyzing the minutiae of collars and pleats and waistlines, and we then show pictures of our chosen items to our dressmaker, who tries, to the best of her abilities, to imitate them.

Bronia wears no makeup; her dresses, invariably of flowery calico prints, hang loosely around her body; and she wouldn't know how to put on a pair of nylon stockings. She never opens the newspaper, and her speech is dotted with sighs and muttered invocations. "She's a bit primitive," my mother says to me in collusive tones. "So superstitious. She doesn't wash when she menstruates." But when my mother is pregnant, and Ciocia Bronia tries to divine from cards whether it will be a girl or a boy, my mother waits for the verdict with her eyes shining. As for me, I believe it absolutely—although I no longer remember whether it turned out to be right or wrong.

I feel a great trust in Ciocia Bronia—in the clothes she makes for my dolls, and the bread dunked in coffee with milk she feeds me in the morning. But I know that I don't have to listen to her as I listen to my mother, and I know too that she looks on me as a finer creature, that she's already deferential to me. "My kitten, my princess, my golden one," she intones, and then I feel singled out for special attention—but I am also infused with a gentle, disinterested love, almost as if I were its source.

When I am about seven, Ciocia Bronia gets married to a man I don't like and moves to Breslau, where I don't like to visit; it is still a city of rubble, and her husband starts pinching my breasts as soon as there is anything to pinch. My mother thinks Bronia should be happy; and I believe that in her quiet, peaceful way, she is. After all, she had never really expected to have a husband, to be a mistress in her own house. For her, this is an achievement, and it is one with which she rested content.

Ciocia Bronia remains devoted to our family even across the unimaginable distance of the Atlantic. In Canada, we get badly spelled letters from her, in which she pleads for some news from "her darling Eva;" but I never write. There is no way, I know, that I can convey the nature of my new life to her, and besides, she is one of the many affections that are only causing me the pain of nostalgia, and that I therefore try to numb or extract from myself like some gnawing scruple, or splinter lodged in a thumb.

My father almost never mentions the war; dignity for him is silence, sometimes too much silence. After a while, he finds it difficult to talk about many things, and it is not until the events have receded into the past that he recounts a few stories from those years—by that time so far removed that they seem like fables again, James Bond adventures. How will I ever pin down the reality of what happened to my parents? I come from the war; it is my true origin. But as with all our origins, I cannot grasp it. Perhaps we never know where we come from; in a way, we are all created ex nihilo.

Before they had to hide in their forest bunker, my father had a narrow escape. This was when the roundups of Jews were intensifying in his town, and the Wydra brothers—there were three of them—were considered a prize catch because they kept eluding the gestapo so successfully. So when a German truck filled with Jews being transported to a nearby concentration camp passed my father on the road one day, one of the people on it couldn't contain himself and stupidly shouted out, "There's a Wydra!" The German in charge of course stopped and ordered my father to get on. None of the people on that truck came out of the war alive. My father did because, as the Germans stopped the truck for the night and herded people into some house reserved for this purpose, he noticed a door that was a crack open and slid through it. Then he was out in the back and he started to run, toward the forest ahead. Within minutes, there were loud barks of dogs pursuing him. But he ran fast, and once he was in the forest, he managed to throw the animals off his track. The area was unfamiliar, and he wandered through the snow until dawn, when he found himself on the edge of the woods again. Approaching him was a figure of a peasant. My father couldn't know whether the presence of the peasant meant rescue or death—but by that time, he couldn't walk anymore anyway. He had to trust the figure. The peasant turned out to be all right; he took my father into his house—situated next to the concentration camp to which the transport was being taken. Then, word was sent to my mother of my father's whereabouts, and she came to fetch him in a cart. For the next few days, she told me, my father had a cold.

When they hid in their bunker, my father had to come out each night to forage for food. Sometimes, he would make his way to the village church, where the priest would give him some bread. But one night on the way back, he was grabbed by two young Ukrainians—strong and drunk—who told him they were going to take him to the gestapo. They each took him by the arm. But as they were crossing the bridge of a local river, my father—"strong as a bull"—threw them off violently, letting them fall against the bridge's railings (he makes a violent gesture with his powerful arms as he tells me this), and then jumped into the river, though it was half iced over at this time of the year. He stayed in the freezing water, diving under the ice repeatedly for an hour or so, until he was quite sure that his pursuers had given up and gone away. "Ach," my father finishes, making an impatient gesture with his hands, as if to throw off these memories. What does it matter? It happened, it happened, what can you make of it?

My mother wants me to know what happened, and I keep every detail of what she tells me in my memory like black beads. It's a matter of honor to remember, like affirming one's Jewishness. But I don't understand what I remember. To atone for what happened, I should relive it all with her, and I try. No, not really. I can't go as near this pain as I should. But I can't draw away from it either.

When I am much older, I try to get away more. Surely, there is no point in duplicating suffering, in adding mine to hers. And surely, there are no useful lessons I can derive from my parents' experience: it does not apply to my life; it is in fact misleading, making me into a knee-jerk pessimist. This is what I tell myself, and for a while I have a policy of keeping my mother's stories at a long arm's length. But once, years later, in a noisy cafeteria in New York, I meet somebody who knew my parents in their town before the war. It is the only such person I've ever met—she has located my parents, on this other continent, by a series of flukes, and now she wants to talk to me. It is also the first time I get some glimpses of how my parents—whose history has always made them archetypal in my eyes—have a particularity, even within this metastory. This woman is different from my mother: divorced, working on her own, tougher. Her daughter is as different from me as I can imagine—a saleswoman who takes dance lessons and doesn't care a whit about the past—and this also comes as a surprise. We should be more like each other; we have been molded by the same Thing. The mother has a photograph of herself and other young women—including my mother's sister. They stand on a tiny bridge in a frozen landscape, in coats with fur collars, looking older than their age, their heads cocked in an innocent gesture of coquetry. So that's what she looked like; yes, a little like Alinka. But the image adds so little information; there is no way to penetrate the veil this way either. My parents' old friend, though, tells me a story while we're having lunch in the Union Square cafeteria that I have never heard: when my parents finally had to run for the bunker, she recounts, my mother, who had had a miscarriage, was too weak to walk through the snow all the way. My father ended up carrying her on his back, kilometer after kilometer. Another image for me to store, another sharp black bead added to the rest. As I listen, I lower my head in acknowledgment that this—the pain of this—is where I come from, and that it's useless to try to get away.

When I am a child, my father teases me once by asking who I would choose—him or my mother—if they were to get divorced. Then, seeing the terror on my face—they fight often and I think he really means it—he says, "Don't worry, after everything we've gone through, our marriage is as strong as the Chinese Wall. Nothing is going to break it." My soul, even then, twists with the wrenching complexity of this knot.

Every two weeks or so, my mother takes me to the library to provide for my next fortnight's reading. Every time, I anticipate the event as if it were a trip into Sesame itself. The library is located in a narrow, old street, in an ancient building, which one enters through a heavy wooden door. The interior is Plato's cave, Egyptian temple, the space of mystery and magic, on whose threshold I stand a humble acolyte. It is yellowly lit, smoky with dust and respectful whispers, and behind the counters, which stop the customers from entering farther, it reveals deep, ceiling-tall rows of shelves. When your turn comes, one of the guardians of the mysteries—most of them bespectacled women in black, satiny versions of a nurse's uniform—approaches for a consultation. My mother mentions some author or title she's interested in. And as for me—what might I want to read next? An adventure story? A boarding school novel? Something historical? The very thought of these possibilities makes the next two weeks a terrain of potential pleasure. The guardian then quietly vanishes into the cavernous interior, to emerge with a stack of musty, yellow-paged volumes. I open them; I sniff their aged smell; I read a few words; some of them have illustrations at which I look greedily; then I have to choose from the riches of Araby.

I come out, usually into the dim evening streets, enchanted with what awaits me, and as soon as I come home, I pounce on one of the volumes. Then there's the prospect of reading for the entire evening. My parents are worried that I read too much—it's not restful; it'll strain my eyes—and sometimes I sneak under the table in the hope that they won't notice what I'm doing. Sometimes they don't.

The boarding school novels, usually French, feature wicked girls who skip school and sneak out at night to do God knows what; I'm fascinated by them, but it's always the quiet, *bien pensant* girls who seem to end up with a boyfriend, so I conclude that I should wish to be like them—though I feel regret for giving up, even in my imagination, the titillating possibilities of badness. There's a book by an Italian writer called *Heart* about people so pathetic— deaf, blind, destitute—and children so filled with pity and kindness that I weep uncontrollable tears over the stories. There's Jules Verne and *Alice in Wonderland,* and *Doctor Dolittle,* and *Quo Vadis?*—all of this very different from the reading we're assigned at school, about boys and girls spending summers on a collective farm, being helpful to their hardworking mothers, or competing to do even more work than their two-week plan calls for—reading that I know not to take seriously from the teacher's voice. "And what did you learn about the value of work from this story?" she asks the class with cheerful peremptoriness—and we answer in jaded tones, as if we were just disposing of a silly duty.

But this is not true of my library books, whose contents I take at face value and with complete suspension of disbelief. Like all Polish children, I am given lots of books by Sienkiewicz—the laureate of Polish nationalism—even though they might be considered strong fare by some standards. His historical novels about the travails of Poland's medieval empire, its triumphs and defeats, are populated by proud Polish beauties—I am particularly fascinated by one tall, pale, dignified countess to whom the hero is irresistibly drawn because of the strange restrained power he senses within her—by incredibly cruel Prussian knights clopping through the landscape in heavy metal armor, and by scenes of battle and torture. There are frequent descriptions of people being impaled on a stake or having their tongues cut out, or their eyes gouged, that are quite impossible to extract from my head once they've been put there.

Sienkiewicz's *Quo Vadis?* should teach me a lot about Roman history and the beginnings of Christianity, but I read it mostly for its hints of a whole other knowledge—sex. Its scenes of Roman orgies don't yield all that much detail but they're enough to stimulate tantalizingly pleasurable images, which fill my head at bed-time—fantasies of bare-breasted women feeding grapes to reclining men and people bathing each other languidly, behind which I feel something else I can't get to, but which go round and round until I lull myself to sleep.

Then, by some oversight or mistake, I am handed Boccaccio's *Decameron*—which I begin to read like any other book, until I realize what incredibly saucy material I've stumbled on. Of course, I don't "understand" what I'm reading about: but there must be a foreknowledge of sex as there is of other things, for Boccaccio's scenes of hermits giving in to fleshly temptresses and his casual couplings set my blood afire; it is a kind of *tęsknota,* I suppose, though of a different kind.

But it is books that describe milder, less remote experiences—worlds closer to my own—that really matter to me. One day, I open *Anne of Green Gables*—and for the next few months I'm hooked. I ask the librarian frantically when the next volume might arrive; I'm anxious if there's too much of a pause between them—I can't be left hanging in suspense about whether Anne will become a teacher or not. My conversation is full of Anne's bons mots and news from her daily life—that her friend, Diana, is tragically dying, that Gilbert invited her for a walk, that she got some dresses with bouffant sleeves for her birthday and was absolutely ecstatic. As long as I'm reading, I assume that I am this girl growing up on Prince Edward Island; the novel's words enter my head as if they were emanating from it. Since I experience what they describe so vividly, they must be mine.

Like so many children who read a lot, I begin to declare rather early that I want to be a writer. But this is the only way I have of articulating a different desire, a desire that I can't yet understand. What I really want is to be transported into a space in which every-thing is as distinct, complete, and intelligible as in the stories I read. And, like most children, I'm a literalist through and through. I want reality to imitate books—and books to capture the essence of real-ity. I love words insofar as they correspond to the world, insofar as they give it to me in a heightened form. The more words I have, the more distinct, precise my perceptions become—and such lucidity is a form of joy. Sometimes, when I find a new expression, I roll it on the tongue, as if shaping it in my mouth gave birth to a new shape in the world. Nothing fully exists until it is articulated. "She grimaced ironically," someone says, and an ironic grimace is now delineated in my mind with a sharpness it never had before. I've grasped a new piece of experience; it is mine.

The yellowed pages I take out of the library draw me into them as into a trance—but only on the condition that they create a convincing mimetic illusion. I feel subtly cheated by *Alice in Wonderland,* because it is all pretend, a game, and of what interest is that? My reading is all mixed up, and it's not so long after I read *Alice* that I'm given *War and Peace.* This is something I should read carefully, my parents convey to me, a classic, something very important—but the usually discouraging invocation of duty has no effect on me this time. I don't notice that *War and Peace* is a book, something I'm reading. Surely, this is just life.

It is a beautiful, sunny day in Cracow, and I'm holding my mother's hand as we stroll toward our favorite park—Park Krakowski. But in the middle of this relaxed saunter, the tone of her voice changes as if she wanted to tell me something very important. "You're grown up enough now to understand this," she says. "It's time you stopped crossing yourself in front of churches. We're Jewish and Jews don't do that." It doesn't come as that much of a surprise, really. Of course, I've known we're Jewish as long as I can remember. That's why everyone died in the war. But the knowledge has been vague, hazy; I didn't understand its implications. I feel almost relieved at having it officially confirmed.

The sense of being Jewish permeates our apartment like the heavy, sweet odor of the dough that rises in our kitchen in preparation for making hallah. The Jewishness lives in that bread, which other people don't seem to make; it's one of the markers of our difference. But until I'm seven years old, I cross such markers regularly; I keep the distinctions blurry. Indeed, insofar as I acquire any explicit religious education, it's Catholic. It's hard not to. Catholicism is everywhere: it's the atmosphere I breathe. "Jesus, Joseph, and Sainted Maria," my mother says in a humorous tone, when she's exasperated, or when things get out of hand. On the street, we often see nuns in their cowls and priests in graceful long soutanes, and I know by the respectful looks people give them that they're special, exempt from ordinary rules. My friends, with whom I play on the street or at the tiny local playground, are much concerned with the question of sainthood. Danuta Dombarska, an earthy, blond girl who lives in the next building to us and is one of my best friends, informs me earnestly one day, while we are waiting our turn at the swing, that she wants to be a saint when she grows up. St. Veronica, maybe, or St. Teresa. Her eyes grow dreamy; this is clearly a pleasurable, romantic fantasy. "I don't want to be any sort of saint," I tell her firmly by the time we're on the swing. I don't know whence this conviction comes, but it's very strong. Being a saint means lying down in a white dress, perhaps on a cross. I don't like this supine position. I want to roam the world and have adventures. Or maybe it's that I don't believe in saints, as I don't "believe" in what goes on when we attend church on Sunday. Yes, I go to church with Danuta and other kids quite often; my parents, until that official announcement, don't stop me. They're not, after all, believers themselves, and they don't want to make my young life unnecessarily difficult. Let her go and play with the others is their implicit message—and that's how the whole thing feels. It's a kind of charade, made more satisfying by all the trappings of seriousness—as if one got to play house on a very grand scale. I like the gray-stone, curvy Baroque facade of our neighborhood church, and its incense-smelling interior. I kneel down with the others, and I sing the beautiful anthems; I get a particular thrill when some clear, strong voice emerges from the unison crowd. And once, as we kneel in a row to receive the priestly benediction, the priest puts his hand on my head and, looking worriedly into my face, tells me that if I want to ask him anything, I should come in and talk. I guess he knows I don't belong.

I guess I know it too. For all these Sunday forays, and the fun of going to church at Easter, dressed up in a nice dress and carrying a basket filled with candied bunnies, I assume that in spite of the gratifyingly earnest looks I and the other children put on for such occasions, everyone knows this isn't really real. So it comes as a surprise to me when one day Danuta talks to me about God—his goodness, his intolerance of sin, his forgiveness—and her face again takes on that dreamy, deeply earnest look. Then I realize she means it. God is as real to her as her neighbors; I look at her with some awe—perhaps, after all, she knows something I don't?—but I have no images of God that are mine, that I've been taught to visualize or love.

Our maids make more concerted efforts to infuse me with some Christian feeling. The first of these is a fresh country girl, shy and fawnlike, but after being with us awhile, she starts coming into my room when my parents are out for the evening, and, curling up beside me on my bed, tells me stories of saints' lives and of Jesus Christ. During one of these sessions, she informs me that she wants to save my soul and give it to Jesus. I guess I'm impressed enough by this, or perhaps a little scared—will she really change me some-how?—that I tell my parents about it, and after that the stories stop.

Another maid takes me to Cracow's great churches, particu-larly St. Mary's, a forbidding edifice in the middle of the city with a Gothic spire and famous medieval sculptures inside—angular, wooden, anguished figures of Christ in a coffin, surrounded by St. Mary and the apostles, which impress me with their contorted postures of deep suffering. Maybe it's this maid who tells me that I should cross myself in front of a church, which from then on I conscientiously do, even when we pass one on the tramway. Most of the other riders cross themselves too—a small, surreptitious gesture across the chest, repeated throughout the car and accompa-nied by quick, conspiratorial glances.

In the house, we have a Christmas tree every year, and I get gifts on St. Nicholas's Day; my parents do this not as a gesture of assimilation but so my sister and I won't feel left out of the sur-rounding festivities. I don't see any incongruity between this and the Passover dinner—the only Jewish ritual we observe at home. They are both exceptional occasions, both holidays. Even after my mother unchristens me, the Christmas tree continues. But it's easy enough for me to stop the other rites. The confirmation of Jewishness straightens things out. So being Jewish is something definite; it is something that I am. Though Jewishness, until now, has been filled with my mother's tears and whispers in a half-understood tongue, when she finally speaks of it directly, she conveys that it is something to be proud of—something to stand up for with all one's strength. "They'll tell you that you are worse than them," she says, "but you must know that you are not. You're smart, talented—you're the equal of anybody."

The subject of anti-Semitism now comes up frequently, but when my parents—mostly my mother—speak of it, there is anger rather than shame in their voices. "After all we've gone through they still hate us," my mother says bitterly. "Can you imagine something so primitive? It's something they drink in with their mother's milk." "Primitive" is a much more damning term than "immoral" or "evil." Primitive means "vulgar, unenlightened"—something nobody would want to be. Anti-Semitism is a darkness of the mind, a prejudice—rather than a deviation from moral principles. Altogether, such principles don't seem to have much of a hold over Polish imaginations. Poland is a Francophile culture, and people around me judge each other by their intelligence and style (to say that someone is "stupid" is the most definitive and frequent dismissal one can issue), by how elegant, or charming, or clumsy, or witless they are, rather than by their rectitude or lack of it.

Anti-Semitism comes under the heading of barbarian stupidity, and that makes me feel immediately superior to it. The signs of such stupidity, however, are everywhere. My father comes home one day reporting on a fistfight he got into when someone on the street said to him that "the best thing Hitler did was to eliminate the Jews"—that classic line so conveniently brought out whenever a Pole quickly wants to express a truly venomous hatred. On another occasion, my mother comes home incensed; Pani Orlovska, the mother of my friend Krysia, and a "better" person—she is educated and a doctor's wife—wanted to know, in the intimate confidence of their friendship, whether really, really, it was true that Jews mixed in some Christian blood with their matzo for Passover. "And this is an intelligent person?" my mother says furiously. But somehow the anger does not become wholesale enough for my mother to stop seeing Pani Orlovska, or even liking her. There are other parts to Pani Orlovska, after all, as there are to all the people who have drunk anti-Semitism with their mother's milk, but among whom we live in friendship and even intimacy, and with all the complexities of affection and impatience that those bring.

I gradually come to understand that it is a matter of honor to affirm my Jewishness and to do so with my head held high. That's what it means to be a Jew—a defiance of those dark and barbaric feelings. Through that defiance, one upholds human dignity. This is no Sartrean, conscious conclusion on my part, of course, but an outgrowth of some basic pride that is as strong in me as it is in most children. It seems a simple affirmation of justice, of rightness, of reason that Jews are human the way other people are human. After all, I see that with my own two eyes, and I'm too young yet to believe that the emperor is wearing clothes. Besides, maybe I don't want to be riven from my non-Jewish friends—not yet. I don't want to suspect the worst of them, don't want to look out for how they'll hurt me, to be on guard. My mother warns me: there's an anti-Semite in every Pole; be careful; even the most educated among them are superstitious about Jews; even the best will betray you. But this is where I stop heeding her. I sense that if I want to keep my dignity, I cannot act suspicious, cannot wait for slights as if I knew they were going to come. Besides, I do not feel they will come. I cannot believe that the friends with whom I play so happily look on me as a dark stranger.

Still, there are incidents. One day, Julita, who's almost a friend, though not quite—she is too haughty, too beautiful, too earnest— passes me a note in class. "Is it true that you are of Hebraic faith?" she writes me. "I'm a Jew," I answer on a piece of paper, confused by her strange locution. But from that day on, I hate her, and cherish dreams of revenge. Someday I'll be more beautiful, more famous than she. Then she'll see.

My pride receives a more serious wound—because it's more

intentionally inflicted—in an incident involving Yola, a spoiled, timid little girl who counts as a friend among a small group of companions I hang around with, but whom we tease quite mercilessly and with considerable inventiveness. We concoct whole gothic stories for her benefit, complete with notes hidden in the ground, boxes with odd objects, and suggestions of ominous dangers. I don't know whence these fantasies spring, or why Yola—perhaps it's because she is so credulous and easily frightened—becomes the object of such inperious cruelty. After a while, though, she can help herself no longer; she tells her father. Our little cabal is summoned to her house. We stand in front of Yola's father, heads hung down in some form of remorse—but it is me he singles out. "It was you who thought this up, right?" he says, while I shake my head no. "I know you," he continues nevertheless, looking at me with utter disdain. "You are the leader of this. You little Jew." It's the gleam of malicious satisfaction in his eyes—as if he were tightening the right screw—that registers like a cold touch and that I can never forgive. From then on, Yola and I ignore each other with the consistency and pretended indifference of seasoned diplomats—a difficult feat, since we live in the same neighborhood and see each other frequently.

In 1957, prayers and religion classes begin to be instituted in Polish schools. This signals a shift in the political balance of power; in the constant tug-of-war between church and state, the church, for the moment, has won a substantial victory. So now, after the morning roll call, the class stands up and, led by the teacher, recites the Lord's Prayer—the Polish version of it, which includes a special plea for the Virgin Mary's intercession. Then we betake ourselves to the schoolwide assembly, where every day we sing the Internationale, whose stirring melody never fails to fill me with the requisite inspirational feeling.

I'm too young to appreciate the delicious political comedy of this juxtaposition. Indeed, it's with a not altogether unpleasant sense of righteousness and heroism that I stand silently while others recite the Lord's Prayer. This is what I have been instructed to do by my parents: show respect by standing up, but do not compromise yourself by actually saying the words. I feel a great self-assurance about this gesture. I'm upholding human dignity through it. And because I know I'm in the right, I'm doubly surprised when one day a group of kids I don't know very well runs after me and starts pummeling me and shouting, "Out with the Yids!" In the melee, several of my friends quickly come to my aid, dispersing the assault, and it is to them that my feelings turn. Of course, I would be defended. The others are just stupid, primitive. My sense of trust is undiminished. Justice is justice. Truth is truth. At eleven, this is what every fiber in my body wants to believe.

Soon after these watershed events begin, Marek is accused of stealing by his schoolmates and gets into a ferocious scrape with them—a scrape in which he too is called ugly, anti-Semitic names. There are low-voiced discussions between his parents and mine, and they warn us that things may get bad. But we should know that we're as good as anybody—maybe better. I don't like these speeches, in which I hear a false, sententious tone, but the introduction of religion in schools, greeted by most Poles with joy as an anti-Soviet triumph, is taken by many Jews as an official mandate for anti-Semitism, and people are worried.

My own fledgling ideas of Jewishness, however, receive a more comical test. It is about this time that my parents go for a longish trip to Russia, leaving my sister and me in the hands of a maid, neighbors, and friends. And it is during their absence that Alinka begins to attend religion classes after school. She's only seven, and remembering my parents' tolerance of my own childhood Catholic foibles, I decide that she might as well go. Until, that is, I find her, one evening, kneeling in front of the light switch, hands clasped, eyes turned piously upward, reciting an evening prayer. What are you doing? I inquire. Well, the priest told the class to pray in front of holy pictures, she explains. Such pictures are a feature of every Polish home I know—usually cheap imitations of Raphael's *Madonna and Child,* or some other variation on the subject—and people use them as icons in front of which to kneel in prayer. The light switch is the closest thing to such pictures that my sister could find in our bare-walled apartment. I don't know why her very pragmatic solution strikes me as a sacrilege, as going too far. Passive participation is one thing, but she seems to be falling for the whole thing; she's taking it seriously.

I know it's up to me to provide firm guidance here, but I'm baffled as to what it should be, so I decide to take the very adult action of calling Marek's mother to solicit her advice. I feel very grown up indeed as I ask our downstairs neighbors if I can use their telephone, and dial it myself for the first time ever. I explain the situation to Pani Ruta breathlessly and ask her what I should do. "Leave her alone," she says in her husky, humorous voice. "What harm is it doing her? She can't understand these things yet."

Well, I should have known. Pani Ruta's tolerance on the subject of Jewish observance is even more extensive than my parents'. Her family was assimilated enough so that they could "pass," using "Aryan papers" during the war and living through it in relative comfort in their Cracow apartment. And she's not only irreligious but naughtily irreverent. My parents, for all their conscious disbelief, fast on Yom Kippur; they observe the dietary prohibitions of Passover. They do so partly out of respect for the dead—but partly because these central injunctions, for all their postwar secularism, still have the powerful force of taboos. But violating taboos is precisely what Pani Ruta likes to do, and one time during Yom Kippur, when everyone else is praying at the synagogue, she takes me to a restaurant and does the most shocking thing possible—she orders pork cutlets for herself and me. "You're an intelligent girl," she says. "You don't have to go along with these superstitions." I'm flattered, of course, and I eat my pork cutlet with a tingling sense of my own sophistication. Yes, I'm the kind of person who will defy superstition and convention. Of course. But I feel a bit uneasy too; the defiance seems too deliberate, as if it were calculated to betray. I don't think my parents would be happy about it, and I don't tell them of the incident until much later.

My family goes to the synagogue only once a year, on the High Holidays. The day on which this happens is a disruption of everything ordinary, a small journey into a hermetic otherness. The morning begins in a solemn mood; we all put on our best clothes, and my parents kiss my sister and me formally—not in affection, but as if they were stamping on our foreheads the seal of an impersonal legacy. For this day, we cease being their children and become something both larger and smaller. Then we begin the long walk to the synagogue—a walk that takes us gradually farther away from the familiar streets and into a sleepy, becalmed realm, the Jewish Quarter. Here the houses are white and low, the streets narrow and winding, and almost nothing stirs, except sometimes through the first-story windows we see a figure of a bearded man.

The synagogue itself has a Moorish facade with tiled mosaics and a portico with toylike, miniature arches. There's a courtyard adjoining it, where people who haven't seen each other all year exchange greetings with commiserating nods and talk in grave, sad voices. These meetings are commemorations of all their dead, as well as religious rituals, and everyone respects the mood.

Once the service starts, the children are left to their own devices outside, but from time to time, I go in to see my parents. I enter through a low-ceilinged, musty, long, damp corridor; on one side, there are hundreds and hundreds of candles, flickering dimly. They've been placed here to honor the dead, and I feel how many of them there are: an endless procession, and someone is always adding more. Then the interior, so dark that the men—they are all men downstairs—become spectral silhouettes, marked by the swaying movement of the white tallithim. An irregular arrhythmic hum, so unlike the music of the Catholic church—this is more rapt and more private—rises and falls in the darkness. Peering, I make out my father's figure, and I approach him eagerly. I want a little attention from him. But he barely notices me; he takes my hand without interrupting his chant, and I feel painfully that he has become inaccessible to me. Then I go upstairs to where the women are praying and sit next to my mother; she at least smiles at me, but she also soon returns to her book.

Across the lawn from the main temple, there's a tiny white building, no bigger than the space of a large room. I never know what its uses are, so when it's opened one day, I'm almost fearful to go in. When I do, I stand still with wonder, for what I see is a circle of men, dressed in long, black coats, moving round and round in a drunken, ecstatic dance. They're paying no attention to the few spectators who have gathered around them; their eyes are raised toward the Torah, which they pass on from hand to hand as tenderly as if it were a baby. "Hasidim," somebody tells me. I don't know what that means, but I feel I've come upon something even more mysterious than the main synagogue.

One day, as I sit quietly under the one tree in this gnostic garden, a bee stings me on the back of my neck. At first, it seems like just an ordinary sting, but then my limbs swell alarmingly, I break out in a rash, and I can hardly breathe. My parents, terrified, rush me to a doctor, who offers a diagnosis: I'm heavily allergic to bee sting. Such an allergy gets worse with every injection of the venom. If I get stung again and don't get help immediately, I may well die.

I don't know why, but this sting under the leafy branches of the synagogue tree becomes my private transaction with Mystery. I've been injected with a bit of my own mortality; I've received a strange sign.

The rest of Cracow, the city of my daily life, is a place not of mystery but of secrets. Mystery only deepens as you go further into it, but secrets give themselves up unto the light. Cracow to me is a city of shimmering light and shadow, with the shadow only adding more brilliance to the patches of wind and sun. I walk its streets in a state of musing, anticipatory pleasure. Its narrow byways, its echoing courtyards, its jewellike interiors are there for my delectation: they are there for me to get to know. The quiet street that takes me to my music teacher's is nearly always empty and almost strange in its placidity. It's as if no one lived here, as if time stopped serenely and without fuss; but then, a breeze blows, making the sky clear, and the street is enveloped in warmth. In the park where I play with my friends, there are winding paths that let us out onto the wider, more lucid avenues, and a weeping willow by the pond that is just about the most graceful thing I know: it's so melancholy, and melancholy is synonymous with beautiful. My friends and I play near that tree, jumping rope or drawing in the sand.

In the winter, the streets become covered with ice and snow, and when I'm still small, my mother takes me to school on a toboggan, which she pulls by a rope. Later, I transport my sister, bundled up in layers of clothing till she looks like a cuddly round animal, by the same method. When we both grow a little older, we take our toboggan to a hill near our house, crowded with children climbing up and sliding down, and we return home exhausted in the falling dusk.

The city is full of history, though I don't experience it as that. To me, it's natural that a city should be very old, that it should have cavelike cafés with marble-topped tables, medieval church spires, and low, Baroque arcades. Age is one of the things that encloses me with safety; Cracow has always existed, it's a given, it doesn't change much. It has layers and layers of reality. The main square is like a magnetic field pulling all parts of the city together. It's heavy with all those lines of force and pinned into place by the long Renaissance building in the middle with the ancient name of Sukiennice. Its stony, echoing interior served as a merchants' market for some centuries; now it's a mart of sorts as well, with the arcades inside selling such things as Polish folk crafts and millinery goods. But it's the enormous cobblestoned square in front of Sukiennice—a square that enlarges outward in the diagonal lines of Renaissance perspective—that I really like. Occasionally, there are a few musicians playing old, sentimental melodies on accordions and violins, and always there are the pigeons—hundreds of them, swooping down for the crumbs they know they'll get from people who come here to feed them and to rest for a quiet spell. All around this expanse is the beating heart of the city; rows of pastel-colored buildings, a bookstore, a wood-paneled, medicinal-smelling pharmacy, some cafés, and narrow streets radiating outward, holding their many-layered secrets.

My father frequents one of the cafés—The Varsovian—regularly, and sometimes I go in with him and watch him in animated conversations with his acquaintances. They are mostly male, and they congregate there during the day. Whenever you drop in, there is a group to join. A cup of strong, black coffee, contentious discussion, and they are happy. My mother takes me to older places, where we eat yummy ice cream from elegant, tall glasses. Sometimes she treats herself and me to a taxi ride home, and then she asks me not to tell my father about this extravagance.

From the age of seven on, I am allowed to set out by myself on certain circumscribed routes. I can go to Krysia's place—it's within walking distance—or take the tramway to Marek's. Marek's apartment is my second home; we visit each other, with or without our parents, constantly. I am fascinated by the fact that he has grandparents—elderly people, though in robust good health, who mostly stay at home and to whom great deference is due because of their age. Marek's father has an ulcer, and he often stands against the living-room stove to heat away the pain. It's understood that Pani Ruta doesn't like him much, and that everyone is allowed to make fun of him. Marek and I, after our afternoon snack of rye bread and bitter chocolate, are usually allowed to retire to "the third room"—the Bergs' apartment is bigger than ours—where we invent endless conversations and games. Once, when I come in, Marek greets me with the announcement—clearly, he has prepared this carefully—that the reason he loves me is because some women are good and some are beautiful, but I am the only one he knows who is both good and beautiful. At eleven, I'm stopped dead in my tracks by this declaration, I think it's so gallant and romantic. I lower my eyes modestly, the way a woman who's both good and beautiful should, but afterward, in our tousles and sex games, I resist him less coyly and allow him—though semisecretly, even from myself—to be more affectionate toward me.

Sundays, aside from being visiting days, are for strolling on the *Planty*, the broad, tree-lined park-boulevards, which used to form the border of the old city. On that one free day, the *Planty* are full of people promenading slowly, and sometimes my parents run into their friends and chat for a while, their voices lowering if the exchange takes place in Yiddish. Then I pick up some delicious gossipy remarks, such as "Well, he's not handsome, but he's good to her; she's a smart woman," or, "He was nervous about something, no? Something about that deal, or is it her again?" But even if we just walk along without anything in particular happening, the *Planty* are full of enchantment. There's the Esplanade restaurant, where we sometimes stop for dinner and where I always order the same thing—borscht with delicious meat-filled croquettes, their dough both soft and crispy, and a breaded veal cutlet. Why look any further if you've discovered complete satisfaction? When I play queen with my friends and get to ask for anything at all I want, I request breaded veal cutlets. But these dinners have more than a gustatory charm: they make me feel that I'm on a sort of stage, where I can observe and be observed. With the hum of voices and waiters bustling about, I feel as though I'm participating in a grown-up, public drama, and I try to sit up straight, nod my head graciously and discreetly, like the adults round me, and make mental notes on the other people in the restaurant, the way I'm sure everyone else is doing.

Then sometimes on our walks we stop at the goldfish pond, and I fall right into magic. My parents and I step onto a gracefully curving, miniature bridge made just to my dimensions, and then I stare and stare into the pond. The transparent water is filled with hundreds of tiny fish, which are not gold at all but red—and which shimmer and quiver with quicksilver motions like creatures brought to life by a genie. Even my father, who usually has no use for pretty things, stands looking into the water with an appreciative smile.

The *Planty* are another space of happiness, and one day something strange and wonderful happens there. It is a sunny fall afternoon and I'm engaged in one of my favorite pastimes—picking chestnuts. I'm playing alone under the spreading, leafy, protective tree. My mother is sitting on a bench nearby, rocking the buggy in which my sister is asleep. The city, beyond the lacy wall of trees, is humming with gentle noises. The sun has just passed its highest point and is warming me with intense, oblique rays. I pick up a reddish brown chestnut, and suddenly, through its warm skin, I feel the beat as if of a heart. But the beat is also in everything around me, and everything pulsates and shimmers as if it were coursing with the blood of life. Stooping under the tree, I'm holding life in my hand, and I am in the center of a harmonious, vibrating transparency. For that moment, I know everything there is to know. I have stumbled into the very center of plenitude, and I hold myself still with fulfillment, before the knowledge of my knowledge escapes me.

My sister becomes a tomboy and a leader of children as soon as she is old enough to run around by herself. From our little balcony, we see her literally leading files of neighborhood kids in various exploits, like snail gathering and tree climbing. Once, my mother gets an enormous bill from our little local patisserie: it seems that Alinka brought fifteen or so children to the establishment, and with the generosity of a born leader, allowed them to order whatever their hearts desired. Sometimes she brings her companions home—ragamuffins she has befriended somewhere, and they run riot in our apartment, till my mother forbids her to bring anyone without her permission. But Alinka is a more willful customer than I—she doesn't obey so easily, doesn't feel the need I do to be "good." Perhaps this is because my mother was ill a lot when she was small, and she was practically brought up by our maids, so the sense of filial obligation and guilt does not flower in her so fully.

Whatever the reasons, in our family's division of archetypal labor, she is the difficult child, I the easy one. She is also supposed to be less pretty than I, though her dark hair, enormous blue eyes, and symmetrical features should stare this perception right out of countenance. Or it may be because my features have more of that irregularity—pouty lip, oblique cheekbone, slightly slanty eyes—which the Poles value as an ideal of feminine beauty.

Pure myth, all this, but the myths run deep, and we believe them ourselves, for years and decades to come. Still, in spite of such divisions, and though we fight and make each other cry, and I sometimes knock on the top of her scalp energetically in an effort to "beat some brains into her head," and she sometimes gets under the piano and bites my leg when I practice because it's so boring to have me play scales while she has nothing to do, we are sisters, sisters. My mother often dresses us in identical outfits, and then we feel the deliciousness of our doubling. We play tickling games in which whoever laughs first is the loser, and I put away rarities like raisins for Alinka and reproach my mother when she gets angry at her. It's only during summer vacations that I balk at her presence—I want to run around with my friends, with Marek, and I don't want her to slow me down. Then, one summer we become separated: my mother gets very ill and has to go to a sanatorium for several months, and she gives us away to different people. I am to spend my vacation with Marek and his family, and Alinka goes to some private establishment where several children are taken care of by a sort of governess. This is the summer of my most intense romance with Marek; we sleep in the same room, and I suffer the agony and the ecstasy of longing; we embrace and kiss and roll around on the floor until Pani Ruta feels called upon to give me a talk on womanly restraint. I forget all about my family for that July and August, but when we come back to Cracow and I enter our apartment, Alinka runs up to me silently and embraces me as if she wanted to fold herself into my body. She is pale, and for the first time I see the mark that will always be the telltale sign of her unhappiness—a muted but distinct greening of the delicate skin near her ears and nose. "They treated her very badly there," my mother tells me softly, and as Alinka cleaves to me wordlessly, I feel as though I'm holding another person's soul in my hands.

My mother and I are climbing the stairs to the Orlovskis', where I am to spend the day playing with Krysia. Krysia is deemed a highly appropriate friend for me to cultivate, because she is from a "better family." Krysia's mother comes from an upper-class, almost aristocratic background; her father was a well-known architect. Krysia's own father is a doctor. They belong to the prewar haute bourgeoisie—a status that continues to be respected in Poland's supposedly classless society. In most people's minds, coming from an old lineage counts for more than high position in the Polish

People's Republic; it is certainly better than being an influential party apparatchik, for example—though an apparatchik may have more money, a bigger apartment, and sometimes even, wonder of wonders, a car. Of course, party apparatchiks are compromised from the beginning by their political associations. But even aside from that, lineage gives a solidity, a depth that such newly minted success cannot bestow; it implies a moral uprightness and the dignity of not having to prove yourself, of being somebody to begin with—and being, by the still preindustrial standards of this particular society, is far preferable to striving.

There is dignity and uprightness to Pani Orlovska's very bearing. She is a tall woman dressed with a resolute dowdiness; she wears shapeless sweaters, thick stockings, and sensible, block-heeled shoes. Her face, framed by beautiful white hair, tightly pulled back in a bun, is long, plain, and extremely attractive—I suppose because of her clear blue eyes, which she focuses on people with an energetic concentration. She uses no makeup and tells me that I should wash my face with the hardest laundry soap—it's the best thing for one's complexion. Cracow, roughly, is Poland's Boston, to Warsaw's New York, and Pani Orlovska is a sort of Boston bluestocking whose class confidence is evident in her very lack of ostentation. She greets us at the door cheerfully and says to my mother, "So you'll leave her to us for the day?" "Till four o'clock," my mother decides, but Pani Orlovska says, "Let her stay for dinner. They like to play with each other so much," and my mother, smiling with pleasure, agrees. Then I'm ready to enter the eccentric Orlovski microcosm.

The Orlovskis' apartment dates from the prewar days and is larger than the quarters of most people I know. It has not only two bedrooms—one for the children and one for the parents—but also the "little salon," with its old-fashioned chaise longue and a big grand piano, and the doctor's office, which Krysia and I occasionally enter on our tiptoes, and which contains all kinds of intriguing, gleaming silver instruments, with their elongated edges and sharp ends now rendered satisfyingly harmless.

The afternoon progresses through several stages. First,

Krysia and I are allowed to go off on our own to play. Krysia could be pretty, with her blond hair and blue eyes, but there is something severe about her even when she is a child; her lips make a determined, thin line and her manner is brusque. Her mother calls her a porcupine, because she recoils from being hugged instinctively, as if she were an adult with an over-developed sense of privacy. She plans our games methodically, but they're always interesting. To begin with, she shows me how to draw—a skill at which I'm singularly talentless, so I look on with wonder at the horses whose flaring manes and knobby knees emerge with such accuracy from a few movements of her pencil. Then, we go through her "botany" notebooks, in which dried plants are carefully attached to the pages and described in her neat, round handwriting, and she tells me about the various properties of weeds, trees, and flowers. When we are a bit older—about ten—she gets a small telescope, which she installs in the attic, where she spends long night hours observing the stars. This is a pastime I much admire; it's something a boy might do naturally, but in a girl it takes imagination and daring. Her mother encourages Krysia in this; perhaps she will become a scientist.

After a few hours of undisturbed play, Pani Orlovska takes us into the "little salon" for an afternoon snack of tea and hard, bitter chocolate, which is considered to have some healthful properties, and for questioning. How am I doing in school? And what about my playing? Sometimes, we are joined in this interlude by Pani Orlovska's mother, who resides in the little salon, and whose plump softness and curly white hair give her an unmistakable resemblance to her long-haired French poodle, Kiki. She is usually dressed in a long, embroidered brocade robe, and she seems to do almost nothing all day long aside from sitting on the sofa and petting Kiki, who never goes far from her. She seems to me oddly contented for someone suffering from such advanced age, and I can't figure out the explanation for this—though maybe it is connected with her being what my mother calls *dama,* which means, approximately, a grande dame.

Often, in the course of these leisurely afternoons, there is a musical interlude. I've started taking piano lessons recently and since Pani Orlovska considers herself the discoverer of my talent, she also takes it upon herself to be its nurturer and guardian, and she likes to hear me play so that she can check on my progress. And sometimes, as a special treat, and a didactic demonstration, Krysia's older brother, who is also preparing to be a pianist, is summoned to play for us—in order to show me what I can do if I practice enough, what marvels await me when I grow older. Robert, who is eighteen—glamorously grown up—and in the last year of music high school, isn't a real pianist yet, and even I can hear the studied laboriousness that prevents the music from lifting out of his hands. Still, he plays such adult music as Chopin's scherzos and Beethoven's late sonatas, and I am awed by having such big pieces performed for me in such intimate proximity. And there are moments, after he completes a difficult arpeggio or a particularly beautiful passage, when his rather sallow, birdlike face rises above the keyboard as if he were observing his own handiwork with triumphant approval. Then I feel the power that music bestows. Everyone listens intently. Is he improving? Will he be the great pianist the family hopes to produce?

Robert waits for Pani Orlovska's permission to retire. His mother's authority over him is pretty complete, and he does not go out of the house without telling her his exact plans and agreeing on the hour of his return.

But Pani Orlovska's position changes subtly in the presence of her husband, as does the atmosphere of the whole household. He appears only when dinner is on the table and immediately covers the gathering with tension. He is a beefy, balding, unsmiling man whose every utterance carries some hidden provocation. He criticizes the soup for not having enough salt, the napkins for not being folded properly; all of this is implicitly directed at his wife, who answers him with a forced courtesy; but she is clearly on the defensive.

I always know that the tension is not really about the salt, but it is not until I'm twelve or so that my mother tells me what the matter is. Dr. Orlovski has a permanent mistress, "a painted blonde," whom he supports in some nearby apartment and who is practically his second wife. "I don't know why she puts up with it," my mother adds. Such arrangements are common enough in Poland, and tacitly understood by all parties. But in Pani Orlovska's case, the situation doesn't accord with her dignity; it throws some odd light on her, on what she might be as a woman, rather than as an impressive personage.

Nevertheless, in my mind Pani Orlovska possesses a kind of female authority that I admire, and that I recognize in many vivacious and strong-minded women around me. I want to grow up to be like them, animated and sturdy and smart.

So does Krysia; she would like nothing better than to become like her mother, but this, in postwar Poland, turns out to be a difficult trick to accomplish. Once I leave, I don't see the Orlovskis for eighteen years; when I finally visit again, Pani Orlovska is little changed. Her skin covers her high cheekbones tightly, her white hair is beautiful, and her blue eyes are as clear and intelligent as ever. In her seventies, she has begun to write, and has completed a novel about Helen Keller; it has a romping, spirited tempo and a high-minded optimism. I'm having some romantic troubles at the time, and Pani Orlovska, looking straight at me, gives me advice as in the old days: "A woman should be strong; she should love with her mind; let men love with their hearts." I look at her wonderingly, and, unexpectedly, she laughs at her own wisdom.

Robert, who is now in his forties, still reports his every move to his mother. He has never married, nor become a pianist. He is a well-known music critic instead, but he drops whatever he is doing to drive his mother across town, or help her move some piece of furniture. Dr. Orlovski never emerges from his office during my stay, and he is referred to only most obliquely. I notice that he does not appear in the numerous photographs of her wedding that Krysia shows me.

As for Krysia, the porcupine, it seems that her reserved little heart was a loyal, affectionate organ. After I left, she composed a poem about our friendship and the weeping willow in Krakowski Park, where we used to play so often. She also acquired a map of the American continent, and stuck pins along the route of my family's journey from Montreal to Vancouver, as she imagined me in such strange and exotic places as Quebec or Manitoba. Surely, the trip was grander in her imagination than in my reality. But by the time of my return visit, she has grown into a corpulent matron complete with three children. Like so many of my Polish peers, for several years after she got married, she lived with her husband and their first child in the old Orlovski apartment. Then they were lucky enough to get a place of their own in one of these boxy prefab buildings that give the peripheries of cities from Cracow to Marseilles and Bangkok an oddly reiterative look. The electricity in this Polish version of modern housing goes out often, and the hot water can never be relied on. Krysia, in all of this, is harassed as her mother never was—harassed by her job as a lab assistant, by the housework in which her husband never helps her, by the endless queues in which she has to stand to accomplish the simplest household shopping. Harassed, but proud—of her children, of her husband, of her vaguely Swedish rugs and the vaguely Danish furniture. As we try to tell each other of our lives, I can see that she can't make out the sense of my story: that I am divorced, that I live on my own in a New York apartment, that I travel all over the place, that I have ambitions to write. Well, I often can't make sense of my own story either. What a strange sort of creature I've become! But as I listen to Krysia, I know that I couldn't any longer give up the freedom that often weighs so heavily on me, like a burdensome gift for which I can't find sufficient use. I couldn't, after all, exchange it for the weights around Krysia's life.

By the time I visit her, Krysia drives a little Fiat, which is her proudest possession. More than anything else, the car makes her a part of the great, modern world. I get into it with her on one occasion, so that she can drive me around Cracow. She is parked on some ancient cobblestone street, and, as she starts up the motor, I see her making that well-remembered surreptitious sign of the cross. Then we look at each other and smile at the crosshatched ironies that have brought us to this place.

. . .

Being sick, just a little, is an indolently enjoyable state. The fever puts you in a dreamy half-trance in which images emerge unsummoned and the inside of your head is a place sufficient unto itself. You get to lie all day long under the cozy goose-down quilt and read to your heart's content, or play cards with adults, who become especially attentive to you. It's especially nice if my sister gets sick at the same time, because then our beds are pushed close together and we can play cards or dominoes or wrestle with each other. Sometimes, after the lights are put out, I say to Alinka, "I'm not Eva, I'm Eva's ghost," but I scare myself by this almost as much as I scare her; perhaps I am a ghost. Perhaps I'm just imagining that I'm me. In the dreamy state when my temperature goes up a few degrees, I am such stuff as dreams are made on.

When I'm a child, I get sick frequently. For one thing, I staunchly, resolutely, and consistently refuse to eat. For a while, when I'm old enough to invent such categories, I proudly think of this as my first existential protest, but it turns out that an aversion to food is common among postwar children; perhaps we sense some of what we're drinking in with our mothers' milk, what they've had to ingest, and we refuse it as later, my contemporaries all over the world will refuse to ingest the goods offered by their parents' world, will refuse to inherit the earth. But when I'm four years old, all I know is that it is a matter of honor—especially once I've announced that I won't eat—to outwait my parents, not to let them win over me. I sit in front of my plate feeling invincible. My will at this age is, after all, absolute.

Sometimes, when these fits come on, my father puts on strange clothing and a fake beard and tries to distract me with some improvised mimicry, while my mother says, "Open up, Florianska Gate," as she deftly tries to push a spoon into my mouth—Florianska Gate being a familiar arch in Cracow, which used to function as a gateway to the old city. When my protest persists, my parents take me to a specialist in another city, Katowice, for a consultation, and afterward, my mother buys a beautiful white scale, such as you see only in stores, to carefully weigh various prescribed dosages of food. But my resistance is only cured when I fall into what is called "malicious anemia," which, rightly or wrongly, is attributed to my self-willed malnutrition. Then I'm removed from school for a whole year and made to lie in my bed under the quilt all day long, and moreover, every week a doctor comes to give me some painful injections of vitamin B. This is no fun at all, and I finally agree to accept food, which from then on, I begin to consume with a perfectly healthy appetite.

When I get a cold or the flu, Dr. Otto, our family doctor, comes promptly over with his enormous leather bag. He chats with my mother for a while, drinks a cup of tea, and only then takes out his beautifully curving stethoscope, which I like because I know it won't hurt me. Then he writes out his prescription, *recepta*—a word whose musty crispness makes me think of yellowing old paper.

My mother tells me how, in her own childhood, she was cured of some awful illness by a peasant passing through their town, who made a mysterious concoction of herbs for her to bathe in. For most of my sister's and my illnesses, these are the standard remedies: every time you're in bed, you get *kogelmogel*—a creamy, thick, sweet mixture of egg yolk, sugar, butter, and cocoa. That's almost worth being sick for in itself. For a sore throat, a vodka compress, made by soaking a piece of cotton cloth in vodka and wrapping it around your neck, which has first been rubbed with Mother's face cream to prevent chafing by the alcohol. For serious flus, you get *banieczki,* or "cuppings." This particular procedure is usually performed by Ciocia Bronia. While I wait uneasily, lying on my stomach with my arms over my head for protection, she pours a tiny drop of alcohol into one of the little glass cups, which are really shaped more like vases. She lights a match, quickly heats up the container, and then I hide my face in the pillow as with a small shock of burning heat the cup is applied to my back, where, with a sizzle, it suctions the skin up into its interior. Then you have to lie still for several minutes, until Ciocia Bronia begins to pull the cups off, each one accompanied by a plop of released flesh, as if the skin had temporarily become inanimate matter.

The point of most such remedies is to generate as much heat and rest as possible, on the old idea that a sick body is cured by being coddled and by conserving energy. When my mother gets seriously ill, she goes to a sanatorium—one of those Oblomovian institutions where the body is brought back to its equilibrium by being submerged in a variety of warm waters and encouraged to take the prone or at least the reclining position. But at some juncture in my childhood, my mother, who prides herself on being a modern woman, begins to take us to Dr. Gren, who is known for his advanced and highly unorthodox methods of treating children, supposedly picked up during his years in America—whence most advanced things unquestionably originate. His kind of medicine makes for a radical change in my and my sister's childhood—for he introduces us to the invigorating merits of cold. Now, when I get a sore throat, I'm supposed to eat as much ice cream as I can; for the flu, I get dunked in a hot bath, followed by a pail of cold water. This is supposed to be done several times, but as usual, my mother colludes with me in fudging a little, and after about two alternations I jump out of the tub into the merciful embrace of the dry towel. Though we follow Dr. Gren's stern prescriptions, they go against the grain.

But it's not till I come to the land of progress where Dr. Gren supposedly got his education that I'm confronted with the idea of health as effort. Run, swim, do aerobics, I am urged by every cultural loudspeaker. Run harder, run faster, run more every day. Keep moving, keep on the move. Expend energy. Build your body up so that it's as hard as a board, as muscular as an athlete's, as invulnerable as a steel machine. Don't stay in bed too long, my doctor tells me when I get the newest strain of flu; it's slightly shameful to be sick, anyway, and probably slightly psychosomatic. I follow the directions; occasionally, I put on my sneakers and go out for a run to prove to myself and others that my body parts are in good working order. Once in a while, I go to a health club, that place where people, with a look of high seriousness on their faces, attach themselves to various contraptions and put successive parts of their bodies into strenuous motion. They are smooth, well-preserved, middle-class bodies for the most part—for class affects even how we get to look and age—and their healthy glow does credit to the machines and their own elaborate exertions. But I keep remembering the more indolent sensuousness that stood for health in my childhood, and I marvel at the eagerness to drive the body to the limit—as if one's flesh could be properly castigated that way, and the danger of passivity exorcised, like a deadly sin.

Once a week, I am woken up early in the morning by sounds of peasant calls coming into the window from the street below. "Fresh vegetables, fresh cream, butter, eggs, young chickens . . . ," they shout out in strong, hoarse voices, elongating the vowels in a sing-song lilt.

I jump out of bed, drawn to all this bustle, and a bit later, my mother and I emerge into the street, which for the day has been transformed into an improvised market. Peasant women, with their long, wide skirts and kerchiefs on their heads, stand or squat on the pavement in front of their array of wares. Some of them have unplucked chickens hanging from a string around their necks, so that the dead birds sway with the movements of their large, many-skirted bellies. I always feel relieved when my mother buys a chicken that's dead. Sometimes, chickens are brought to our house alive, and then our maid closes the kitchen door and I hear horrible, high squawks which then, just as horribly, cease. Once, I come into the kitchen too soon, and, unbelievably, a chicken without a head runs toward me at full speed. I stare at it as if it were the Medusa's head before beating a retreat; the chicken seems furious about being dead, furious enough to do something horrible to me.

Other sellers hold out little nubbins of cool butter and thick sour cream to be tasted. "Doesn't madame want to taste it? Mine is fresh and not expensive," a woman encourages us as we pass by. My mother stops at some of the improvised stands—though *stand* is a euphemism, since the displays are mostly set out on pieces of newspaper spread on the pavement. With relish, we taste the sweet, fresh butter, or a stinging white radish, or smooth sour cream, and after much choosing and bargaining—this involves pretending to be in a huff and walking away to the next stands—we choose the best goods available on this stretch of the street, which my mother packs into her net shopping bag.

These produce sellers, who at dusk drive back to their villages in horse-drawn carts, constitute one of the rare pockets of private enterprise surviving within the cracks of our highly systematic System. So do our maids, who sometimes stay with us for a few months, sometimes for a few years. Both come to us courtesy of Polish peasants' orneriness, and the persistence of old bourgeois ideas. After the war, when the Russians attempted to collectivize Eastern Europe's farming, they found Polish peasants' resistance too powerful—and, they knew, potentially too violent. The collectivization succeeded on only a small percentage of the land, and many farms remained privately owned, providing us with our vacation cottages, our weekly infusion of fresh food, and a supply of young country girls who come to the cities with no profession or way of making money, and who prefer working in somebody's house to laboring on the assembly lines in the newly sprung-up factories.

From my mother's point of view, a maid is a necessary part of a lady's equipment. Everybody has one. But maids also fill in the great technology gap created by the Five-Year Plans, in which conveniences for the housewife do not occupy a position of high priority. Our household, like most others, is innocent of electrical appliances, and it takes pretty hard labor to keep it in shape. Once a week or so, the maid waxes the parquet floors in the first and the second rooms, and then polishes them by walking on two pieces of felt, her feet splayed and digging in hard. Once every two weeks, she undertakes the enormous project of doing the laundry—and then the apartment is transformed into a vaporous bathhouse of steam, soapy water, and expanses of white material being rubbed energetically against the washboard. Afterward, my mother and I stretch the sheets and the quilt cases between us by pulling their ends in opposite directions, to get them ready for ironing.

When we get a fridge—my parents bring it from their trip to Russia—everyone comes over to inspect it. It's placed in the first room, the only one in which there is enough space, and there it sits like a gleaming white, vertical boat. It seems less an object of utility than one of admiration, and we don't use it much, or give up the habit of putting milk and butter on the balcony for the night.

To most of our maids, my mother is part "madame," part friendly counselor, and they alternately bicker, work together, and fall into their appointed roles of mistress and servant, insofar as such social separation is possible in the revealing proximity of our snug quarters. "I told you to have dinner on the table at two. I told you to knock on the door before coming in," my mother admonishes the maid, with whom only that morning she was peeling potatoes. No wonder that her tone in these exchanges does not have the proper hauteur; it's hard to maintain self-importance in such circumstances.

Hanka is the maid who stays with us the longest. She is a slim, attractive young woman who wears her blond hair in a smooth roll close to the nape of her neck, whose eyebrows are plucked in an arching line, and whose dresses are stylishly tight. She comes to our house when Alinka is still an infant, and becomes as attached to my sister as Ciocia Bronia was once to me. She often feeds Alinka in the morning, takes her to the park, scolds her when she misbehaves, and reads her bedtime stories. Altogether, Hanka is more of a friend than most of these cohabitants of ours. She's a lively, affectionate young woman who is eager to learn the ways of the city and the "modern world." She is cheerful; she usually sings as she works in the kitchen, and my mother, who has a nice, mellow voice, often joins her, in a rhythmic accompaniment to their tasks. At other times, Hanka and my mother discuss "feminine" matters—I can always tell when such subjects come up from the coyness of their voices and smiles. At some point, my mother lends Hanka a book that fascinates me too. It is called *For Women*, and is illustrated with sly, curvy cartoons of women extending their spike-heeled legs, exhaling rings of cigarette smoke, or shaping their lipsticked mouths into a wicked, vampy moue. The book's purpose is to give advice on how to be glamorous, sexy, and constantly seductive. I find its tone—so arch, so suggestive—irresistible and cannot refrain from repeating some of its bons mots to Marek: "What are women for? So that men will have someone to persecute," I quote to him while we're waiting for a movie in a theater lobby, but my attempt at feigning coquettish sophistication backfires as I notice the people around us suppressing their smiles and I end up blushing hotly. Hanka turns to this book for guidance often and then consults with my mother on whether the advice she gleans from it is quite respectable. Should she wear a skirt with such a long open slit? What about that cigarette holder, would it look good on her? Her boyfriend gave her some nylon stockings with seams in the back, and she shows them to my mother with some pride. My mother listens to the tales of those boyfriends with a sort of older woman tolerance, though once both of them seem worried. Hanka might be pregnant, I infer, and I also gather that my mother thinks this would be disastrous; the boyfriend should marry Hanka first, otherwise he'll surely vanish.

Other maids come and go too quickly to become more than a collection of quirks and idiosyncrasies. There's an elderly woman, always wearing a handkerchief on her head, who pretends to be deaf for a long time—until she is caught eavesdropping on my parents behind the door. There is another one, a tiny person whose outlines are indistinct because she is swathed in so many layers of skirts, underskirts, sweaters, and aprons, who refuses either to undress or to put out the light in the kitchen at night because of some strange superstition whose nature she can't divulge.

It never occurs to my parents, or to us, that our apartment may be too crowded or that we may be suffering from invasion of privacy. After all, we have more space than many people we know, and there are often additional visitors who spend the night on the couch in the first room. I'm usually unsure who they are: my father's acquaintances from the world of his business dealings, or maybe relatives of some people my parents knew before the war. They stay as long as they need to—sometimes several days, sometimes longer. For a while, a young man comes to our house every Friday and sometimes stays overnight. He is Jewish, and he lost both his parents during the war. Now he lives in an orphanage, and my parents invite him in the old Jewish tradition of taking in needy strangers on the Sabbath. He doesn't seem cheered by these occasions, though, and he bites his fingernails and looks unrelievedly depressed throughout dinner.

There is always the heat of human proximity in the apartment, but it never seems uncomfortable to me. Seeing people so up close, in their intimate, unguarded behavior, is the very stuff of life, and I like to discuss the small daily events with my mother and to hear them converted into the witty, reflective, insightfully malicious gossip that is her characteristic tone.

In the evenings, I try to stay awake as long as I can, listening to the adult talk in the first room. Visitors often drop by, and the conversation veers from common acquaintances to food prices, politics, maids, movies, books. Everyone in this little circle seems to read the same books—often they are passed on from person to person like rare treasures—and the conversation about them is as impassioned and intimate as other gossip. Was she right to marry him, or to leave him? What could she have done instead? Voices rise in animated discussion, giving me the satisfying feeling that characters in books are contiguous with real people, a colorful addition to the gallery, and grist for my curiosity about human motives and feelings. It all weaves in and out, and I fall asleep with the sense that I am immersed in a stream, and that when I wake up, there will be more stuff, more talk, more life.

I know that something has happened as soon as we file into the main school auditorium. The various classes enter in an unusually orderly, hushed fashion; even some of the older boys who have a reputation as troublemakers and near hooligans aren't whistling or throwing paper balls at each other. The stage is empty except for a lectern and two conspicuously placed flags—Poland's and the Soviet Union's. When the principal himself appears, we look at each other uneasily. This must be something big. He asks us all to stand up. Then he gives us the stunning news: Joseph Stalin has died. This is both very abstract and nearly unbelievable. On the one hand, since Stalin wasn't really a mortal, but a great granite monolith in the middle of our lives, he shouldn't have died. On the other hand, aside from surprise, one can't feel much about the death of a granite monolith. He'll just live in a mausoleum from now on, instead of the Kremlin. But the principal is determined to bring the tragedy of it home to us. His voice trembles; he's clearly shaken. He reminds us of Stalin's heroism during the war, of his special love for children, of his great friendship for our nation. Without him, we'll feel leaderless, unguided, orphaned. All we can do is try to live up to his great Communist ideals, to carry forward Stalin's dream of bringing equality and justice to all oppressed people all over the world.

After the speech, the whole auditorium breaks out into the "Internationale"—sung more gravely, slowly than usual. Then the flags are lowered to half-mast, as we observe several minutes of silence. By the time we return to our separate classrooms, there is hardly a dry eye in the crowd, and for several minutes the teacher lets us sit in silence, while people variously sniffle, let tears run down their faces, or cry with open abandon. For some reason, though, I'm not crying. I'm holding myself upright, and have an illogical sense of pride in my own resistance. I hardly know why, but I don't think it's right for me to mourn the passing of Stalin. I don't think he was a friend of mine. I think my weeping classmates are sissies.

I don't exactly know how I've acquired these sub-rosa convictions. Politics infiltrates daily lives in the most porous ways. It is another one of those whispered, half-secret subjects, like Jewishness, and as with Jewishness, we kids pick up reverberations of half-finished political phrases like bat signals. The neighborly huddles around Radio Free Europe broadcasts are usually accompanied by undertone commentary: "So, well, are they going to go in there this time?" "Don't worry, that's not something they'll go to war over." The very mention of the word *war* sends me into a small panic, and my parents calm me down each time. "Nobody wants war again," they say. "Nobody who has lived through it. Even the Russians won't let it happen, not for a long time." The bookshelf attached to my parents' bed holds the collected works of Lenin and Stalin. But I've never seen them taken out or opened, and even when I'm very young, I know they are not like other books, there to be read, but because we're supposed to have them—maybe in case there is a police inspection, as there once is.

Disbelief in all symptoms of official life is, of course, so taken for granted that nobody needs to talk about it very much. Politics, like religion, is a game, except almost no one—no one we know, anyway—seems to believe in it. Poles don't need demystifying philosophies to doubt all sources of power and authority. Nose-thumbing the system is a national pastime, and every second street-corner exchange is a deconstruction. But, in this anarchic country, my parents are surely among the more anarchic citizens; my father is the person who didn't register for work with the other Jews during the war, and he's certainly not going to join the Party, or buy into a set of clumsily concocted ideas about Five-Year Plans and the New Man. His attitude toward such matters is of a piece with the way he jumps out of the tramway while it's still moving, and with his high speeds on the motorcycle. On May Day, when all employees are required to participate in the enormous parade, in which tanks and soldiers alternate with regional costumes and wreaths of wheat celebrating Poland's peasant power, my father is one of the first to sneak off. He spots us at some appointed place, makes a beeline out of the file, and then we quickly move through the crowd of onlookers to go for a walk on the *Planty*.

For both my parents, the sense of disaffiliation is radical enough that they do not feel the drive to develop an opposing ideology, or to join in patriotic or nostalgic discussions about the "real Poland," which some of their non-Jewish friends, after a few glasses of vodka, mistily lament. They don't have reminiscences of the underground resistance, from which Jews were mostly pushed out, and they were not engaged in the bitter fight for Poland that took place between the nationalists and the Communists after the war. On this political map, they do not figure: they are the ones whom nobody wanted. "Politics," my mother is given to saying, "it's all a dirty business." Politics is what has habitually tried to crush them; and this Poland, after all, is not quite their Poland. As with the troubled subject of Jewishness, my parents don't want to instill too many political lessons in me too early, though they some-times warn me not to repeat an anti-Russian joke or some fragment of a discussion in school—such as the conversation that takes place one day when we receive the news that a friend has just been sent to Siberia. Several people gather in our apartment to console the exiled man's wife. The mood is grim, but nobody seems to be shocked or outraged. "Ten years," someone informs a new arrival who hasn't heard yet, and he nods his head compassionately and resignedly. "Maybe they'll reduce it to five," someone offers to the weeping wife, mentioning stretches of time that sound like eternity to me. I don't understand what this is about; I don't know why Pan Gorczawski, a jolly, handsome man, has to go to an awful place called Siberia. "The bastards," somebody says, but everyone ac-cepts this event with a sort of fatalism that pervades their relations to the larger world. That's how things are; it's useless to protest or rail when you can't do anything about it.

So I know better than to believe anything I'm told about political matters. In the newspapers and magazines, the Soviet Union is portrayed as a sort of parent country, the center toward which the whole world leans. In nearly every issue of my favorite journal, *Cross Section,* there are pictures of blond Russian girls in flower wreaths, gleaming with health, or of women in scarves stand-ing near tractors, smiling broadly against expansive fields. On the radio, there are soulful Russian songs, and at the movies I see the bravery of Russian soldiers in battle. I can't help being affected by all this optimism and heroism and brave, clear eyes and good cheer. I love the melodious, songlike sound of Russian language and pictures of men dancing Cossack dances. The Russians have spirit, flair, soul.

But then there are secret police, and Siberia, and the Party, which is half joke, half dirty word. If Russia is a parent, it's a harsh one—like one of those fairy-tale stepmothers, perhaps, who are bent on stuffing their hapless children down the well. When I mention to Pani Ruta that I heard Moscow is supposed to be beauti-ful, she tells me that Russia is like a girl who wears perfume to cover up the fact that she is dirty. Moscow has been gussied up for show, and it covers up the sores in the rest of the country. Pani Orlovska hopes that the United States will be the first to send a rocket into space. "They'll show them, you'll see. They'll teach these barbarians," she says vehemently, and if I'm a bit surprised at this total and frank inversion of the received pieties, it's only because she's so impassioned about a matter of politics.

And if Russia is the center, it is a heavy and leaden center, a sort of black hole sucking bright energy into its sinister recesses. From people who have been there, I hear tales of fantastic poverty, of informers and fear. On the other side of the world, whirling in interplanetary space like an enormous flying saucer, is America—another ambiguous land of vague fears and desires. On the newsreels before the movies, when the name Eisenhower is mentioned, it is in sharp, dark tones, and usually in association with an announcement of some military maneuver or warlike intentions. America is always getting ready to go to war, in contrast to those Soviet tanks, which are always wreathed in flowers and peaceful intentions. In a magazine, I read an article on lynching in the South and another one on the poverty of American workers. I also read *Uncle Tom's Cabin,* which makes me weep with frustration at the injustices perpetrated upon Tom and his family; perhaps—this is what people sometimes say—America is a cruel place full of cold-hearted people.

But everyone also knows that America is the place where all the better things in life—cars, dollars, chewing gum, ballpoint pens—are endlessly available, even, my parents assure me, to those supposedly downtrodden workers. Sometimes we get material proof of American wealth, as when we receive a parcel from a friend of my parents who somehow had the great good luck—everyone agrees it's good luck—to end up there. Hysterical with excitement, we slash through the ropes tying the cardboard box and begin to pull out such wonders as a large box of cocoa with foreign words written all over it, a nylon slip for my mother, and then, best of all, two dresses, also made of nylon, with lace trimmings and beautifully gathered in at the waist, for my sister and me. For a while, Alinka and I are the envy of the entire neighborhood, and we preen and prance as if we were from America ourselves. Then we see an American movie—my first—in which a very handsome man with the exotic name of Kirk Douglas, mostly seen on a horse, pursues an Indian maiden till, at the end, he spots her walking— naked!—into a virginal pool of water and hops in right after her, so that they swim together in a brightly bucolic, Technicolor embrace. Her walk, discreetly filmed in long shot from the back, and the subsequent resolution, are destined to become indelibly imprinted on my memory, if only because of the collective shudder and gasp that arise from the audience as the pair softly lower themselves into the water. Nakedness, at that historical moment, is not a frequent feature of the Polish cinema.

Later—this also causes a small sensation—a well-known music critic on the radio takes the bold step of playing a song, called "Rock Around the Clock," on which he gives a long and learned disquisition (this is music of the oppressed races, we're given to understand, and thus politically correct and edifying). The electric, sexy excitement of this piece of music is totally unlike the plaintive lyricism of the songs I usually hear on the radio—mostly Polish and French. And, as I hum "Rock Around the Clock" in my sadly unhoarse voice, I can't quite believe that a country from which so many terrific things come can be as glum as the newsreels would have it.

At school, I get two political educations, one superimposed on the other like two transparencies conflated into one photograph. First of all, there is this business of learning Russian. From the fifth grade on, Russian courses are compulsory. This should be no big burden, according to speeches by the principal and other personages, because learning the international language of Communism is something we should naturally want to do. The only problem is that the teachers assigned to this task prove uniformly unenthusiastic. In the other courses, discipline is rather strict. Each day we may be called on to recite a fragment of a memorized passage, or to answer questions in front of the class—although, of course, one can always count on the help of one's classmates, who mouth or mimic the answer if they see you getting stuck. But in the Russian course, this never seems to happen, and after taking us through some lackadaisical exercises, the teacher chats with us—in Polish—about other things.

In the history courses, the textbooks we read present an endless succession of class wars, a heroic pageant of the oppressed triumphing over the oppressor: poor, dispersed Polish knights fighting the Prussian juggernaut in the fourteenth century, peasants rebelling against cruel feudal landlords in the eighteenth, workers rebelling against the cobra grip of their bosses in the nineteenth—and from then on, it's smooth going for the writers of these texts, for history becomes equivalent to the stirring progress of the Polish Communist party, from its beginnings as a struggling, hounded voice of true morality through its rise as the triumphant and ever-improving—no, Communism isn't perfect yet, but it's capable of self-criticism—knight-errant of universal Morality and Truth, and culminating, in the seventh grade, with a memorization of Marx's Communist Manifesto.

I don't know the exceedingly complex historical and ideological arguments that one could level at this version of history, but I know that my teachers don't believe it. Through the approved conceptual grid, they show us glimpses of a different picture. That king, who supposedly oppressed his subjects so tyrannically . . . really, a teacher throws in, he was a great Polish patriot, he installed a decent sanitation system and brought Italian architects to build some of the most beautiful buildings in Europe. His wife, Queen Jadwiga, was so religious and good to the poor that she was considered a saint.

From this, I can infer several things: apparently, in this teacher's book, being a patriot and being religious are good things, and apparently, he wants to convey this to us. When he tells us such things, his voice gains more warmth, and he leans forward at his desk, giving us to understand that this is between him and us—he's telling it to us straight. In other words, the history books leave out important things. I should disregard them, I should look for the truth elsewhere.

Still, such images and ideas, and underimages and half-spoken phrases, float safely enough in the atmosphere; the coexistence of the official and the popular wisdom, and the disparity between them, is part of a whole package, an accepted order of things. Then, abruptly, everything changes. In 1956, Poland's president, Bierut, who is almost as much a fixture on the scene as Stalin—he has been around ever since I can remember—dies during a visit to Moscow. This gives rise to many jokes about how for a true Communist going to Moscow is so deeply moving that you're bound to get a heart attack. No one believes for a moment that a Polish premier just happened to die in Moscow of natural causes. Bierut's funeral is honored by processions all over the country, and this time, my toughness is not given a fair chance, because over the crowds massively and slowly moving along Cracow's streets, the knell of Chopin's Funeral March sounds through the loudspeakers, and the solemnity of the music gets all mixed up with the occasion, so that I feel as if I'm in mourning, even though I know that Bierut was a friend of Stalin's and therefore no friend of ours. But I also sense something else in the air—a sort of anticipatory tension, an uncertainty about what might happen next.

Soon thereafter, the tension thickens. I don't exactly know what's going on—no one is telling me—but I sense that some dangerous, rumbling upheaval is coursing through our lives. One day, when I come to school, everything has been turned topsyturvy. The portraits of Lenin and Stalin adorning the walls of every classroom have been torn down, and in their place, long ribbons of paper are affixed to the wall, with slogans, scrawled in crayon, proclaiming things like POLAND FOR THE POLES and WE DON'T WANT SUCH FRIENDS—things that should never be said in the open, out loud. The classrooms are in complete disarray, with overturned chairs and a broken window. I'm intimidated by the daring that wreaked this havoc. Our homeroom teacher sternly delivers a diktat about "hooligan behavior," which will be severely punished. But I sense that something much more serious is going on here than the standard transgressions—like overturning the inkwells, or stealing the notebook in which grades are recorded—that incur the equally standard pedagogical displeasure. The teacher's voice, under the familiar words, sounds earnest—as if she were addressing peers and not just childish pranksters. In the hallways, I see older students talking in groups—sometimes with teachers joining in—as if they had important business to accomplish.

Then the tension is turned up another notch. It is as if everyone's attention is concentrated not on daily life but on something that will happen, and in this concentration, the air becomes even denser, heavier. In ominous voices, people begin to say awful words: "tanks . . . ," "pogrom . . . ," "civil war." There has been some violence in Poznan, and every hour rumors and numbers run like a drumbeat through the street. "They shot into the crowd . . . they killed fifteen . . . twenty-five . . . fifty. . . . They're singling out Jews. . . . No, that's not true, don't panic. . . . If it spreads to Warsaw, it's all over. . . ." Communications between Poznan and the rest of Poland have been cut off, and so there's no real news, only the nervous snatches of conversation in hallways and on the street, but it's enough for me to be filled with terror. The worst might actually happen. My friends and I hold a frightened conference about what we would do if shooting began on the streets, if bombs started falling out of the sky. We talk about this in lowered voices, exchanging what bits of knowledge we have gathered on the subject, and we come to the conclusion that in the dread event, it would be best to hide in the basement; people survived the war that way, down below, where the bombs cannot reach you. The only problem is food. We've all read stories of provisions running out, gradually, so that first people did without sugar in their tea, and then had only one meal of soup a day, and then . . . "Hunger was the worst," my mother has often told me. "May you never experience it." Some people are already preparing for this new eventuality. Zosia's parents, in whose house the discussion takes place, have bought enormous bags of flour and sugar. On the way home, in Cracow's gray dusk, I see sinuous queues of people forming in front of our neighborhood store. They are lining up for provisions. That means it might start any day.

In a panic, I run home and begin to plead with my parents to go out and buy some food. But for some reason, they are remarkably calm. "Don't worry, there won't be a war," they say, and my father even laughs at me. "And if there is, flour and sugar won't help you," my mother adds. Still, I plead with them to do something; what if we have to stay in the basement for weeks? Finally, my parents relent and send down the maid—or pretend to—to get some supplies.

Then, suddenly, the mood changes again. They have let somebody named Gomułka out of something like prison, and he'll now replace Bierut. Everyone seems to be glad about this, though I'm a bit confused about how somebody who has been in prison can suddenly come out and run the country. It's not that I think that in order to be upstanding, you have to respect the law. After all, just about everyone we know seems to play tricks on the law, and then boast about it to boot. Still and all, there's some cognitive disjunction in accepting a lawbreaker as the leader of the country. The Party's head is the law, the force that supervises the arrests I occasionally read about, of people who got rich by stealing some government goods and who, I surmise, just got carried away and took too much, or else weren't smart enough to get away with it. Surely they haven't let one of these familiar gamblers, congenial though they are, be in charge! But no, I gather there's something different going on here. People's voices, when they talk about Gomułka— still in those undertones—sound surprised and sort of hopeful. "Well, look, look, who would have thought that they'd let him out . . ." "Maybe they've learned something . . ." "Well, well, we'll see what this means . . ." Then Gomułka becomes the first secretary, and on the radio I begin to hear new kinds of phrases: "We must examine the past honestly," an earnest voice says. "This is a painful time for all of us . . ." "We must have the courage to admit our mistakes without losing faith . . ." "Comrade Stalin was a great leader, but there are many things coming to light . . ." I am arrested as much by the voices that say these things as by what they say— voices in which the usual "I'm the mouthpiece of truth" resoluteness is replaced by the more hesitant tones of uncertainty and persuasion, as if the speakers were sharing some difficult thoughts with their listeners.

"Well, who knows, maybe something will change," my mother sighs, though she doesn't sound as if she'd bet on it. Nevertheless, for the first time I feel as though the winds of the wider world, against which my parents are usually so indifferent or guarded, have been allowed to waft in through our window—and that this is a large change in itself.

It turns out that for us, the winds of change are real enough, for they sweep in the policies that will carry us, like acorns picked up in great numbers by a large breeze, across the ocean. The events I've witnessed happen so early in my life that my Polish political consciousness is left in its fledgling state, just beginning to discern the lines of force within which our individual lives are held. It seems, though, that my political unconscious is by then set firmly in place, as if that botched business of crude and contingent events entered the psyche as deeply as the first memories of our mother or father. Once, in the midst of all this turmoil, my father—no patriot he—shouts "Long Live Bierut!" out of his sleep, in a voice that implies a salute. I don't know what dream has provoked this uncharacteristic obeisance, and the line becomes a family joke. Years later, after I learn what these events meant in the more remote way of books and from the distant safety of a place where they matter little and could never happen—long after I find out that they were triggered by Khrushchev's twentieth Communist Congress Party speech and de-Stalinization, and that Bierut probably committed suicide in Moscow, and that Gomułka was a leader of a "deviationist" Communist faction I dream of Stalin in vivid, Technicolor detail. In my night vision, Stalin, looking very much like himself in his greenish, high-collared uniform, stands on a high podium in an immense hall to which my sleeping self refers as the Hall of the People. The room is filled with rows upon rows of ceremoniously dressed soldiers representing different ethnic groups. Women come up to the great leader to ask him to make them fertile. But I—small, lost, and without a uniform—know that I have to escape. I start maneuvering my way out, between sabered Cossacks in their red shirts, until I get to the exit—and then, I begin to run. For my life. Though when I wake up, I can't for the life of me figure out what I am running from, or how Stalin—a personage known to me as evil, but known only from photographs and movie footage—came to be so pertinaciously lodged in my brain.

When I am eight years old, I am taken for my first music lesson. Pani Grodzinska, the teacher who has been picked for me and Marek, is a homely, elderly woman with gray hair pulled back tightly in a bun, and her apartment is thick with rugs, dust particles swirling through the air, and a profusion of porcelain figurines covering every available surface. But in the corner of this bibelot paradise stands a majestic, black, quiescent beast—a grand piano. It may be the first such object I have seen this close up—and with its graceful curves, its shiny black surface, its lightly held massiveness, it strikes me as almost alive. When Pani Grodzinska sits down to play a simple melody for me—well, it's instant love. That such beauty can emerge from under one's fingers! Pani Grodzinska, as she begins to play, alters from a homely woman to someone whose movements become as harmonious as the sounds she is summoning. As soon as I hear this simple melody, I know that I want to be able to bring forth sounds like that, to attain such an adult combination of ease and command.

Piano lessons are part of my parents' ambitions for giving their children the better things in life. Musicians in Poland have sacred beast status; great pianists or violinists are endowed with the glitter of stardom and the prestige of high art. But playing an instrument is also a part of a good upbringing, of becoming properly middle class, and the adults in our circle—especially the Jewish ones—all seem to decide simultaneously that their children should not go without this advantage. Besides, who knows, maybe there's a prodigy among us? Having musical talent is an avenue of success open to everyone; if one of us turns out to have sufficient quantities of it, we may achieve that meteoric ascent from ordinariness to fame and glamour that all of us, not so secretly, dream of.

Marek and I embark on our musical education in tandem, and as the first step toward God knows what unknown heights, we are taken for a "hearing test"—something apparently advised by experts as a way of testing a child's potential "musicality." For an hour, we are led through such paces as singing fragments of melodies, repeating the pitch of notes played for us on the piano, clapping out rhythmic patterns, and trying to identify similarities between different intervals. Marek gets over all of these hurdles with flying colors; I have the humiliation of failing most of them. I do not have a good ear.

Later, though, one of my music teachers will tell me about the importance of "inner ear"—the ability to hear feelingly. In this, I turn out to be better. Music seems as lucid to me as books, as that moment in the park when everything was rolled into one, as the times when I feel a brimming love for my sister or for Marek. It speaks to me about everything in pearly, translucent sounds.

Of course, like any self-respecting child, I balk at practicing. To begin with, Pani Grodzinska doesn't let me play at all; instead, she wants me to practice letting my arm fall loosely on the keyboard, to achieve that state of relaxation that is considered at the time the sine qua non of pianistic technique. This is extremely dull, and so are the five-finger exercises I have to go through endlessly before I am rewarded with anything that sounds like a melody—though the monotonous scales I'm supposed to repeat till they become automatic are sweetened somewhat by the fact that I practice them with Marek. But as soon as I am given even fragments of real pieces—a simple transcription of a theme from a Beethoven symphony, or a movement of some Kuhlau or Clementi sonatinas—I plunge into them with enthusiasm. I don't wonder about what they should sound like—I seem to know. By the end of the first year or so, Pani Orlovska, who is a trained musician herself, pronounces that I have Talent.

My teacher seems to think so too, and my "Talent" gradually begins to take on a sort of existence of its own; it becomes almost an objective entity—something that belongs to me but that is also outside of me, a valuable possession to which I have an obligation and which I have to nurture carefully. "You're only a child, but God gave you a golden apple," Pani Orlovska tells me, looking down at me sternly with her cool blue eyes, "and that means you have a duty. It's a sin to waste a gift. Discipline, you must have discipline. You must practice two hours a day. With the exception of Sunday." From then on, my idea of grace is fulfilling your talent completely, and my only idea of sin is misusing that gift. The dread of not becoming completely what you can be is so strong that sometimes in later life it will paralyze me. How horrible to do the wrong thing, the thing that doesn't express your essence—and how horrible to fall short of your powers, or to discover that they might be more meager than their seemingly limitless potential!

But for a long time, I don't worry about such possibilities. I'm filled with a quasi-mystical belief that my Talent is essential and complete. Else why would I play as if the music emanated from inside me, as well as from outside? Eventually, it is agreed that I should be passed on to Pani Witeszczak, a teacher who has the reputation for being particularly good with young people and who has nurtured some well-known Polish pianists. She is not a beautiful woman, but although I am at first intimidated at the prospect of playing for so exalted a personage, I soon find something peacefully reassuring about the mildness of her brown, owllike eyes and her understanding smile. During my lessons, Pani Witeszczak's mother, who is extremely old and frail, and who used to be a music teacher herself, lies on the sofa near the piano under a thick pile of quilts and occasionally offers some observations. The apartment is also shared by Pani Witeszczak's son, and later his wife and their baby. Everyone in the household moves and speaks softly and treats each other with a sort of respectful tenderness. Much later, I learn—from one of her son's novels—that Pani Witeszczak is a very religious person, and that during the war she sheltered several Jews at great risk to herself.

Although she never raises her voice, and is unfailingly kind, Pani Witeszczak exercises great authority over me. She is the first in a sequence of music teachers to whom I owe the closest thing I get to a moral education. In this intimate, one-to-one apprenticeship—an apprenticeship mediated through the objective correlative of music—they teach me something about the motions and the conduct of my inner life. When Pani Witeszczak attempts to convey to me what tone to use in a Bach invention, or the precise inflection of a theme in a mazurka, she is trying, indirectly, to teach me the language of emotions. "Music is a kind of eloquence," she tells me. "Ask yourself what it says here. See? This is like someone pleading. And here someone is getting angry, more and more angry, and trying to persuade somebody else, who is not listening."

It is that speech that Pani Witeszczak tries—by cajoling, by explaining, by guiding my hand—to tease out of me. Like all teachers in Poland at that time, she emphasizes the importance of tone, and I soon find out why: tone, I discover, is something about which I cannot lie. If I do not feel the kindling of a fire as I play, my tone betrays me by its coldness; if I do not feel the capricious lightheartedness of a scherzo, my tone turns wooden in spite of my best attempts to feign playfulness. By some inexplicable process, the precise nuance of what I feel is conveyed through my arm to my fingertips, and then, through those fingertips, to the piano keys, which register with equal precision the slightest swerve of touch and pressure. I gradually learn, though, that expressing this musical speech involves a paradox. For if the spirit is to flow into the keys through the conduit of my arm and hand, it has to move in the other direction as well—from the keys into my arm and soul. Pani Witeszczak's ideal is to make the music sound as if it were playing itself. It is to that end that one has to relax, relax as much as possible—relax one's arm and one's self, so that one can become the medium through which the music flows as naturally as melting snow in the spring. "Relax," she keeps saying. "All you have to do is let the music be itself." But there is a further twist of the paradox—for such freedom, such receptivity can be achieved only through the rigor of controlled technique, if I don't have to worry about just how I'll execute the next passage, and whether I can manage a jump or a trill. One's fingers can become boneless conduits only if they've been made very strong first. Music may express the deepest truths, but it expresses them through a material medium, and in order to say what I want, I need to bend the physical medium of my arms and fingers to my will. To that end, Pani Witeszczak insists on the virtues of strict, daily discipline. My mother is to keep a log of how much I've practiced each day—and if I haven't fulfilled my contract, I'm painfully reproached. "If you want to be a pianist," she tells me, "you have to decide to be like a nun. It takes total devotion. You have to make yourself strong." I try to imagine such single-minded dedication, but for now, I believe all too much in my God-given powers and my inner ear. I don't, however, believe in work. Effort, scales, time at the piano—I suffer through them with a very bad grace. Surely, such mere exercises are for the plodders, for lesser talents than me. Perhaps this large streak of self-indulgence is fostered by my parents, who coddle me to the best of their ability.

Or perhaps I am picking up notions about flair, and panache, and sparks of inspiration—tonalities of character that are the true Polish values, and that are encouraged by my peers and my schoolteachers, not to speak of the Romantic poetry we read. There is a romantic undercurrent to much of the education I get. What counts in a written composition—whether it's about our last school excursion or a poem by Mickiewicz—is a certain extravagance of style and feeling. The best compliment that a school exercise can receive is that it has *polot*—a word that combines the meanings of dash, inspiration, and flying. *Polot* is what everyone wants to have in personality as well. Being correct and dull is a horrid misfortune. "The good," in our eyes, is not a moral entity at all but spontaneity, daring, a bit of recklessness. Marek, in my mind, has *polot*. So did those Polish cavalrymen, about whom we hear so often, who went out to meet German tanks when the Nazis invaded. Chopin's A Major Polonaise coming over the loudspeakers in the last heroic moments of the Warsaw uprising, as bullets and grenades ricocheted through the streets—that is a gesture that captures the essence of *polot*. And *polot*, of course, is absolutely necessary in music; without it—without the flair, and the melancholy, and the wildness that ignite the sounds with fire and tenderness, you can practice all you want, and you won't come anywhere near greatness.

Music—philosophers have known its dangers—inspires me with such grandeur that I think I know what inspiration is about. As I progress to pieces by Mozart or Chopin or Beethoven, I begin to feel in possession of enormous, oceanic passions—anger and love and joy and grief that surpass merely being angry, or happy, or sad. "I know how anyone in the world feels," I confide in Marek once. "Anyone at all." "Who, for example?" he asks. "For example, a slave in America." I have just read *Uncle Tom's Cabin* and have wept over Tom's trials. "Or a murderer." Marek is perplexed. "How could you know what a murderer feels?" But I am convinced I could; a murderer, after all, is a human being with emotions, and I understand all emotions, no matter how raging or large. If I can express the passions contained within a Beethoven sonata or the Chopin Berceuse, then I know everything about being human. Music is a wholly adequate language of the self—my self, everyone's self. And I am meant to speak this language; life wouldn't be complete without it. Music begins to take the shape of Fate, or Destiny—a tremendously powerful magnet toward which my life will be inevitably moving.

My mother, in the meantime, conscientiously takes me to concerts so that I can hear some pianists who have achieved the blessed condition of greatness already. When the Chopin Competition comes around in 1955, we stay glued to the radio, following the play-offs like a five-act drama and supplementing our musical curiosity with every bit of gossip and information we can garner about the contestants. The announcements of the prizes, though, are greeted with skepticism and even indignation. Once again, they are "political," meaning dishonest. "The first prize was patriotic, the second diplomatic, the third one strategic, and the fourth one fair," goes an immediately circulated joke—for these honors are given, respectively, to Polish, Russian, Chinese, and French pianists. By popular consensus, the Frenchman should have won the first prize—but it is also the general understanding that the jury was never free from that ugly pressure which distorts everything, even music, from the start.

In 1958, though, a musical event takes place that has the symbolic meaning of transcending immediate politics. For the first time since the war, Arthur Rubinstein comes to play in Poland—and his arrival provokes an outbreak of high excitement, patriotism, nostalgia and pure sentiment that art still has the power to induce here.

His long absence was a protest against anti-Semitism, but now he is awaited as a native son. He is the greatest in the world, he is Polish, and he plays the piano in the high Romantic tradition—as it really should be played. In Cracow, people spend the night on makeshift beds in front of Symphony Hall, so they can beat others to the tickets when the box office opens in the morning. My father, who as always prefers shortcut methods, waits until the evening, and then somehow maneuvers us through the onrush of the crowds, past the ticket takers, so that we are propelled into the auditorium, whose aisles are filled with people crowding right up to the stage and being squeezed ever tighter as more people arrive.

The hall is so overheated that two people faint during the concert and have to be carried out. But nothing interrupts the audience's breathless attention to Rubinstein's every note. His tone—warm, pliant, utterly "natural"—is the real stuff. It bespeaks an empathy that never violates the music—never interrupts its fluidity with a harsh or a wooden sound. As for me, I am fascinated by the way he raises his eyes, a beatific smile on his face, as if to focus on some point in his mind and breathe the music in, receive it from some outside source. The concert progresses through tiers of excitement. When, at the end of the first half, he plays the A Major Polonaise, with its heroic, revolutionary echos, the audience spontaneously breaks out into a shout of *"Wiwat! Wiwat!"*—which is simultaneously a toast and a salute of camaraderie and celebration.

After the official program is finished, there are two or three of the usual encores—but the audience doesn't have any intention of letting Rubinstein go. People begin shouting out names of pieces they want him to play and, inclining his elegant head, the pianist stands on the stage listening to the requests, and then sits down and plays again and again and again, as if this were a family reunion, and he too didn't want to leave this packed and overheated hall. But finally he indicates by a gesture of the hands that this is the end, that he can't go on anymore—and then the audience, as if moved by some unanimous impulse, rises and starts up the song *"Sto lat, sto lat,"* which means "May he live a hundred years," while the pianist stands there, visibly moved, bowing his head and blowing kisses. Then, exhausted and exhilarated, the crowd moves slowly out. We've had our moment of collective euphoria; we've had our catharsis.

How absurd our childish attachments are, how small and without significance. Why did that one, particular, willow tree arouse in me a sense of beauty almost too acute for pleasure, why did I want to throw myself on the grassy hill with an upwelling of joy that seemed overwhelming, oceanic, absolute? Because they were the first things, the incomparable things, the only things. It's by adhering to the contours of a few childhood objects that the substance of our selves—the molten force we're made of—molds and shapes itself. We are not yet divided.

Once, in New York, I met a Russian artist who tried to explain to me why his compatriots are so despondent when they get to America. Like most self-respecting Russian artists who end up emigrating, he was a pretty active dissident. And yet, he told me, his eyes filling with a revealing fire, he felt convinced that Russia was the greatest—really, the only—country in the world. "We defeated the Germans in the war, we had the greatest literature in the world, we had the greatest culture. It was such a pride," he said intently. I looked back intently, trying to understand. National pride? It seems, for our globe, a terribly old-fashioned sentiment. I hardly know what it means.

No, I'm no patriot, nor was I ever allowed to be. And yet, the country of my childhood lives within me with a primacy that is a form of love. It lives within me despite my knowledge of our marginality, and its primitive, unpretty emotions. Is it blind and self-deceptive of me to hold on to its memory? I think it would be blind and self-deceptive not to. All it has given me is the world, but that is enough. It has fed me language, perceptions, sounds, the human kind. It has given me the colors and the furrows of reality, my first loves. The absoluteness of those loves can never be recaptured: no geometry of the landscape, no haze in the air, will live in us as intensely as the landscapes that we saw as the first, and to which we gave ourselves wholly, without reservations. Later, of course, we learn how to be more parsimonious: how to parse ourselves into constituent elements, how to be less indiscriminate and foolish in our enthusiasms. But if we're not to risk falling into that other absurd, in which we come unpeeled from all the objects of the world, and they all seem equally two-dimensional and stale, we must somehow preserve the memory and the possibility of our childish, absurd affections. Insofar as we retain the capacity for attachment, the energy of desire that draws us toward the world and makes us want to live within it, we're always returning. All we have to draw on is that first potent furnace, the uncomparing, ignorant love, the original heat and hunger for the forms of the world, for the here and now.

"Basia and I were talking about you, and we were wondering about whether you were going to get married," I say to Pani Konek shyly. Pani Konek smiles and tells me that we shouldn't worry, in fact a very interesting man has asked her to get married, though she doesn't know what her answer will be. I nod, feeling shy and flattered to be having this conversation with one of my teachers at all. After Pani Witeszczak, she is my favorite teacher, perhaps because she teaches my favorite subject—literature. In her class, I've learned how to recite poetry out loud, and how to "write beautifully"—that is, with smoothness of style and fanciful similes that show high flights of the imagination. And now, she has invited me for this walk on the *Planty,* where she's talking to me as to a grown-up, about the high calling of literature, and this admirer of hers, who unfortunately lives in another city.

Pani Konek teaches at the Cracow Music School, which I've been attending for two years—ever since it has been decided that I should be trained as a professional pianist. I've always liked going to school. At the beginning of the year, I like buying the smooth navy blue fabric from which our dressmaker will make my school uniform—an anonymous overdress we're required to wear over our regular clothes in order to erase economic and class distinctions; I like the feel of the crisp, untouched notebooks, and dipping my pen into the deep inkwell in my desk, and learning how to make oblique-angled letters. It's fun to make up stories about the most eccentric character I know, or about the shapes icicles make on the winter windows, and to try to outwit the teacher when you don't know something, and to give dramatic recitations of the poems we've memorized—though once, I suffer the humiliation of hearing my voice come out in a high squeak instead of the low and sorrowful timbre appropriate to the poem's dark and tragic content.

But music school is even better than the neighborhood school I went to earlier. It's a venerable old institution that combines a basic curriculum with a full musical education, and it is situated in an old gray-stone building, which you enter through a dark corridor leading to a tall wooden doorway that makes a great ceremonial screech when you open it. Inside, the atmosphere is warm with sounds of violins, flushed kids running around the narrow, parqueted hallways, and the heat of competition. We still wear that democratic uniform, which hides the inequities of dress, but the degree of everyone's "talent" is gauged constantly. Everyone knows that little Marysia—angelic looking with her pale skin and blond curls—is sensitive and has a beautiful tone, but she is too frail (that's because her parents are so old) ever to become a great pianist. Everyone knows that Piotrek—though you wouldn't think it, looking at his chubby body and unprepossessing face—has got all the fire and impatience and irrepressible drive to deserve the respectful looks reserved for the future greats. I seem to have something too—a quality of feeling—as Basia enviously tells me whenever we play new pieces for each other.

Basia becomes my best friend at the music school, and though she envies my piano playing, in everything else I am the admirer. She is beautiful in a "classically Slavic" way—with black hair plaited into a thick braid at the back of her head, sloe, brown eyes, and a face that is all high cheekbones and oblique angles. She knows that she is beautiful, and that things will go well for her in life, and this gives her great self-confidence and charm. To me, she seems the acme of sophistication. She is a professor's daughter, and she flirts with the students who come to her house, and who are college boys;

moreover, she is not only very smart and one of the best students in our class but she has the excitingly bohemian ambition of becoming an actress.

Basia and I often walk home from school together, and we talk about everything—music and the books we read, and that strange feeling, like an itch, but not quite, that comes over us at night when we think of boys or of the Roman orgy scenes in *Quo Vadis?* "But you shouldn't think about such things when you have your period," Basia tells me authoritatively. "Why?" I ask. "Because you'll get sick," she tells me, making it all sound mystifying and ominous, like meeting a black cat on the street. Then, one day she brings me an arcane bit of revelation. Her father, she tells me proudly, knows about a very famous man named Freud, and this Freud, who her father thinks was very wise, said that girls of our age are in love with our fathers and therefore want to kill our mothers. "But I don't want to kill my mother, I love her!" I protest, wide eyed with wonder at such ideas. "You may think you love her, but right now, deep down, you hate her. That's what Freud said," Basia tells me with her usual self-assurance.

This startling information—for I take it as such—makes enough of an impression on me that I feel I have to confess it to my mother in order to unburden myself of it. "Do you know that I am at an age when I am in love with my father and I want to kill you?" I therefore ask her, watching anxiously for her reaction. "And who told you so?" she inquires. "Basia," I say, and she smiles. "I don't think you really want to kill me, do you?" she says, and, reassured, I reply, "No, I don't really, but maybe I just don't know it." I might never think of Freud again—at least not until I find myself in a country where I'm forced to think of him all the time—but that evening, as I listen from my bed to my parents' conversation, I hear my mother laughingly repeat to my father what I had told her that afternoon. I burn with a sense of betrayal and utter shame. Now my father knows. How can I look at him again?

For a while, Basia betrays me too. One summer, she goes away to a scout camp for young Communists, and though I write her almost every day, she doesn't answer. I miss her terribly, and I don't understand how she can forget me like that; after all, we pledged friendship to each other, and friendship is serious, deep—something to which one ought to be forever faithful. When she comes back, we are polite to each other, but it isn't the same. She is running around with a different, classy crowd, and she sometimes sports the red scarf worn by the Young Pioneers. My parents don't allow me to join such groups of future comrades—and as I once observe Basia talking animatedly with a cluster of her new friends, I am pricked with pain and envy. "I don't think she cares about me anymore," I confide to Marek gloomily. "Don't worry, I'm your best friend anyway," he reassures me. "We'll be friends forever."

But as the time of our departure approaches, Basia remembers our friendship again. Once again, we have long talks; she makes me promise that I won't forget her. Of course I won't! She passes a journal with a pretty, embroidered cloth cover to my fellow classmates, in which they are to write appropriate words of good-bye. Most of them choose melancholy verses in which life is figured as a vale of tears or a river of suffering, or a journey of pain on which we are embarking. This tone of sadness is something we all enjoy. It makes us feel the gravity of life, and it is gratifying to have a truly tragic event—a parting forever—to give vent to such romantic feelings.

It's only two years later that I go on a month-long bus trip across Canada and the United States with a group of teenagers, who at parting inscribe sentences in each other's notebooks to be remembered by. "It was great fun knowing you!" they exclaim in the pages of my little notebook. "Don't ever lose your friendly personality!" "Keep cheerful, and nothing can harm you!" they enjoin, and as I compare my two sets of mementos, I know that, even though they're so close to each other in time, I've indeed come to another country.

When I leave, Basia writes me often. She is becoming more arty and bohemian every day. She is learning English, translating some stories from that language; she is beginning to act in some student productions and experiment with abstract designs for Christmas cards. I envy and admire her even from Canada; after all, she's becoming exactly what she wanted to be, while I'm becoming a strange kind of creature I never meant to turn into. After a while, though, our correspondence stops. It is only when I go back to Poland many years later that her mother, whom I locate at her old address, tells me with a combination of anger and contempt that Basia gave up a promising career in physics and has become an unsuccessful actress who plays small roles in provincial towns. I don't dare contact her; I don't dare to see what has remained of our girlish romanticism—and our girlish romance.

I am afraid that my mother and I are occasionally guilty of reducing the high Romanticism of the music I play to the stuff of pulp romance. Sometimes, as we take our walk through the park, we fantasize together about how I will play on the stages of the world, in a long, blue taffeta dress—for some reason, it's exactly this dress that satisfies both our desires—and how audiences all over the world will applaud. In my mind, there is a further delectable sequence to this scenario, which I play over and over again. In this part, the concert is over and I am on the stage, surrounded by a circle of men in dark tuxedos—men pale with admiration, who have come to pay me homage because they have been so moved by the high and essential human passions I've expressed in my playing. Far from summoning images of nunlike devotion, music in my mind has a definitely erotic tinge. It comes out of the very same place whence arise my night thoughts about Marek and those new longings that Basia and I talk about.

A performance, of course, is the peak toward which all such feelings gather, and in which—music's fatal lure—they are sometimes almost fulfilled. In my first year at the music school, Pani Witeszczak decides that for the year-end concert we'll really wow them with Haydn's D Major Concerto, in which she will accompany me on a second piano.

This is my first public performance, and I approach it with all the serenity of inexperience. I simply don't know that I'm supposed to be nervous. During the afternoon, I take a nap unmarred by any twinges, and all through the student concert, while I wait my turn,

I giggle with my friends and comment on various students' playing. Then it is time to run backstage, and when I emerge to face the packed auditorium from the other side, I feel such a heady joy that I know nothing can go wrong. I am both half-conscious and hyper-conscious as I play—a state of grace in which my fingers seem to become deliquescent, pure instruments of my will, and in which I am not really playing but listening to the lovely music as it pours out. When it's over, and after I bow to the applause in a haze, Pani Witeszczak looks at me and strokes my hair; it's a happy moment.

But this is also the last time that I enjoy such an innocent calm. From then on, performing becomes more self-conscious, more problematic and difficult. I begin to develop various techniques to staunch my nervousness; I eat chocolates before performing to stoke up my level of energy; later, I take a book backstage and try to read some philosophy. I know that if I can concentrate on a passage from Plato—he is my preferred reading on such occasions, though he would presumably condemn the overheated excitement I'm trying to rein in—I'll be all right.

I acquire another trick of concentration during a tour on which I am sent with a group of students and some supervising teachers. We are taking culture and the flower of socialist Poland's youth to the provinces. In towns such as Bydgoszcz and Kazimierz, we stay in dirty dormitories with no private bathrooms and no toilet paper; we eat in those grim workers' cafeterias which dot the Polish land-scape and in which for very little money you can get a piece of dry bread and some greasy food on a poorly washed plate. Neverthe-less, this counts as being "on tour," and the glamour of the very idea makes me nervous about the technically difficult piece I'm to perform—Weber's Rondo Brilliante. I pace up and down the jerky corridor of the train and bite my fingernails until the teacher accompanying us, to keep me calm, tells me to sit down and go over the piece in my head, note by note, imagining what both hands are doing. If you can get through the entire piece that way, she says, then you can be certain that you can play it on the piano itself. I soon find out how hard it is to accomplish this Zen act of playing purely in the mind, without the reality and the resistance of physical matter. But I also discover how much playing occurs in the mental act. Yes, if I can have the self-control to imagine all the sounds in my head, then the mind will translate them into the physical act somehow.

Still, when I come out on the stages of the various bare school auditoriums where I am supposed to repeat the same piece evening after evening, each time matching my own best form, I am nervous. My childish fearlessness is gone, and I can no longer count on a state of grace. From now on, I'll have to get to that synthesis of will and receptivity by the more difficult route of full consciousness. I'll have to acquire a new kind of self-knowledge; I'll have to work harder.

The time I work the hardest is shortly before I leave. The school has decided to make an exception of its policy—usually, it resists making "stars" of us—and has allowed me to give a whole recital by myself. This is a daunting prospect—to get through so many pieces without losing my nerve and concentration—and in preparation, I start practicing like a dervish. I practice till my fingers hurt, I practice to make absolutely sure that I won't shame myself, I practice till Pani Witeszczak gets worried and tells me to let up. Perhaps I also practice to ward off the moment of departure; as long as I'm still getting ready for the concert, I don't have to think about leaving.

I am more terrified than I've ever been as I sit backstage waiting to come out, and I get through the program not in that hypnotic trance of my first performance, but through sheer focusing of mind and will. Afterward, though, I have my full reward. My friends are particularly generous with praise, and, to top it all off, Robert, Krysia's older pianist-brother, comes to tell me how well I've done and kisses me in an unmistakably adult way. For a moment, music, admiration, and sexuality all come together, just like they're supposed to.

The last person I say good-bye to before I leave is Pani Witesz-czak. For the first time within our acquaintance, I come to her house not for a lesson but to sit at the table and have tea and cake and talk. "What will you miss the most?" she asks me kindly. "Little things,

I think," I tell her. "The napoleon pastry from our bakery. Not knowing what's in *Cross Section.*" Then, as I let the question sink in, it comes upon me that I'll miss much more than that, and I say, "Everything. Cracow. The school. Basia. You. Everything." Pani Witeszczak strokes my hair to let me know that she understands, and from then on I don't talk much, because I can't stop myself from crying. It turns out that this is the person and the room I can least bear to leave; after all, it's here that I've felt most intimately understood; it's here that I've felt most intensely all my hopes for the future; it's here that I've acquired perhaps the only ideal I'll ever really understand—the ideal of an equilibrium between effort and pleasure, between mind and passion, between receptivity and power.

"You're so delicate, like a mimosa," Pani Witeszczak tells me, looking at me with her mild, intelligent eyes. "Delicate plants are more difficult to uproot and transplant. For a while, you'll feel like a plant with its roots exposed. You'll have to learn how to protect yourself." Her mother tries to stop her, but Pani Witeszczak says, "Why? She should know what's happening to her." Then the floodgates really open, and I allow myself to cry without stopping. When I finally have to leave, I hold on to Pani Witeszczak hard, and I say, "I'll be back, you'll see." "Of course you'll be," she says very gently, but I know that neither of us believes it.

It is an autumn afternoon in 1958, and we are all going, dressed more formally than usual, to the Bergs' house. We are going to say good-bye. I am unprepared for this. I have not accepted the knowledge that Marek is about to leave "forever"—for that is how I understand it.

As soon as I enter the apartment, though, I am jolted into an instant recognition of departure, finality, the end. The apartment has been transformed from a place in which people have lived cozily and for a long time into a space from which they are fleeing—that image of lives being torn and uprooted that will be, from now on, imprinted on my retina with quickening regularity. The familiar rooms, which used to be warm and muffled with their thicknesses of furniture, now echo with emptiness and the wooden crates that line the hallway. There are some trunks and suitcases, and there are people awkwardly standing about. We don't exactly know how to behave. What are the ceremonies for such departures—departures that are neither entirely chosen nor entirely forced, and that are chosen and forced at the same time?

But such leavetakings are becoming more frequent. In 1957, the ban on emigration, under which most of the Polish population lives, is lifted for Jews. Anyone who is Jewish can now automatically get permission to leave for Israel—and everyone who is Jewish is confronted with a decision. To leave or not to leave now becomes the main subject of conversation. Most people we know decide immediately, and the exodus begins. The Rotenbergs leave; the Taubes leave; the Leitners leave. Our personal world is changing; it begins to seem less and less possible to be Jewish and of our class—that is, definitely Jewish, non-Communist, without a particular stake or significance in the society—and to remain.

The Bergs have held out longer than most. They are assimilated enough to feel that Poland is their real home, and the grandparents especially are loath to leave the comfortable apartment where they have spent most of their lives and the city to which they are entirely accustomed. Israel doesn't seem like a friendly prospect by comparison. "What will we do there?" they ask sadly. "We'll never get used to it, it's too late." Separating the family seems out of the question; the decision has to be made for all, and eventually, after countless and anxious discussions, they take the momentous step: they're going to leave, like the others, though they do it without much enthusiasm, and only because it seems impossible to stay. It will be different being Jewish in Poland from now on, in this once again depopulated landscape; it will be increasingly difficult for the children. The exodus is extremely large, and only Jews who are involved in the life of the culture, or are part of the Communist elite, remain—until 1968, when most of them too are forced out by an "anti-Zionist" purge. But for the less important, even if they've never given much thought to their Jewishness, there is, after a while, almost no choice.

My parents have no doubts about the matter. Poland is home, in a way, but it is also hostile territory. They tried to get out once before, shortly after the war, when some Jews were given exit visas, but didn't succeed. The question is not whether to leave, but for where.

Marek knows exactly what he wants. He wants me to follow him to Israel. When we come in on that last day, he beckons me into the "third room" and tells me that this is a serious moment, and I should allow him to kiss me in front of the others: we should not act like timid children anymore. His voice is in fact so serious, and so full of urgency, that I say yes, he may—though when it comes to the point, we're both so nervous that his kiss lands awkwardly on my chin. Before we leave the Bergs' apartment, he shakes my father's hand, and, looking him straight in the eye, tells him that we must come to Israel, because I am supposed to be his wife. I have believed this also; like music, Marek has been a part of my Destiny. But I fear that my Destiny is going to take an abrupt swerve; I fear that we are going to end up in Canada.

This possibility arises because of a letter we receive, out of the blue, as far as I can make out, from somebody named Mr. Rosenberg whom my parents knew before the war and who lives in a place called Vancouver—or "Vantzo-ouver," as we pronounce it. This man, whom my father helped in some way at the beginning of the war, offers to sponsor us as immigrants to Canada, which, he writes, is the real land of milk and honey, the land of opportunity, the place where you can grow rich and be happy. For my father, this is an irresistibly alluring vision—to become a man of means in the American way, a man of substance. We don't have the remotest idea of what we might find or do there, but America—Canada in our minds is automatically subsumed under that category—has for us the old fabulous associations: streets paved with gold, the goose that laid the golden egg. There is also that book about Canada from the war. And, my father reminds my mother, whose impulses really draw her toward Israel, in Canada there is no war, and there never will be. Canada is the land of peace. In Israel, there's a constant danger of war, and they take even girls into the army. Does she want her daughters to end up on a battlefield? Does she herself want to go through a war again?

I understand the force of this argument, but still, the thought of a place called Canada fills me with a sort of horror vacui. I don't want to leave Poland at all; I hardly see how I can be extracted from all of this, from everything I've experienced so intensely. But if leave we must, I want at least to go to a place that is beginning to be familiarized by the presence of a few friends, a place I've heard called our "real home." Once the Bergs leave, they send us bulletins of new impressions and adventures. At the airport in Italy, where they stop over for a few days, there was an automatic escalator, and the grandmother was so terrified that finally they had to carry her down. There are so many oranges there, and they are so cheap and large and fresh that after eating their fill and more, the Bergs are actually getting tired—imagine that!—of this great luxury. Apparently, one can get tired of just about anything.

Then, brief flashes from Israel: they are learning the language in special courses; they are in little settlements in the desert. Conditions are harsh; there is lots of sand and little water, and they are living like pioneers—but they love this country, this country which is their real home. Yes, Pani Ruta, of all people, has become a patriot. For all the hardship, she wouldn't want to live anywhere else. This is where Jews can feel that they are in their own place, at nobody's mercy; it is wonderful to be building it and fighting for it together.

Before we're sure where we'll end up, my mother, who is worried about my future as a pianist, writes to no less a figure than Ben-Gurion, a cult hero who is also "one of ours," to inquire whether I'll be able to get piano lessons if we come to Israel. This is the kind of gesture she knows how to make; the gesture of a person who does not have enough power or standing to go through the normal channels of influence but who can cut through the rules and appeal to some grand personage's ordinary humanity, to what's similar in everyone. "Just remember, everyone is human, everyone has the same feelings," she often tells me. "You should never be afraid of anybody."

In Ben-Gurion's case, her resourcefulness pays off, for within several weeks, a letter typed messily on onionskin paper and signed by the premier of Israel himself, arrives at our address. The letter is no bureaucratic form either; it is lengthy and sounds as if it were written by an actual person. Be assured, Ben-Gurion tells my mother—or perhaps someone from his office does—that your child, if she is talented, will receive all the attention she deserves. We do not like to let talent go to waste in Israel; there are excellent music teachers here, and, if necessary, she'll get a scholarship. We'll take care of her. This is a splendid response; we wouldn't be lost in a country whose premier himself cares enough to write a letter to us. Israel begins to sprout a few tendrils in my imagination. In my internal geography, it's closer than Canada, the journey to it less unthinkable. Somehow, one could get from here to there.

But for a long time, my parents hesitate—and then sway in favor of Canada. Once the decision is made to go there, persuading the authorities that they should allow us to follow our choice will take two years. It is a period during which we almost literally live out of our suitcases, during which my father, as the result of wanting to emigrate, loses his job, during which I am taken in and out of school—during which the matrix of ordinariness begins to dissolve in the suspended, provisional state of waiting.

The sense of impending loss makes me want to hold on to what I've had with all my might. I stoke up the images of Marek—they are not memories yet, he is too much alive within me—as if my will could make him materialize. Immediately after he leaves, I take to my bed for a week and plunge into fits of unstoppable tears, ending up in the dull thud of migraines that will visit me from now until our own departure. Then I begin to make weekly pilgrimages to the Bergs' building, as if standing in front of it could prevent their afterechos from vanishing. And every day—religiously—I go through a ritual fantasy about Marek. In this repeated scene, I am older, perhaps about nineteen, and I've managed, somehow, to come to Israel. I am disembarking from a ship, and there, on the shore, I see Marek. We begin running toward each other, and then—finally, at last—we fall into each other's arms, and hold on to each other for minutes on end, wordlessly. The fantasy ends there, and then I am returned to the street I'm walking on and a state of ashen deprivation. Fantasy is a sapping strategy, but for a long time I can't stop recycling it again and again, like a helpless somnambulist; after all, this is a fantasy not of something unreal but of something I once had—and could have had—and this knowledge strengthens the vividness of that ritual scene, and my repeated disappointment.

As it happens, the fantasy, with some inevitable variations, comes nearly true. Marek and I have our reunion—though by that time I have imagined this meeting so often that I can hardly believe in its face-to-face reality. Even a fulfillment of a fantasy, it turns out, is different from a fantasy of fulfillment.

I am standing at the prow of the ship, watching the water tear away in a diagonal, forever repeating, forever receding line. For days, nothing but the sea. The Atlantic is mostly gray and not beautiful in this early April, but it's so immense, so without end, that it makes me anxious to contemplate all of it, and I have to concentrate on the manageable straight rip within the water's surface.

The first time I saw the sea was one summer, when we came to vacation on the Baltic coast—and its vastness stilled me into an enormous awe and peace. Now, it makes me restless. As soon as the *Batory* pulls out of the harbor, and I begin to explore its decks and its interiors, I plunge into a state of near-feverish excitement, in which all the pain of the last few weeks and all my calm are obliterated.

"What's come over you?" my mother asks. "You never used to be like this."

I don't know what's come over me, but I find it difficult to keep still, and I don't want to stay near my parents any more than I have to. I fight with them and stalk off in fits of stubborn sulkiness.

This transitory tempest follows months of bureaucracy and disarray. Our exit visas have been obtained by a combination of legal maneuvering and bribing the requisite officials with adequately large sums, paid out in the illegal foreign currency that my father has wisely stowed away. We have even obtained a special permit to take my piano out of the country, although it belongs in the vast category of objects one is supposed to yield to the national treasury. This should be some consolation, but I do not think my piano will be of much use to me in that no place to which we are journeying. The only information I have about Canada comes from an article in *Cross Section*, which described it as a "cultural desert," a country in which no one cares about fineness, or music, or art. I have shown this article to my parents in an implicit accusation. They are taking me to a cultural desert! What am I going to do there?

As the day of the departure approaches, wooden crates begin to fill up our apartment, packed with our quilts and clothes and china. The new tenants—whoever they are—come to look over our furniture, which they want to buy from us. Then the police arrive, to inspect the crates for any possessions we might be trying to take out illegally. More bribes—and, as an extra, I'm told to play the piano for them. My playing has never been used as a currency of exchange before, and I chafe under the order.

As I wander around Cracow with my friends in the last few days, everything becomes heightened: some song we sing together, a movie we go to see, some playful or affectionate remark. By myself, I burst into tears as I pass a nondescript patch of garden, which, it turns out, holds a bit of myself, or a creek in which I used to play. Ordinary streets become luminous with the light of loss. "Look," I tell my sister as we take the tramway to the train station. "Look, remember. You may never see this again."

I don't think my parents approve of this effusion of sentiment. "Do you think you'll want to come back here?" they and their friends have asked each other, and the answer almost invariably comes back as "What for? What is there to miss?"

Perhaps in another few years I might have come to feel the same way; perhaps the abstract issues of a collective identity would have developed an intimate logic that would have propelled me outward; perhaps. But for now, I hardly have an identity, except that most powerful one of first, private loves. So as my homeroom class gathers at the train which will take us to Gdynia, and from there to the great unknown, I only know that I want to stay, stay with them. The Orlovskis come into the train compartment with us, and Robert once again kisses me in a way that makes us both blush. Then they are told to leave the train, and I stop crying, as if the fluid current of life had suddenly stopped flowing. For the rest of the trip, I am overcome by dullness that is like Lethe.

There is nothing dull about being on the ship, though. Everything around me seems so elegant and glamorous that I feel I have been transported right into a sparkling, complete fictional world, perhaps like something in *Anna Karenina.* There is a bar, where people sit on high stools in languid poses and drink many-colored liquids early in the afternoon. The chandeliers in the main common room glitter in the evenings, and in the dining room we're always seated at a table covered with a gleaming white tablecloth, and we get foods I've never seen before—olives and bananas and even a pine-apple for dessert.

This is more of the great world than I've ever seen, and I wander up and down the decks, observing the people around me, and practicing nodding my head with gracious dignity as I pass strollers I've seen before. The *Batory* is carrying many emigrants, and sometimes we exchange our anxieties and fragments of infor-mation about the place we're going to. There is, for example, Irena; she is the focus of the ship's gossip mill, and she completes the novel I'm temporarily living in perfectly. In fact, she could be Anna herself. She has dark hair, cut short with bangs over her forehead; green eyes, slightly aslant; well-defined cheekbones; and almost olive skin. For the first few days, she had kept to herself, though she always had her German shepherd with her. Then, when the *Batory* stopped in Copenhagen, a handsome Dane came on, and since then they're always seen together. The Dane is her ideal counterpart—tall, slim, blue-eyed, blond. Except for some smiles and brief words they teach each other, they are silent: they don't know each other's language. I assume they are lovers, but there is also some extra secret attached to them—I can tell from the harsh, envious looks people give them, and from the invisible circle of exclusion that is always drawn around them.

There is also a group of kids who every day meet in the lounge or around the swimming pool. There is Lila, the authoritative figure among us, because she is older, and because of her evident strength and good sense. Lila's parents were killed during the war, and she grew up in an orphanage. Now, she is being adopted by some distant cousins in Canada, whom she has never met. She is facing her new fate with a kind of open-eyed stoicism. She has been a good student, and she has wanted to study physics at the university; that's exactly what she'll do in Canada. She'll let her cousins help her for a while, but she won't be dependent on anyone. Then, there's Janek—the central magnet drawing me toward this group. He is also older than I—about sixteen—and he has dark sandy hair that falls over his forehead in a strip and a nonchalant manner that includes smoking cigarettes with a great deal of deep inhaling and ferocious stamping out in the ashtray. Janek grew up with his mother, about whom he speaks resentfully; I gather that she was an alcoholic, and she was not kind to him when he was a child. He's going to Canada to join his father, whom he has never seen; he left Poland during the war, before Janek was born. In Janek's mind, the father stands for everything that is exciting and good and great. It will be "capital" to go hunting with him in the forests near which he lives; it will be "capital" to live in a small pioneering outpost in the part of Canada named Ontario. It's practically a Karl May adventure.

Resourceful Lila has organized English lessons for our passage, so that, as she puts it, we don't seem like "dumb peasants" when we arrive. She has a textbook, and each day she tries to take us through a few sentences. " 'Cannot' is an exception to the rule," she is now saying. "You can write it as one word, unlike other negative verbs. Or you can say 'can't.' " Usually, I would absorb this stuff easily, eager to pick up some new tidbits of knowledge. But now I can't concentrate; I don't want to let the sounds in. "I don't think I like English," I tell them miserably, and Janek says, "Barbarian.

Primitive." I'm a little cheered up by his teasing and wait till we can go off by ourselves for a while. I know that what I'm doing qualifies as "running after boys," but I don't care. I'm in a fog, and the rules, for now, don't hold. When the sun comes out, throwing a midday glitter over the waves, I turn toward the sea hypnotically, full of a discomfiting, longing feeling. *Tęsknota.*

My parents have also made friends on the ship, with a couple who are a few cabins down from us and who are going to Montreal. The Berensteins seem lucky in comparison with us, because they have real relatives there, who have prepared an apartment for them and have promised to find Mr. Berenstein a job. They often come to our cabin and speculate on what their new lives will hold. "You needn't worry," Mr. Berenstein, a jolly, somewhat pudgy man keeps reassuring my parents, "all of ours have done very well there." But I see that my father worries nevertheless and keeps pinching the flesh of his upper arms nervously.

The journey—it takes twelve days altogether—works up to several climaxes that make me feel as if I'm not quite myself, and temporarily existing in a denser, more artificial medium than what I've known as ordinary life. First, Irena and the Dane single me out to play Cupid. They have heard me practice the piano in the lounge, and now Irena asks me to play something just for them. I go through some Chopin mazurkas and turn around to see them staring at each other with an absorption that has made them forget me entirely. I play some more, and by the time I turn around again, they're gone; but I don't mind this unusual lack of attention.

Two days before we arrive in Canada, great preparations begin for the Captain's Ball. I've been asked to participate in the evening's program of entertainment, so I put on my best dress, and look carefully in the mirror while my mother combs my hair into something that I hope has a casual elegance.

The dining room has been transformed into a big bauble of color, streamers, and glittering lights. When my turn on the program comes, I am not nervous at all—because all of this is happening out of time, out of space. I am, for a moment, a figure of my own fantasy, and I play my appointed role as if I were in the movies.

After the program is over, and the orchestra launches into dance music, the captain himself, straight and resplendent in his uniform, comes to our table and, bowing smartly, asks me to dance. My heart, at this, knocks hard against my ribs, but he leads me through the lively polka and then a waltz with such assurance that I don't seem to be able to make a wrong step.

As the last attraction before the evening's end, the emcee announces a contest that entails dancing with a Ping-Pong ball between the partners' foreheads. The couple who can keep their balance longest, without letting this round object slip, wins.

The floor quickly fills up with pairs trying, through variously ridiculous contortions, to achieve this feat, and then, just as quickly, begins to thin out, as couple after couple loses the ball. The last pair, of course, is Irena and the Dane. They move across the floor smoothly, holding against each other very straight, as if something as silly as a Ping-Pong ball couldn't be an impediment to their union. By now I know their secret: she is going to Canada to join a husband who, by marrying her, has made her emigration possible. So everyone stops laughing and watches silently as this perfect shipboard romance plays itself out before us with such unashamed recklessness.

The next day, as soon as I wake up, I know that something has changed. Then I realize that the ship's sideways shifting, to which I have become accustomed, has ceased. Today, I remember, we come to our first stopping place, called Halifax.

When I come out on deck, I see a bit of a world that returns all my sense of loss to me like a sudden punch in the stomach. The sea has narrowed to a gray, wide waterway, on the shores of which I can make out muddy land, some marshlike vegetation, and a few isolated houses. We are informed over the loudspeakers that we have entered the St. Lawrence Seaway. I don't know what kind of body of water that is, or how it cuts into the continent we are so eerily approaching. There is something about the sight that is ineffably and utterly different from the watery landscapes I'm used to. Maybe it's the air, maybe the enormous width of this inland channel, maybe the distribution of the houses on the shore, dropped into the land at odd intervals, like lonely sentries. Then the foghorn sounds, and the ship comes to a stop. We seem to be in the middle of nowhere. On the shore, there is nothing but a long, wooden building. The sailors throw a plank for crossing. It's cold.

As I observe these proceedings, I notice Janek walking toward the gangplank, a suitcase in each hand. I run after him; I call his name; he turns back confusedly, and acts as if he doesn't know who I am. A tall man is standing on the other side of the bridge, and Janek is moving toward him slowly, like someone who both wants and doesn't want to reach his target. I watch Janek approach the tall man and put his suitcases down; I watch the man draw his son impetuously toward himself. I watch them walk off together, the suitcases now in the man's hands. Janek is not going to turn back.

My private disappointment, however, is soon drowned out by the buzz of much more interesting news. Irena is refusing to leave the ship. Her husband has come to meet her and is waiting for her to disembark, but she won't, and she is detaining the whole ship while they negotiate. For the next several hours, the husband paces back and forth on the cement platform on the other side—a short, corpulent figure, with a blond mustache, condemned in this melodrama to play the role of a satyr to the Dane's Hyperion. Irena, intermittently, is seen to pace the deck, the German shepherd obediently at her side. She is smoking a cigarette and never looks at the man who is no more than a few yards from her.

"She's holding out," somebody reports. "Who can blame her. Why should she live in a godforsaken Canadian village with somebody like him."

"He says Canada has a legal system," another bulletin informs us. "He says he wants his money back for the ticket. And for the dog's, too."

Lila comes up to me, and we discuss the situation for a while. "Of course, she married him just because she wanted to get out of Poland" is Lila's authoritative opinion. "But now that she's made her bed, she should sleep in it. Which doesn't mean she can't sleep in others," she concludes archly.

By midafternoon, the ship's loudspeakers begin to summon

Irena, repeating her name in more and more peremptory tones. She has half an hour to make up her mind. At dusk, the whole ship gathers to watch her fur-coated figure step down the gangplank and walk on without looking at her husband, who turns with an angry movement and follows her into the wooden building.

The melodrama over, the crowd disperses to its private affairs, and I wander into the lounge—where I see something that stops me in my tracks. The Dane, all alone in the room except for a chaos of overthrown furniture, is doing a sort of furious dance with a chair, which he is about to throw at the wall. He notices me, though, and stops himself in midmovement. For a moment, we stare at each other expressionlessly. His face is flushed, he smells of alcohol, and his eyes are the brightest, clearest blue I've ever seen.

I think of Irena and the Dane in later years, and I try to accomplish the difficult trick of imagining a plausible reality for these half-real imagos. Has the Dane become Claus von Bülow? Or did he go back to Denmark, to his wife and job? And what of Irena? Is she now baby powder's Basia Johnson? I meet women like her often in my adult life—attractive, charming Polish women who come to "America" to seek their fortunes. They are usually impressively resourceful, with the spunk of those who play the game for all it's worth, because there's so little to lose and so much to gain. They are unhesitant in using their sexuality to advance themselves in the world, and they often marry for money or take lovers who can assist them in their careers. They do so with the self-confidence of women who are used to being the object of desire and who can clearhead-edly separate strategy from feeling. I admire this gambling wit, which, with the moralism I've acquired in America about sex and the sentiments, I could never imitate. But not all of them, of course, end up with prosperous mates or court settlements of $390 million. Perhaps Irena is a comfortable hausfrau in a Canadian town, the vivacious foreigner who runs her household efficiently and grows pansies and sweet peas in her garden. I know those women too, women whose bravado is more hidden and whose secret personali-ties come out only infrequently—women whose odd fates zigzag throughout the continent in idiosyncratic patterns. There are models for immigrant fates, as for all others, though I doubt that any of them feels entirely natural to those who live them.

But I have no map or model in my mind as I stand at the railing disconsolately, and the *Batory,* after having waited for Irena's decision, begins moving again. The next morning, standing with my parents and my sister in a crowd at the ship's prow, I discern the outlines of massive, gray shapes against the cloudy sky. Closer still, the shapes resolve into buildings, tall and monolithic to my eyes. Montreal. It actually exists, more powerful than any figment of the imagination. We look at the approaching city wordlessly. The brief *Batory* interlude is over, and so is the narrative of my childhood.

Part II

EXILE

We are in Montreal, in an echoing, dark train station, and we are huddled on a bench waiting for someone to give us some guidance. Timidly, I walk a few steps away from my parents to explore this terra incognita, and I come back with snippets of amazing news. There is this young girl, maybe my age, in high-heeled shoes and lipstick! She looks so vulgar, I complain. Or maybe this is just some sort of costume? There is also a black man at whom I stare for a while; he's as handsome as Harry Belafonte, the only black man whose face I know from pictures in Polish magazines, except here he is, big as life. Are all black men this handsome, I wonder?

Eventually, a man speaking broken Polish approaches us, takes us to the ticket window, and then helps us board our train. And so begins yet another segment of this longest journey—all the longer because we don't exactly know when it will end, when we'll reach our destination. We only know that Vancouver is very far away.

The people on the train look at us askance, and avoid sitting close to us. This may be because we've brought suitcases full of dried cake, canned sardines, and sausages, which would keep during the long transatlantic journey. We don't know about dining cars, and when we discover that this train has such a thing, we can hardly afford to go there once a day on the few dollars that my father has brought with him. Two dollars could buy a bicycle, or several pairs of shoes in Poland. It seems like a great deal to pay for four bowls of soup.

The train cuts through endless expanses of terrain, most of it flat and monotonous, and it seems to me that the relentless rhythm of the wheels is like scissors cutting a three-thousand-mile rip through my life. From now on, my life will be divided into two parts, with the line drawn by that train. After a while, I subside into a silent indifference, and I don't want to look at the landscape anymore; these are not the friendly fields, the farmyards of Polish countryside; this is vast, dull, and formless. By the time we reach the Rockies, my parents try to pull me out of my stupor and make me look at the spectacular landscapes we're passing by. But I don't want to. These peaks and ravines, these mountain streams and enormous boulders hurt my eyes—they hurt my soul. They're too big, too forbidding, and I can't imagine feeling that I'm part of them, that I'm in them. I recede into sleep; I sleep through the day and the night, and my parents can't shake me out of it. My sister, perhaps recoiling even more deeply from all this strangeness, is in a state of feverish illness and can hardly raise her head.

On the second day, we briefly meet a passenger who speaks Yiddish. My father enters into an animated conversation with him and learns some thrilling tales. For example, there's the story of a Polish Jew who came to Canada and made a fortune—he's now a millionaire!—on producing Polish pickles. Pickles! If one can make a fortune on that, well—it shouldn't be hard to get rich in this country. My father is energized, excited by this story, but I subside into an even more determined sullenness. "Millionaire" is one of those fairy-tale words that has no meaning to me whatsoever—a word like "emigration" or "Canada." In spite of my parents' protestations, I go back to sleep, and I miss some of the most prized sights on the North American continent.

By the time we've reached Vancouver, there are very few people
left on the train. My mother has dressed my sister and me in our
best outfits—identical navy blue dresses with sailor collars and gray
coats handmade of good gabardine. My parents' faces reflect anticipation and anxiety. "Get off the train on the right foot," my mother
tells us. "For luck in the new life."

I look out of the train window with a heavy heart. Where have
I been brought to? As the train approaches the station, I see what
is indeed a bit of nowhere. It's a drizzly day, and the platform is
nearly empty. Everything is the color of slate. From this bleakness,
two figures approach us—a nondescript middle-aged man and
woman—and after making sure that we are the right people, the
arrivals from the other side of the world, they hug us; but I don't
feel much warmth in their half-embarrassed embrace. "You should
kneel down and kiss the ground," the man tells my parents.
"You're lucky to be here." My parents' faces fill with a kind of
naïve hope. Perhaps everything will be well after all. They need
signs, portents, at this hour.

Then we all get into an enormous car—yes, this is America—
and drive into the city that is to be our home.

The Rosenbergs' house is a matter of utter bafflement to me. This
one-story structure surrounded by a large garden surely doesn't
belong in a city—but neither can it be imagined in the country. The
garden itself is of such pruned and trimmed neatness that I'm half
afraid to walk in it. Its lawn is improbably smooth and velvety (Ah,
the time and worry spent on the shaving of these lawns! But I will
only learn of that later), and the rows of marigolds, the circles of
geraniums seem almost artificial in their perfect symmetries, in their
subordination to orderliness.

Still, I much prefer sitting out here in the sun to being inside.
The house is larger than any apartment I have seen in Poland, with
enormous "picture" windows, a separate room for every member
of the family and soft pastel-colored rugs covering all the floors.
These are all features that, I know, are intended to signify good

taste and wealth—but there's an incongruity between the message I'm supposed to get and my secret perceptions of these surroundings. To me, these interiors seem oddly flat, devoid of imagination, ingenuous. The spaces are so plain, low-ceilinged, obvious; there are no curves, niches, odd angles, nooks or crannies—nothing that gathers a house into itself, giving it a sense of privacy, or of depth—of interiority. There's no solid wood here, no accretion either of age or dust. There is only the open sincerity of the simple spaces, open right out to the street. (No peering out the window here, to catch glimpses of exchanges on the street; the picture windows are designed to give everyone full view of everyone else, to declare there's no mystery, nothing to hide. Not true, of course, but that's the statement.) There is also the disingenuousness of the furniture, all of it whitish with gold trimming. The whole thing is too revealing of an aspiration to good taste, but the unintended effect is thin and insubstantial—as if it was planned and put up just yesterday, and could just as well be dismantled tomorrow. The only rooms that really impress me are the bathroom and the kitchen—both of them so shiny, polished, and full of unfamiliar, fabulously functional appliances that they remind me of interiors which we occasionally glimpsed in French or American movies, and which, in our bedraggled Poland, we couldn't distinguish from fantasy. "Do you think people really live like this?" we would ask after one of these films, neglecting all the drama of the plot for the interest of these incidental features. Here is something worth describing to my friends in Cracow, down to such mind-boggling details as a shaggy rug in the bathroom and toilet paper that comes in different colors.

For the few days we stay at the Rosenbergs', we are relegated to the basement, where there's an extra apartment usually rented out to lodgers. My father looks up to Mr. Rosenberg with the respect, even a touch of awe due to someone who is a certified millionaire. Mr. Rosenberg is a big man in the small Duddy Kravitz community of Polish Jews, most of whom came to Canada shortly after the war, and most of whom have made good in junk peddling and real estate—but none as good as he. Mr. Rosenberg, who is now almost seventy, had the combined chutzpah and good luck to ride on Vancouver's real-estate boom—and now he's the richest of them all. This hardly makes him the most popular, but it automatically makes him the wisest. People from the community come to him for business advice, which he dispenses, in Yiddish, as if it were precious currency given away for free only through his grandiose generosity.

In the uncompromising vehemence of adolescence and injured pride, I begin to see Mr. Rosenberg not as our benefactor but as a Dickensian figure of personal tyranny, and my feeling toward him quickly rises to something that can only be called hate. He has made stinginess into principle; I feel it as a nonhuman hardness, a conversion of flesh and feeling into stone. His face never lights up with humor or affection or wit. But then, he takes himself very seriously; to him too his wealth is the proof of his righteousness. In accordance with his principles, he demands money for our train tickets from Montreal as soon as we arrive. I never forgive him. We've brought gifts we thought handsome, but in addition, my father gives him all the dollars he accumulated in Poland—something that would start us off in Canada, we thought, but is now all gone. We'll have to scratch out our living somehow, starting from zero: my father begins to pinch the flesh of his arms nervously.

Mrs. Rosenberg, a worn-faced, nearly inarticulate, diffident woman, would probably show us more generosity were she not so intimidated by her husband. As it is, she and her daughter, Diane, feed us white bread with sliced cheese and bologna for lunch, and laugh at our incredulity at the mushy textures, the plastic wrapping, the presliced convenience of the various items. Privately, we comment that this is not real food: it has no taste, it smells of plastic. The two women also give us clothing they can no longer use. I can't imagine a state of affairs in which one would want to discard the delicate, transparent bathrobes and the angora sweaters they pass on to us, but luscious though these items seem—beyond anything I ever hoped to own—the show of gratitude required from me on receiving them sours the pleasure of new ownership. "Say thank you," my mother prompts me in preparation for receiving a batch of clothing. "People like to be appreciated." I coo and murmur ingratiatingly; I'm beginning to master the trick of saying thank you with just the right turn of the head, just the right balance between modesty and obsequiousness. In the next few years, this is a skill I'll have to use often. But in my heart I feel no real gratitude at being the recipient of so much mercy.

On about the third night at the Rosenbergs' house, I have a nightmare in which I'm drowning in the ocean while my mother and father swim farther and farther away from me. I know, in this dream, what it is to be cast adrift in incomprehensible space; I know what it is to lose one's mooring. I wake up in the middle of a prolonged scream. The fear is stronger than anything I've ever known. My parents wake up and hush me up quickly; they don't want the Rosenbergs to hear this disturbing sound. I try to calm myself and go back to sleep, but I feel as though I've stepped through a door into a dark place. Psychoanalysts talk about "mutative insights," through which the patient gains an entirely new perspective and discards some part of a cherished neurosis. The primal scream of my birth into the New World is a mutative insight of a negative kind—and I know that I can never lose the knowledge it brings me. The black, bituminous terror of the dream solders itself to the chemical base of my being—and from then on, fragments of the fear lodge themselves in my consciousness, thorns and pinpricks of anxiety, loose electricity floating in a psyche that has been forcibly pried from its structures. Eventually, I become accustomed to it; I know that it comes, and that it also goes; but when it hits with full force, in its pure form, I call it the Big Fear.

After about a week of lodging us in his house, Mr. Rosenberg decides that he has done enough for us, and, using some acquired American wisdom, explains that it isn't good for us to be dependent on his charity: there is of course no question of kindness. There is no question, either, of Mrs. Rosenberg intervening on our behalf, as she might like to do. We have no place to go, no way to pay for a meal. And so we begin.

"Shut up, shuddup," the children around us are shouting, and it's the first word in English that I understand from its dramatic context.

My sister and I stand in the schoolyard clutching each other, while kids all around us are running about, pummeling each other, and screaming like whirling dervishes. Both the boys and the girls look sharp and aggressive to me—the girls all have bright lipstick on, their hair sticks up and out like witches' fury, and their skirts are held up and out by stiff, wiry crinolines. I can't imagine wanting to talk their harsh-sounding language.

We've been brought to this school by Mr. Rosenberg, who, two days after our arrival, tells us he'll take us to classes that are provided by the government to teach English to newcomers. This morning, in the rinky-dink wooden barracks where the classes are held, we've acquired new names. All it takes is a brief conference between Mr. Rosenberg and the teacher, a kindly looking woman who tries to give us reassuring glances, but who has seen too many people come and go to get sentimental about a name. Mine—"Ewa"—is easy to change into its near equivalent in English, "Eva." My sister's name—"Alina"—poses more of a problem, but after a moment's thought, Mr. Rosenberg and the teacher decide that "Elaine" is close enough. My sister and I hang our heads wordlessly under this careless baptism. The teacher then introduces us to the class, mispronouncing our last name—"Wydra"—in a way we've never heard before. We make our way to a bench at the back of the room; nothing much has happened, except a small, seismic mental shift. The twist in our names takes them a tiny distance from us—but it's a gap into which the infinite hobgoblin of abstraction enters. Our Polish names didn't refer to us; they were as surely us as our eyes or hands. These new appellations, which we ourselves can't yet pronounce, are not us. They are identification tags, disembodied signs pointing to objects that happen to be my sister and myself. We walk to our seats, into a roomful of unknown faces, with names that make us strangers to ourselves.

When the school day is over, the teacher hands us a file card on which she has written, "I'm a newcomer. I'm lost. I live at 1785 Granville Street. Will you kindly show me how to get there? Thank you." We wander the streets for several hours, zigzagging back and forth through seemingly identical suburban avenues, showing this deaf-mute sign to the few people we see, until we eventually recognize the Rosenbergs' house. We're greeted by our quietly hysterical mother and Mrs. Rosenberg, who, in a ritual she has probably learned from television, puts out two glasses of milk on her red Formica counter. The milk, homogenized, and too cold from the fridge, bears little resemblance to the liquid we used to drink called by the same name.

Every day I learn new words, new expressions. I pick them up from school exercises, from conversations, from the books I take out of Vancouver's well-lit, cheerful public library. There are some turns of phrase to which I develop strange allergies. "You're welcome," for example, strikes me as a boucherie, and I can hardly bring myself to say it—I suppose because it implies that there's something to be thanked for, which in Polish would be impolite. The very places where language is at its most conventional, where it should be most taken for granted, are the places where I feel the prick of artifice.

Then there are words to which I take an equally irrational liking, for their sound, or just because I'm pleased to have deduced their meaning. Mainly they're words I learn from books, like "enigmatic" or "insolent"—words that have only a literary value, that exist only as signs on the page.

But mostly, the problem is that the signifier has become severed from the signified. The words I learn now don't stand for things in the same unquestioned way they did in my native tongue. "River" in Polish was a vital sound, energized with the essence of riverhood, of my rivers, of my being immersed in rivers. "River" in English is cold—a word without an aura. It has no accumulated associations for me, and it does not give off the radiating haze of connotation. It does not evoke.

The process, alas, works in reverse as well. When I see a river now, it is not shaped, assimilated by the word that accommodates it to the psyche—a word that makes a body of water a river rather than an uncontained element. The river before me remains a thing, absolutely other, absolutely unbending to the grasp of my mind.

When my friend Penny tells me that she's envious, or happy, or disappointed, I try laboriously to translate not from English to Polish but from the word back to its source, to the feeling from which it springs. Already, in that moment of strain, spontaneity of response is lost. And anyway, the translation doesn't work. I don't know how Penny feels when she talks about envy. The word hangs in a Platonic stratosphere, a vague prototype of all envy, so large, so all-encompassing that it might crush me—as might disappointment or happiness.

I am becoming a living avatar of structuralist wisdom; I cannot help knowing that words are just themselves. But it's a terrible knowledge, without any of the consolations that wisdom usually brings. It does not mean that I'm free to play with words at my wont; anyway, words in their naked state are surely among the least satisfactory play objects. No, this radical disjoining between word and thing is a desiccating alchemy, draining the world not only of significance but of its colors, striations, nuances—its very existence. It is the loss of a living connection.

The worst losses come at night. As I lie down in a strange bed in a strange house—my mother is a sort of housekeeper here, to the aging Jewish man who has taken us in in return for her services—I wait for that spontaneous flow of inner language which used to be my nighttime talk with myself, my way of informing the ego where the id had been. Nothing comes. Polish, in a short time, has atrophied, shriveled from sheer uselessness. Its words don't apply to my new experiences; they're not coeval with any of the objects, or faces, or the very air I breathe in the daytime. In English, words have not penetrated to those layers of my psyche from which a private conversation could proceed. This interval before sleep used to be the time when my mind became both receptive and alert, when images and words rose up to consciousness, reiterating what had happened during the day, adding the day's experiences to those already stored there, spinning out the thread of my personal story.

Now, this picture-and-word show is gone; the thread has been

snapped. I have no interior language, and without it, interior images—those images through which we assimilate the external
world, through which we take it in, love it, make it our own—
become blurred too. My mother and I met a Canadian family who
live down the block today. They were working in their garden and
engaged us in a conversation of the "Nice weather we're having,
isn't it?" variety, which culminated in their inviting us into their
house. They sat stiffly on their couch, smiled in the long pauses
between the conversation, and seemed at a loss for what to ask.
Now my mind gropes for some description of them, but nothing
fits. They're a different species from anyone I've met in Poland, and
Polish words slip off of them without sticking. English words don't
hook on to anything. I try, deliberately, to come up with a few. Are
these people pleasant or dull? Kindly or silly? The words float in
an uncertain space. They come up from a part of my brain in which
labels may be manufactured but which has no connection to my
instincts, quick reactions, knowledge. Even the simplest adjectives
sow confusion in my mind; English kindliness has a whole system
of morality behind it, a system that makes "kindness" an entirely
positive virtue. Polish kindness has the tiniest element of irony.
Besides, I'm beginning to feel the tug of prohibition, in English,
against uncharitable words. In Polish, you can call someone an idiot
without particularly harsh feelings and with the zest of a strong
judgment. Yes, in Polish these people might tend toward "silly"
and "dull"—but I force myself toward "kindly" and "pleasant."
The cultural unconscious is beginning to exercise its subliminal
influence.

The verbal blur covers these people's faces, their gestures with
a sort of fog. I can't translate them into my mind's eye. The small
event, instead of being added to the mosaic of consciousness and
memory, falls through some black hole, and I fall with it. What has
happened to me in this new world? I don't know. I don't see what
I've seen, don't comprehend what's in front of me. I'm not filled
with language anymore, and I have only a memory of fullness to
anguish me with the knowledge that, in this dark and empty state,
I don't really exist.

. . .

Mrs. Lieberman, in the bathroom of her house, is shaving my armpits. She has taken me there at the end of her dinner party, and now, with a kind decisiveness, she lifts my arms and performs this foreign ablution on the tufts of hair that have never been objectionable to anyone before. She hasn't asked me whether I would like her to do it; she has simply taken it upon herself to teach me how things are done here.

Mrs. Lieberman is among several Polish ladies who have been in Canada long enough to consider themselves well versed in native ways, and who seem to find me deficient in some quite fundamental respects. Since in Poland I was considered a pretty young girl, this requires a basic revision of my self-image. But there's no doubt about it; after the passage across the Atlantic, I've emerged as less attractive, less graceful, less desirable. In fact, I can see in these women's eyes that I'm a somewhat pitiful specimen—pale, with thick eyebrows, and without any bounce in my hair, dressed in clothes that have nothing to do with the current fashion. And so they energetically set out to rectify these flaws. One of them spends a day with me, plucking my eyebrows and trying various shades of lipstick on my face. "If you were my daughter, you'd soon look like a princess," she says, thus implying an added deficiency in my mother. Another counselor takes me into her house for an evening, to initiate me into the mysteries of using shampoos and hair lotions, and putting my hair up in curlers; yet another outfits me with a crinoline and tells me that actually, I have a perfectly good figure—I just need to bring it out in the right ways. And several of them look at my breasts meaningfully, suggesting to my mother in an undertone that really, it's time I started wearing a bra. My mother obeys.

I obey too, passively, mulishly, but I feel less agile and self-confident with every transformation. I hold my head rigidly, so that my precarious bouffant doesn't fall down, and I smile often, the way I see other girls do, though I'm careful not to open my lips too wide or bite them, so my lipstick won't get smudged. I don't know how to move easily in the high-heeled shoes somebody gave me.

Inside its elaborate packaging, my body is stiff, sulky, wary. When I'm with my peers, who come by crinolines, lipstick, cars, and self-confidence naturally, my gestures show that I'm here provisionally, by their grace, that I don't rightfully belong. My shoulders stoop, I nod frantically to indicate my agreement with others, I smile sweetly at people to show I mean well, and my chest recedes inward so that I don't take up too much space—mannerisms of a marginal, off-centered person who wants both to be taken in and to fend off the threatening others.

About a year after our arrival in Vancouver, someone takes a photograph of my family in their backyard, and looking at it, I reject the image it gives of myself categorically. This clumsy looking creature, with legs oddly turned in their high-heeled pumps, shoulders bent with the strain of resentment and ingratiation, is not myself. Alienation is beginning to be inscribed in my flesh and face.

I'm sitting at the Steiners' kitchen table, surrounded by sounds of family jokes and laughter. I laugh along gamely, though half the time I don't understand what's going on.

Mrs. Steiner, who is Polish, has semiadopted me, and I spend whole days and weekends in her house, where I'm half exiled princess, half Cinderella. Half princess, because I'm musically talented and, who knows, I may become a famous pianist one day. Mrs. Steiner was an aspiring pianist herself in her youth, and she takes pleasure in supervising my musical progress: she has found a piano teacher for me, and often listens to me play. However, the Steiners are fabulously rich, and I am, at this point in my life, quite fabulously poor—and those basic facts condition everything; they are as palpable as a tilted beam that indicates the incline between us, never letting me forget the basic asymmetry of the relationship.

The Steiners' wealth is quite beyond the Rosenbergs', and quite beyond my conception of actual human lives. It exists on some step of the social ladder that jumps clear out of my head, and I can't domesticate its owners to ordinary personhood. Surely, the rich must be different. If I feel like a fairy-tale character near them, it's because they live in the realm of fable. Rosa Steiner is a stepmother with the power to change my destiny for good or evil. Mr. Steiner simply rules over his dominion, quietly, calmly, and remotely. I wouldn't dream of revealing myself to him, of making an imposition on his attention.

This is, of course, only one part of the story, though it is the part of which I am painfully conscious. Stefan Steiner accepts my presence in his domestic life graciously. And as for Rosa, she is, aside from everything else, a friend who understands where I come from—metaphorically and literally—better than anyone else I know in Vancouver. In turn, there is something in her I recognize and trust. She is a vivacious, energetic woman in her forties, beautiful in a high-cheekboned, Eastern European way, with a deep, hoarse voice and with a great certainty of her own opinions, judgments, and preferences. She reminds me of the authoritative women I knew in Poland, who did not seem as inhibited, as insistently "feminine" as the women I meet here. Her views are utterly commonsensical: she believes that people should try to get as much pleasure, approval, money, achievement, and good looks as they can. She has no use for eccentricity, ambivalence, or self-doubt. Her own task and destiny is carrying on the tradition of ordinary life—and she goes about it with great vigor and style. Except for the all-important disparate income, her inner world is not so different, after all, from my parents'. The disparity means that she's the fulfilled bourgeoise, while they've been relegated to aspiration and failure. It is her fulfillment, I suppose—yes, our feelings can be cruel—that reassures me. When I'm near her, I feel that satisfaction and contentment are surely possible—more, that they're everyone's inalienable right—possibly even mine.

Mrs. Steiner's snobberies are as resolute as everything else about her. She too believes there are "better people"—people who are successful, smart, and, most of all, cultured. She envisions her house as a kind of salon, to which she invites groups of Vancouver's elect; sometimes, on these occasions, I'm recruited to raise the tone of the proceedings and perhaps advance my own fortunes by playing some Beethoven or Chopin. The Steiners' house, which overlooks both the sea and the mountains of Vancouver's harbor, is surrounded by large expanses of grounds and garden; inside, there are contemporary paintings, grand pianos, and enormous pieces of Eskimo sculpture. I don't know whether I like any of this unfamiliar art, but I know that's quite beside the point.

Mrs. Steiner takes me to her house often, and I'm happiest there when I'm with her alone. Then we talk for hours on end, mostly about my problems and my life. I'm a little ashamed to reveal how hard things are for my family—how bitterly my parents quarrel, how much my mother cries, how frightened I am by our helplessness, and by the burden of feeling that it is my duty to take charge, to get us out of this quagmire. But I can't help myself, it's too much of a relief to talk to somebody who is curious and sensitive to my concerns. Although her sensitivity has its limits: she cannot always make the leap of empathy across our differences. My mother's voice on the telephone ("She always sounds as if there's something wrong. Sometimes she speaks so softly I have to tell her to speak up.") bothers her. And when my father quits his job at a lumber mill, Rosa is full of disapproval; he has a family to support, she tells me; isn't this a bit irresponsible? Suddenly, I feel the full bitterness of our situation. My father is no longer very young, I tell her; the job was the hardest in the mill. He had to lift heavy logs all day—and he has a bad back, the legacy of the war. He was in pain every day. Rosa is abashed by my sudden eruption, and she retreats. She didn't know all this, she says; of course, I may be right. But there is added irony in this exchange, which isn't lost on either of us: the Steiners own a lumber mill. In the Steiner kitchen, I've heard mention of the problems they've sometimes had with their workers.

Still, I can speak to Rosa frankly; we can hash this sort of thing out. But some of the ease of our exchange vanishes when other members of the family enter the scene. Mrs. Steiner is fiercely devoted to her daughters, and in her eyes they are princesses pure and simple. I believe her; what else can I do? I'm both too shy and too removed from their lives to check out what I think of them for myself. Elisabeth, the older one, has just started going to a small, elite college—a place of which I can only gather that there are

extremely interesting young people there, most of them near geniuses, and that Elisabeth has occasionally taken to wearing odd
garments, like Mexican skirts and black stockings. Elisabeth talks
without fully opening her mouth and swallows the endings of her
words—so that I can understand her even less than most people,
and I find myself saying "I beg your pardon" so often, that finally
it becomes more polite to pretend I know what she's saying than
to keep repeating the question.

Laurie is only two years older than myself, and she tries to
befriend me. She often comes to our house—I invariably fight
embarrassment at its stripped-down bareness—to drive me to the
Steiners', and on the way there she talks about herself. Much of the
time, it takes an enormous effort on my part to follow her fast
chatter and to keep saying yes and no in the right places, to attempt
to respond. I try to cover up this virtual idiocy by looking as
intelligent as I can. But I do gather from these conversations that
Laurie has just been at some international camp in Austria, that she
will travel in Europe the following summer, that her parents differ
from others in giving her affection and care—she has many friends
whose parents try to compensate with money for their basic indifference. Isn't that terrible? I try, at this point, to look properly
sympathetic, but the scale of problems she describes is so vastly
different from what I know, and our mutual incapacity to penetrate
each other's experience is so evident to me, that I harden myself
against her. If I were really to enter her world, if I were really to
imagine its difficulties, I would be condemned to an envy so burning that it would turn to hate. My only defense against the indignity
of such emotion is to avoid rigorously the thought of wanting what
she has—to keep her at a long, safe distance.

In the evening, we sit down to a family dinner and its jokey
banter—an American ritual meant to sharpen the young women's
edges for their encounters with the world and to affirm their superiority in that world. The Steiners, led by Laurie, who is clever and
quick, are teasing each other, each bit of witty attack a verbal glove
challenging the others to up the ante. I feel miserably out of it,
laughing too loud, but knowing that I can't enter the teasing circle.

After all, Cinderella can't get snarky with her half sisters, can she? I can only approve; I can't even implicitly criticize—and this seems almost as basic a definition of my position as the lack of money. Razzing can only happen between equals or else it's a deliberate presumption, which brings attention to inferior status. But I'm too proud to engage in this latter kind.

I've had a nice day in the Steiner household; Rosa and I took a long, brisk walk, we ate an excellent lunch, I played the piano for her and she made some comments, and now I'm sitting at their kitchen table, to all appearances almost a family member. When I get home, I'm terribly depressed. There's a yellow light in the downstairs room where my mother is waiting for me; my father, I know, will have fallen asleep in a stupor of disorientation and fatigue. But when my mother asks me about my day with a curiosity that pains me—she almost never gets invited to the Steiners'—I only tell her what a wonderful time I had.

In later years, I'll come to sit at the Steiners' table often, and look back on the polite and rankled girl I was then and flinch a little at the narrowing of sympathies I felt in my narrow straits. I'll come to know that Laurie might have been jealous of me, might have feared, even, that I would displace her in her mother's affections—but I could not imagine then that I could rouse jealousy in anyone. I'll see how much time and attention and goodwill the Steiners lavished on me, more than in our busy and overfilled lives people can give to each other nowadays. Really, they thought about me more seriously than I thought about myself. Who was I, after all? Eva's ghost, perhaps, a specter that tried not to occupy too much space. They were more generous toward me than I was toward them; but then, a sense of disadvantage and inferiority is not a position from which one can feel the largeheartedness of true generosity.

In *Speak, Memory*, Nabokov makes the poetic, or the playful, speculation that Russian children before the Revolution—and his exile—were blessed with a surfeit of sensual impressions to compensate them for what was to come. Of course, fate doesn't play such premonitory games, but memory can perform retrospective maneuvers to compensate for fate. Loss is a magical preservative. Time stops at the point of severance, and no subsequent impressions muddy the picture you have in mind. The house, the garden, the country you have lost remain forever as you remember them. Nostalgia—that most lyrical of feelings—crystallizes around these images like amber. Arrested within it, the house, the past, is clear, vivid, made more beautiful by the medium in which it is held and by its stillness.

Nostalgia is a source of poetry, and a form of fidelity. It is also a species of melancholia, which used to be thought of as an illness. As I walk the streets of Vancouver, I am pregnant with the images of Poland, pregnant and sick. *Tęsknota* throws a film over everything around me, and directs my vision inward. The largest presence within me is the welling up of absence, of what I have lost. This pregnancy is also a phantom pain.

I don't know what to do with this private heaviness, this pregnancy without the possibility of birth. "She's so loyal," Mrs. Steiner says when I tell her that Mrs. Witeszczak was a wonderful piano teacher. There is a hint of criticism in the supposed compliment; the methods of piano teaching are after all more advanced here, Mrs. Steiner suggests, and I should not cling to the ways of the past. That makes me want to defend Mrs. Witeszczak even more. Not everything there is old-fashioned, not everything here better! But everyone encourages me to forget what I left behind. It wasn't any good back there, our Jewish acquaintances say, why would you even want to visit, they didn't want you anyway. I hang my head stubbornly under the lash of this wisdom. Can I really extract what I've been from myself so easily? Can I jump continents as if skipping rope?

In our highly ideological times, even nostalgia has its politics. The conservatives of the sentiments believe that recovering their own forgotten history is an antidote to shallowness. The ideologues of the future see attachment to the past as that most awful of all monsters, the agent of reaction. It is to be extracted from the human soul with no quarter or self-pity, for it obstructs the inevitable march of events into the next Utopia. Only certain Eastern European writers, forced to march into the future too often, know the regressive dangers of both forgetfulness and clinging to the past. But then, they are among our world's experts of mourning, having lost not an archaeological but a living history. And so, they praise the virtues of a true memory. Nabokov unashamedly reinvokes and revives his childhood in the glorious colors of *tęsknota*. Milan Kundera knows that a person who forgets easily is a Don Juan of experience, promiscuous and repetitive, suffering from the unbearable lightness of being. Czeslaw Milosz remembers the people and places of his youth with the special tenderness reserved for objects of love that are no longer cherished by others.

"Dear Basia," I write, "I am sitting at a window looking out on a garden in which there is a cherry tree, an apple tree, and bushes of roses now in bloom. The roses are smaller and wilder here, but imagine! All this in the middle of a city. And tomorrow I am going to a party. There are parties here all the time, and my social life is, you might say, blooming." I am repeating a ritual performed by countless immigrants who have sent letters back home meant to impress and convince their friends and relatives— and probably even themselves—that their lives have changed for the better. I am lying. But I am also trying to fend off my nostalgia. I couldn't repudiate the past even if I wanted to, but what can I do with it here, where it doesn't exist? After a while, I begin to push the images of memory down, away from consciousness, below emotion. Relegated to an internal darkness, they increase the area of darkness within me, and they return in the dark, in my dreams. I dream of Cracow perpetually, winding my way through familiar-unfamiliar streets, looking for a way home. I almost get there, repeatedly; almost, but not quite, and I wake up with the city so close that I can breathe it in.

I can't afford to look back, and I can't figure out how to look forward. In both directions, I may see a Medusa, and I already feel the danger of being turned into stone. Betwixt and between, I am stuck and time is stuck within me. Time used to open out, serene, shimmering with promise. If I wanted to hold a moment still, it was because I wanted to expand it, to get its fill. Now, time has no dimension, no extension backward or forward. I arrest the past, and I hold myself stiffly against the future; I want to stop the flow. As a punishment, I exist in the stasis of a perpetual present, that other side of "living in the present," which is not eternity but a prison. I can't throw a bridge between the present and the past, and therefore I can't make time move.

The car is full of my new friends, or at least the crowd that has more or less accepted me as one of their own, the odd "greener" tagalong. They're as lively as a group of puppies, jostling each other with sharp elbows, crawling over each other to change seats, and expressing their well-being and amiability by trying to outshout each other. It's Saturday night, or rather Saturday Night, and party spirits are obligatory. We're on our way to the local White Spot, an early Canadian version of McDonald's, where we'll engage in the barbarous—as far as I'm concerned—rite of the "drive-in." This activity of sitting in your car in a large parking lot, and having sloppy, big hamburgers brought to you on a tray, accompanied by greasy french fries bounding out of their cardboard containers, mustard, spilly catsup, and sickly smelling relish, seems to fill these peers of mine with warm, monkeyish, groupy comfort. It fills me with a finicky distaste. I feel my lips tighten into an unaccustomed thinness—which, in turn, fills me with a small dislike for myself.

"Come on, foreign student, cheer up," one of the boys sporting a flowery Hawaiian shirt and a crew cut tells me, poking me in the ribs good-naturedly. "What's the matter, don't you like it here?" So as the car caroms off, I try to get in the mood. I try to giggle coyly as the girls exchange insinuating glances—though usually my titter comes a telling second too late. I try to join in the general hilarity, as somebody tells the latest elephant joke. Then— it's always a mistake to try too hard—I decide to show my goodwill by telling a joke myself. Finding some interruption in which to insert my uncertain voice, I launch into a translation of some slightly off-color anecdote I'd heard my father tell in Polish, no doubt hoping to get points for being risqué as well as a good sport. But as I hear my choked-up voice straining to assert itself, as I hear myself missing every beat and rhythm that would say "funny" and "punch line," I feel a hot flush of embarrassment. I come to a lame ending. There's a silence. "I suppose that's supposed to be funny," somebody says. I recede into the car seat.

Ah, the humiliation, the misery of failing to amuse! The incident is as rankling to my amour propre as being told I'm graceless or ugly. Telling a joke is like doing a linguistic pirouette. If you fall flat, it means not only that you don't have the wherewithal to do it well but also that you have misjudged your own skill, that you are fool enough to undertake something you can't finish—and that lack of self-control or self-knowledge is a lack of grace.

But these days, it takes all my will to impose any control on the words that emerge from me. I have to form entire sentences before uttering them; otherwise, I too easily get lost in the middle. My speech, I sense, sounds monotonous, deliberate, heavy—an aural mask that doesn't become me or express me at all. This willed self-control is the opposite of real mastery, which comes from a trust in your own verbal powers and allows for a free streaming of speech, for those bursts of spontaneity, the quickness of response that can rise into pleasure and overflow in humor. Laughter is the lightning rod of play, the eroticism of conversation; for now, I've lost the ability to make the sparks fly.

I've never been prim before, but that's how I am seen by my new peers. I don't try to tell jokes too often, I don't know the slang, I have no cool repartee. I love language too much to maul its beats, and my pride is too quick to risk the incomprehension that greets such forays. I become a very serious young person, missing the registers of wit and irony in my speech, though my mind sees ironies everywhere.

If primness is a small recoil of distaste at things that give others simple and hearty pleasure, then prim is what I'm really becoming. Although I'm not brave enough or hermit enough to stay home by myself every night, I'm a pretend teenager among the real stuff. There's too much in this car I don't like; I don't like the blue eye shadow on Cindy's eyelids, or the grease on Chuck's hair, or the way the car zooms off with a screech and then slows down as everyone plays we're-afraid-of-the-policeman. I don't like the way they laugh. I don't care for their "ugly" jokes, or their five-hundred-pound canary jokes, or their pickle jokes, or their elephant jokes either. And most of all, I hate having to pretend.

Perhaps the extra knot that strangles my voice is rage. I am enraged at the false persona I'm being stuffed into, as into some clumsy and overblown astronaut suit. I'm enraged at my adolescent friends because they can't see through the guise, can't recognize the light-footed dancer I really am. They only see this elephantine creature who too often sounds as if she's making pronouncements.

It will take years before I pick and choose, from the Babel of American language, the style of wit that fits. It will take years of practice before its nuances and patterns snap smartly into the synapses of my brain so they can generate verbal electricity. It will take years of observing the discreet sufferings of the corporate classes before I understand the equally discreet charm of *New Yorker* cartoons.

For now, when I come across a *New Yorker* issue, I stare at the drawings of well-heeled people expressing some dissatisfaction with their condition as yet another demonstration of the weirdness all around me. "What's funny about that?" my mother asks in puzzlement. "I don't know," I answer, and we both shrug and shake our heads. And, as the car veers through Vancouver's neatly shrubberied and sparsely populated streets, I know that, among my other faculties, I've lost my sense of humor. I am not about to convert my adolescent friends to anti-Russian jokes. I swallow my injury, and giggle falsely at the five-hundred-pound canary.

Happy as larks, we lurch toward the White Spot.

If you had stayed there, your hair would have been straight, and you would have worn a barrette on one side.

But maybe by now you would have grown it into a ponytail? Like the ones you saw on those sexy faces in the magazine you used to read?

I don't know. You would have been fifteen by now. Different from thirteen.

You would be going to the movies with Zbyszek, and maybe to a café after, where you would meet a group of friends and talk late into the night.

But maybe you would be having problems with Mother and Father. They wouldn't like your staying out late.

That would have been fun. Normal. Oh God, to be a young person trying to get away from her parents.

But you can't do that. You have to take care of them. Besides, with whom would you go out here? One of these churlish boys who play spin the bottle? You've become more serious than you used to be.

What jokes are your friends in Cracow exchanging? I can't imagine. What's Basia doing? Maybe she's beginning to act. Doing exactly what she wanted. She must be having fun.

But you might have become more serious even there.

Possible.

But you would have been different, very different.

No question.

And you prefer her, the Cracow Ewa.

Yes, I prefer her. But I can't be her. I'm losing track of her. In a few years, I'll have no idea what her hairdo would have been like.

But she's more real, anyway.

Yes, she's the real one.

For my birthday, Penny gives me a diary, complete with a little lock and key to keep what I write from the eyes of all intruders. It is that little lock—the visible symbol of the privacy in which the diary is meant to exist—that creates my dilemma. If I am indeed to write something entirely for myself, in what language do I write? Several times, I open the diary and close it again. I can't decide. Writing in Polish at this point would be a little like resorting to Latin or ancient Greek—an eccentric thing to do in a diary, in which you're supposed to set down your most immediate experiences and un-premeditated thoughts in the most unmediated language. Polish is becoming a dead language, the language of the untranslatable past.

But writing for nobody's eyes in English? That's like doing a school exercise, or performing in front of yourself, a slightly perverse act of self-voyeurism.

Because I have to choose something, I finally choose English. If I'm to write about the present, I have to write in the language of the present, even if it's not the language of the self. As a result, the diary becomes surely one of the more impersonal exercises of that sort produced by an adolescent girl. These are no sentimental effusions of rejected love, eruptions of familial anger, or consoling broodings about death. English is not the language of such emotions. Instead, I set down my reflections on the ugliness of wrestling; on the elegance of Mozart, and on how Dostoyevsky puts me in mind of El Greco. I write down Thoughts. I Write.

There is a certain pathos to this naïve snobbery, for the diary is an earnest attempt to create a part of my persona that I imagine I would have grown into in Polish. In the solitude of this most private act, I write, in my public language, in order to update what might have been my other self. The diary is about me and not about me at all. But on one level, it allows me to make the first jump. I learn English through writing, and, in turn, writing gives me a written self. Refracted through the double distance of English and writing, this self—my English self—becomes oddly objective; more than anything, it perceives. It exists more easily in the abstract sphere of thoughts and observations than in the world. For a while, this impersonal self, this cultural negative capability, becomes the truest thing about me. When I write, I have a real existence that is proper to the activity of writing—an existence that takes place midway between me and the sphere of artifice, art, pure language. This language is beginning to invent another me. However, I discover something odd. It seems that when I write (or, for that matter, think) in English, I am unable to use the word "I." I do not go as far as the schizophrenic "she"—but I am driven, as by a compulsion, to the double, the Siamese-twin "you."

My voice is doing funny things. It does not seem to emerge from the same parts of my body as before. It comes out from somewhere in my throat, tight, thin, and mat—a voice without the modulations, dips, and rises that it had before, when it went from my stomach all the way through my head. There is, of course, the constraint and the self-consciousness of an accent that I hear but cannot control. Some of my high school peers accuse me of putting it on in order to appear more "interesting." In fact, I'd do anything to get rid of it, and when I'm alone, I practice sounds for which my speech organs have no intuitions, such as "th" (I do this by putting my tongue between my teeth) and "a," which is longer and more open in Polish (by shaping my mouth into a sort of arrested grin). It is simple words like "cat" or "tap" that give me the most trouble, because they have no context of other syllables, and so people often misunderstand them. Whenever I can, I do awkward little swerves to avoid them, or pause and try to say them very clearly. Still, when people—like salesladies—hear me speak without being prepared to listen carefully, they often don't understand me the first time around. "Girls' shoes," I say, and the "girls' " comes out as a sort of scramble. "Girls' shoes," I repeat, willing the syllable to form itself properly, and the saleslady usually smiles nicely, and sends my mother and me to the right part of the store. I say "Thank you" with a sweet smile, feeling as if I'm both claiming an unfair special privilege and being unfairly patronized.

It's as important to me to speak well as to play a piece of music without mistakes. Hearing English distorted grates on me like chalk screeching on a blackboard, like all things botched and badly done, like all forms of gracelessness. The odd thing is that I know what is correct, fluent, good, long before I can execute it. The English spoken by our Polish acquaintances strikes me as jagged and thick, and I know that I shouldn't imitate it. I'm turned off by the intonations I hear on the TV sitcoms—by the expectation of laughter, like a dog's tail wagging in supplication, built into the actors' pauses, and by the curtailed, cutoff rhythms. I like the way Penny speaks, with an easy flow and a pleasure in giving words a fleshly fullness; I like what I hear in some movies; and once the Old Vic comes to Vancouver to perform *Macbeth*, and though I can hardly understand the particular words, I am riveted by the tones of sureness and command that mold the actors' speech into such majestic periods.

Sociolinguists might say that I receive these language messages as class signals, that I associate the sounds of correctness with the social status of the speaker. In part, this is undoubtedly true. The class-linked notion that I transfer wholesale from Poland is that belonging to a "better" class of people is absolutely dependent on speaking a "better" language. And in my situation especially, I know that language will be a crucial instrument, that I can overcome the stigma of my marginality, the weight of presumption against me, only if the reassuringly right sounds come out of my mouth.

Yes, speech is a class signifier. But I think that in hearing these varieties of speech around me, I'm sensitized to something else as well—something that is a matter of aesthetics, and even of psychological health. Apparently, skilled chefs can tell whether a dish from some foreign cuisine is well cooked even if they have never tasted it and don't know the genre of cooking it belongs to. There seem to be some deep-structure qualities—consistency, proportions of ingredients, smoothness of blending—that indicate culinary achievement to these educated eaters' taste buds. So each language has its own distinctive music, and even if one doesn't know its separate components, one can pretty quickly recognize the propriety of the patterns in which the components are put together, their harmonies and discords. Perhaps the crucial element that strikes the ear in listening to living speech is the degree of the speaker's self-assurance and control.

As I listen to people speaking that foreign tongue, English, I can hear when they stumble or repeat the same phrases too many times, when their sentences trail off aimlessly—or, on the contrary, when their phrases have vigor and roundness, when they have the space and the breath to give a flourish at the end of a sentence, or make just the right pause before coming to a dramatic point. I can tell, in other words, the degree of their ease or disease, the extent of authority that shapes the rhythms of their speech. That authority—in whatever dialect, in whatever variant of the mainstream language—seems to me to be something we all desire. It's not that we all want to speak the King's English, but whether we speak Appalachian or Harlem English, or Cockney, or Jamaican Creole, we want to be at home in our tongue. We want to be able to give voice accurately and fully to ourselves and our sense of the world. John Fowles, in one of his stories in *The Ebony Tower,* has a young man cruelly violate an elderly writer and his manuscripts because the legacy of language has not been passed on to the youthful vandal properly. This seems to me an entirely credible premise. Linguistic dispossession is a sufficient motive for violence, for it is close to the dispossession of one's self. Blind rage, helpless rage is rage that has no words—rage that overwhelms one with darkness. And if one is perpetually without words, if one exists in the entropy of inarticulateness, that condition itself is bound to be an enraging frustration. In my New York apartment, I listen almost nightly to fights that erupt like brushfire on the street below—and in their escalating fury of repetitious phrases ("Don't do this to me, man, you fucking bastard, I'll fucking kill you"), I hear not the pleasures of macho toughness but an infuriated beating against wordlessness, against the incapacity to make oneself understood, seen. Anger can be borne—it can even be satisfying—if it can gather into words and explode in a storm, or a rapier-sharp attack. But without this means of ventilation, it only turns back inward, building and swirling like a head of steam—building to an impotent, murderous rage. If all therapy is speaking therapy—a talking cure—then perhaps all neurosis is a speech dis-ease.

My parents, sister, and I have formed ourselves into an assembly line leading from the back alley through the garden and into our basement, where we are depositing an odd collection of items. There is a ratty couch with its stuffing half pulled out, a vacuum cleaner, a stained mattress, some heavy pieces of metal whose provenance is unclear. The objects are dusty, awkward, heavy; but worst of all, they bring with them the onus and burden of demotion. Having to lug such stuff is not a nice, middle-class occupation.

My parents have managed to gather a down payment on a "small stucco house," as it was advertised in the paper—I've combed through such ads repeatedly, trying to decode the nuances of wood and old English manses, and, yes, stucco—and we are now installed in this minimally furnished cell of the American Dream, which also functions as the location of a rudimentary business. Rudimentary, but laden with hope. Lots of the people we've met started out just this way—peddling junk. The very name of this occupation chafes me with its bare roughness. But in the community in which we've found ourselves, "junk" has come to acquire a certain compelling ring. For some people, scrap metal has literally turned to gold, and then into spacious homes with thick wall-to-wall rugs. Mr. Landauer still owns a big junkyard from which he draws fat profits. Besides, if, like my father, you have no money, no language, and no accredited profession, what exactly do you turn your hand to? This basic form of exchange in which the Great Chain of Business begins and ends is a logical way to start out for an immigrant who is starting out with nothing. So my father has acquired a small truck—a rickety, much-used vehicle whose shaking and rattling are an inescapable accompaniment to our first immigrant years, and on which I'll later learn how to drive—and in this noisy contraption, he goes off for the day to unknown destinations from which he brings home this medley discard of suburban life. These items, in our version of free enterprise, then get carried into our basement, from where we try to sell them for sums less small than what my father paid for them.

The whole thing is indeed basic, so much so that I keep looking for a hidden trick. In fact, the transaction is stunningly simple, but its every step is, for my parents, fraught with tension for the stunningly simple reason that our survival quite literally depends on it. We have come to Canada at an odd time—between waves of emigration, when there seem to be no support systems to ease the "newcomers'" first steps. We are on our own, and the most obvious elements of every exchange present themselves as hurdles to be deciphered and mastered. There is, for example, the matter of placing an ad in the paper. For me, this is an entirely new idea.

Advertising in Poland was as impermissible as the private enter-prise it implies, and, given the dismal trickle of noncompetitive goods, beside the point. For a while, I am as puzzled by the long pages of ads in Vancouver's newspapers as I am by the NO TRES-PASSING signs that stop me short of entering forest paths or parts of land that look like they should belong to nobody but nature's gods. In front of these signs, struck by the weirdness of untamed landscape being claimed as private property, I recognize how deeply political doctrine seeps into our perceptions.

My parents have, of course, seen systems come and go. But still, they are uncertain about what one says in an ad here, or how one responds to the phone calls that come in after the ad has been placed. "It's a very good couch," my father assures someone on the other end of the line. "What color?" He looks to my mother for help. "Gray. No, no, green." His voice grows peremptorily, impa-tiently resolute. "The only way to know if you like it is if you come over and see it," he informs the person on the other end.

Sometimes, people do come and descend into the basement to look over the motley goods and negotiate the price. But negotia-tion is a slightly wrong word for what then transpires—for the mode my parents are used to is something closer to bargaining. This highly formulaic dance accompanied all extraofficial purchases in Poland, and it entailed a number of dramatic and commonly under-stood gestures—pretending to take offense at the ridiculously high price being suggested, or, on the seller's part, the absurdly low price being offered, raising your voice at the indignity of 'being taken for a fool, appearing to be on the verge of walking away, and so on. I can hear these gestures in my parents' voices—tricks and foxiness are, after all, the essence of business—and I can hear the misfit between these arias of cajoling and the plain, unbending Canadian voices responding to them. Sometimes—often enough to keep us going—they reach an agreement, and in these early days, every completed transaction is celebrated as a triumph; every one that fails is a minor catastrophe, followed by a spell of depression and self-reproach.

EXILE

. . .

After a year or so of doing business from our house, my parents rent a store from which they'll now sell the goods my father brings in his truck. This is a big step up, and my parents are nervous and excited. But it doesn't turn out to be the beginning of a fabulous success story; my father won't build a furniture empire, won't be a real-estate baron, won't buy fancy new cars every year. Now, both of them spend most of their time in a dark, dusty space filled with old pieces of furniture arranged pell-mell, stacks of mattresses leaning against the wall, some nondescript kitchen utensils, stoves, refrigerators, tools, some used books—a space out of Malamud's *The Assistant,* a space in which you wait for salvation. My mother, as always, is readier to accept whatever situation comes to her, and to find some enjoyment in it. She persuades "clients" to come into the store, soothes, bargains, persuades. By the subdued Vancouver standards, my father cuts a rough figure, with abrupt, unqualified statements and overly resolute movements. He gets angry at stubborn customers and sometimes gets into fights with them—perhaps to re-create some of the old excitement and action of his entrepreneurial-hustling days. In the long intervals when nobody comes in, he reads—at first, with an English-Polish dictionary. For some reason, he begins with a thick novel by Faulkner, which he gets through only by consulting the dictionary on every second sentence. Faulkner seems like the most inconvenient writer on whom to learn English, but by this laborious method, my father acquires a large, if heavily accented vocabulary. My mother, who throughout her life has absorbed languages by quick osmosis, and who through the sheer vicissitudes of history has accreted not only Hebrew and Yiddish but also German and Russian and Ukrainian, picks up English from books, conversation, and the general air, and soon she too speaks with an easy fluency.

But while he learns the language, my father never really catches on to how different the rules are here, to the genteel and rational methods of doing business in Vancouver. It is as if his force, having nothing to pit itself against, turns inward on himself, festering in those quiet, drizzly streets and among people who confront him with such unfailing, unpierceable politeness.

My mother reminds herself and us that my father is the man whose resourcefulness has never failed him, who has never been in a situation he couldn't get out of. But for the first time, he can't find his nerve; he becomes anxious about making small decisions, and anxious that he has made the wrong ones. What has him so afraid, he who was apparently fearless in the face of literally deadly danger? It is, I think, the lack of danger. Without an enemy whom he can outsmart, without a hokum law at which he can thumb his nose, he is left at a loss. The structure of the space within which he moves has changed. It has no obstacles he can daringly jump over, no closed doors he can cleverly open. Everything seems to be open, but where is the point of entry? How do you maneuver when there seems to be nothing to maneuver around? How do you fight when there seems to be no particular opponent confronting you? My father is used to battling fate; here, he is faced with seemingly unresistant amorphousness, a soft medium in which hard punches are lost. He needs more of a T'ai Chi technique, something in which you manage and control your own force, because there is no one else to do it for you. He needs to read about Zen on Wall Street.

Instead, he sinks into a despair that is like lead, like the Dead Sea. "For what is the purpose?" he says when somebody asks him to go to a movie or for a walk. "Why are you torturing yourself like that?" I shout. "What do you want?" The answer is astonishing to me. "I want my peace of mind back," he says. "I've always had peace of mind."

Yes, I think, that's probably true. Through the war, the death of his close ones, through the remaking of his life in Poland, my father had never lost his basic, animal composure, which was made up of an unquestioned will to live and enough vitality to know that the will, one way or another, would prevail. And now, he has been confounded by this amiable Vancouver, by its civility and its shaved lawns. What is it, exactly, that prevents him from becoming rich and successful? It doesn't help to know that we've come to inhospitable conditions, and that my parents aren't exactly starting out the race even, with the odds fair and square. So many people have made good; if you don't, it appears that you have only yourself to blame. This—this corrosive logic—is the other side of the New World dream, the seemingly self-inflicted nightmare in which you toss and turn in gut-eating guilt.

And by what odd quirk of history, I wonder, has it come about that from age thirteen on I have not known what peace of mind feels like, that it strikes me as a phrase from another world. Is it that I come from the war, while my parents were born before it? Is it that I have only struggled with specters—their specters among others—while they have battered themselves against hard realities? Somehow, they retained their reserves of strength as long as the conditions of their existence—even at their most terrible—had to be responded to rather than questioned. It is only the worm of self-doubt that undermines their basic certitude.

"That's really sexy," Penny says appreciatively, as Sharon tries on her slinky, long slip. "You really think so?" Sharon wonders as she inspects herself carefully in the mirror. We've gathered in Penny's bedroom, and we're getting ready for a party—girls acting kittenish for each other, in order to test their appeal to boys. The slips and nylon stockings are followed by lengthy applications of makeup, with serious consultations on the colors of eye shadow, mascara, and lipstick.

I'm flattered at being invited to this intimate, insider gathering, but as usual, I'm sitting at a slightly oblique angle to the proceedings. I don't have a silk slip, don't like to put on makeup, and these elaborate preparations are somehow disturbing to me, as if we were in a harem and remodeling ourselves into a special species—"girls"—so that we can appeal to that other, alien species, boys. They are supposed to come and get us, of course, but only after we have made ourselves into these appetizing and slightly garish bonbons. In the conspiratorial giggles in the room, there is the murmur of an unspoken agreement: we're not going to show them who we are, we're going to show them what they want.

The party itself takes place in the basement "playroom" of somebody's house, and it is a nervous affair. Adolescent boys and girls drift around the room in separate groups, glancing at each other uneasily. There is more suppressed giggling among the girls, who are trying to pretend they're not paying attention to the boys, who, in their little clusters, are doing a more brash, bravado version of the giggle in the form of rattling their beer cans and talking too loudly. Why is there so much giggling and exaggeration and nervousness at this party?

The record player starts to croon Frankie Avalon's sticky-sweet melodies, whose charm I helplessly succumb to, and the nature of the tension shifts. The boys, who now know what to do, begin to cross the room. Somebody asks me to dance, and as the lights go out—more giggling—he rocks me from side to side with careful and exaggerated movements. "He held you very close," one of the girls informs me when the dance is over and I'm returned to my own gender. Her tone puts me on the alert. Did I violate some rule of decorum here? I now look at a pair dancing on the floor more carefully and see that they're engaged in a little tug-of-war, with the girl resisting the boy's full embrace.

I'd like to give myself up to the music; I'd like to dance with that boy again, even though I have no idea how to talk to him, and he doesn't seem to have anything to say to me. I want so much to throw myself into sex, into pleasure. But instead, I feel that small movement of prim disapproval. This is "unnatural," I decide—a new word of opprobrium in my vocabulary, and one that I find myself applying to any number of situations I encounter. So much of the behavior around me seems "unnatural"—strained and overcautious despite the cheekiness. Of course, I'm looking at it from my askew angle—a sure recipe for perceiving the artifice in the seemingly spontaneous. But my own primness is a reaction to a discomfort in the air, a lack of ease between the boys and girls, in which this early sexuality is converted not into friendliness but into coy sexiness. The kids at this party are afraid of making the wrong move. The only exception is slinky Sharon, whose smile and movements carry a hint of provocation, as if in response to the mingled aura of envy and suspicion around her. But Sharon pays a price for her knowledge of her own sexuality; if she's this sexy, then she must be "fast" too, and she has a bit of a "reputation." She'll have a hard time marrying, is the common wisdom.

By the time the party devolves into spin the bottle, I think that I've found myself among a strange tribe of adolescents—in Poland, a relatively unidentified species—and that this is a sad comedown from Marek and the packs of boys and girls I ran with in Cracow. It's certainly a comedown from my fantasies of an adventurous feminine destiny, which usually involved lush romances followed by a "civilized" marriage—meaning one in which it would be understood that both I and my husband could have lovers. I don't know where I got such decadent ideas, especially since they were accompanied by wholly unrealistic images of spacious and elegant apartments in which "civilized" marital arrangements could be carried on. Whatever their genesis, however, spin the bottle is not what I had in mind. As the evening continues, I recede further and begin watching the proceedings as if I were an anthropologist of the highly detached nonparticipant variety. I decide that my role in life is to be an "observer"—making a poor virtue out of the reality that I feel so very out of it.

"Communism is a political philosophy based on the idea that there is no private property and everything should be shared equally between everybody," the teacher tells the class of ninth-graders.

"But isn't Communism evil?" somebody asks. "Don't they kill people over there?"

Mr. Jones—he has a kindly, square face and a crew cut that looks like it's made of horsehair—then has an inspiration. He turns to me and asks me to describe what life in a Communist country is really like.

Really like? Really, I've never seen Communism walking down the street. Really, there is life there, water, colors, even happiness. Yes, even happiness. People live their lives. How to explain? In my classmates' minds I sense a vision of a dark, Plutonian realm in which a spectral citizenry walks bent under the yoke of oppression. The very word "Communism" seems to send a frisson up their spines, as if they were in a horror movie; it's the demonic unknown. Doesn't everyone there walk bent under the yoke of oppression? There is no freedom there!

Yes, there is, I tell them, becoming vehement in my frustration. More so than here, maybe. Politics is one thing, but what good is freedom if you behave like a conformist, if you don't laugh or cry when you want to? My outburst is greeted with stares not so much of hostility as of incomprehension. What odd ideas this foreign student has! The teacher, who is obviously delighted by what I say—he has found an ally in his battle against provincial priggishness—attempts to get some discussion going. Then he interrupts himself and asks whether everyone in the class knows where Poland is. There are negative shakes of the head. No, not everyone does. He points it out on the map, to which the students turn with a dutiful indifference. Obviously, most of them will forget this small square on the map, wedged in between larger blocks of other colors, by tomorrow. "Is Poland a part of Russia?" some especially inquisitive soul asks. Ah—now I understand. There is no point in my getting so excited. Of course, I will not convince these teenagers in this Vancouver classroom that Poland is the center of the universe rather than a gray patch of land inhabited by ghosts. It is I who will have to learn how to live with a double vision. Until now, Poland has covered an area in my head coeval with the dimensions of reality, and all other places on the globe have been measured by their distance from it. Now, simultaneously, I see it as my classmates do—a distant spot, somewhere on the peripheries of the imagination, crowded together with countless other hard to remember places of equal insignificance. The reference points inside my head are beginning to do a flickering dance. I suppose this is the most palpable meaning of displacement. I have been dislocated from my own center of the world, and that world has been shifted away from my center. There is no longer a straight axis anchoring my imagination; it begins to oscillate, and I rotate around it unsteadily.

But being "an immigrant," I begin to learn, is considered a sort of location in itself—and sometimes a highly advantageous one at that. In uneventful Vancouver, I'm enough of a curiosity that I too enjoy the fifteen minutes of fame so often accorded to Eastern European exotics before they are replaced by a new batch. The local newspaper takes me up as a sort of pet, printing my picture when I give a concert at the Jewish Community Center and soliciting my views when I come back from a bus trip to the United Nations, on which I've been sent after winning a speech contest. They want to know my opinions of the various cities I've been in, and I have no hesitation about offering them. "New York is the real capital of the United States," I readily opine. "Washington just has the government. It doesn't have the excitement." I take such attention blithely for granted, so I'm not too bowled over when a local radio pontificator, after meeting me in a group of high school students, tells me he would like to hear my opinion on anything at all; for this purpose, he'll lend me one of the fifteen-minute spots that bring him fame with weekly regularity. At this point in my initiation into the English language, I have an active vocabulary of about six hundred words, but it doesn't occur to me that I should mince any of them. I want to tell Canadians about how boring they are. "Canada is the dullest country in the world," I write in the notes for my speech, "because it is the most conformist." People may pretend to have liberal beliefs, I go on, but really they are an unadventurous lot who never dare to sidestep bourgeois conventions. With the hauteur that can only spring from fourteen-year-old innocence, I take these observations to be self-evident, because they are mine. And it doesn't occur to me, of course, that my audience might be offended at being read such stern lessons; after all, I'm simply telling the truth.

I never hear myself in this performance, because I don't know how to find the radio station on which this bit of cultural commentary is being broadcast. But I'm told by someone who hears the program that my host had some very flattering things to say about my little diatribe. Apparently, Vancouverites, as most people, like to see themselves held up in an askew mirror—perhaps any mirror, for that matter. As for me, it is my first lesson in the advantages of an oblique vision—and in the sharp pleasure of turning anger into argument.

Once we find our way back from school, my sister and I begin to dawdle home slowly, looking at window displays on the way. Our walk takes us up Main Street, a ramshackle, low-built part of town that seems a no place, thrown up randomly, without particular order or purpose. There are sprawling parking lots, patches of narrow, wooden houses, and nameless one-story cement structures, which look as haphazard as if the city itself has turned into a junk-yard here. But there are also some window displays—which I'll later recognize for the poor, wrong-side-of-town affairs that they are but which now have the power to mesmerize us with their unfamiliar objects. At this stage of our acquaintance with Western life-styles, Alinka and I can spend several minutes discussing a Tupperware casserole dish, or a blouse with a fetching embroidered collar.

Vancouver's Board of Commerce reputation, boasted of by its citizens frequently, is that it is the second most beautiful city in the world after Rio de Janeiro. This is because Vancouver too combines the usually incompatible elements of ocean and mountains in a picturesque juxtaposition. The craggy Rockies come to the end here and, from some angles of vision, seem to plunge dramatically right into the watery expanse. It is the prevailing opinion of human-kind that this is beautiful, breathtaking. But my soul does not go out to these spectacular sights, which reject me, because I reject them. I want my landscapes human sized and penetrable; these mountains look like a picture postcard to me, something you look at rather than enter, and on the many cloudy days they enclose Vancouver like gloomy walls. Within this forbidding natural frame, Vancouver circa 1960 is a raw town, not much older than the century, and with an outpost flavor still clinging to it. Downtown consists of a cluster of low buildings, with some neon displays flashing in the daytime, which hurt my head because I'm so unaccustomed to them. There are few people in the commercial area, and even fewer on the endless net of residential streets that crisscross each other in eerie quietness.

I walk through those streets not seeing anything clearly, as if a screen has fallen before my eyes, a screen that obscures and blurs everything in my field of my vision. I miss the signals that say "city" to me: the varying densities that pull people toward a common center of gravity, the strata of human, as opposed to geological age. The pulse of life seems to beat at low pressure here. The city's unfocused sprawl, its inchoate spread of one-family houses, doesn't fall into any grid of mental imagery, and therefore it is a strain to see what is before me. A few years later, when I am taken to my first football game, I have the same experience of my sight going awry. Since I don't know the rules of the game, and don't know what to look for, I can never see where the ball is. You can only keep your eye on the ball, it seems, if you have a rough a priori idea of its trajectory. Even on those days when the sun comes out in full blaze and the air has the special transparency of the north, Vancouver is a dim world to my eyes, and I walk around it in the static of visual confusion.

It is when we go into the larger repositories of consumerism— the army and navy store, or the neighborhood supermarket—that my vision becomes most entropic. Confronted with ten varieties of soap or toothpaste, I stand paralyzed, my capillaries tightening into a panicky headache. Just how am I to know which is the real thing, the Platonic toothpaste? Slowly, though, we try to unravel the new hierarchy and order of things. We look at ads on TV carefully, hoping to gather clues as to whether Colgate or Crest is better. We receive the message that more dentists recommend Colgate with full seriousness, and from then on are loyally committed to this brand.

As we gather confidence, even though it's not accompanied by money, my mother, Alinka, and I begin to enter more fashionable department stores, through which we drift as through the circles of Limbo. The profusion of objects at Hudson's Bay—Vancouver's shopping mecca—throws me into a yearning and revulsion that are simultaneous and correlative with each other: perhaps this is what used to be called a state of lust, or more generally, sin. Ah, to have money to buy these leather purses, these rayon blouses, these sweetish perfumes! We spend useless hours trying on dresses in wrong sizes, just to see how they look. When some item goes on sale, we get excited: perhaps we can afford it. We rarely can. Nevertheless, we finger and look, trying to distinguish leatherette from leather, costume jewelry from real silver. But the things threaten to crush me with their thinghood, with their inorganic proliferation, with their meaninglessness. I get headaches at Hudson's Bay; I come out pale and depleted.

After battering myself again and again on the horns of lust and disgust, I begin to retreat from both. I decide to stop wanting. For me, this is a strange turn: my appetites are strong, and I never had any ambitions to mortify them by asceticism. But this new resolution is built into the logic of my situation. Since I can't have anything, if I were to continue wanting, there would be no end to my deprivation. It would be constant, like a never-ending low-level toothache. I can't afford such a toothache; I can't afford to want. Like some sybarite turned monk who proves his mettle by placing himself in seductive situations, I can now walk between taffeta dresses and silk lingerie without feeling a shred of temptation. I've become immune to desire; I snip the danger of wanting in the bud.

By the same sleight of consciousness, I'm becoming immune to envy. If I were to give vent to envying, there would be no end to that either. I would have to envy everybody, every moment of the day. But with my new detachment, I can gaze at what my friends have as if they lived in a different world. In this spatial warp in which I have situated myself, it doesn't make any difference that they live in big houses with large yards and swimming pools, and cars and many skirts and blouses and pairs of shoes. This way, I can be nice to my friends; I can smile pleasantly at their pleasures and sympathize with their problems of the good life. I can do so, because I've made myself untouchable. Of course, they might be upset if they guessed the extent of my indifference; but they don't.

There is something I can have though, with no cash or down payments, or being to the manner born: I can have internal goods. Well, I've always wanted those, but never as much as now. If I can't possess experience in actuality, maybe I can encompass it in the spirit. If I know everything, if I understand everything, then even though I can't have a house with a patio opening out onto a swimming pool, or a boyfriend whom I like, in some other way I can have the entire world. Like Thomas Wolfe, I dream of reading everything in the library, starting from letter A. And like Ben Franklin, whose name I've never heard, I start devising programs of self-improvement. On my daily walk to school I plunge into grandiose plans for perfecting myself. I decide—and this neat schema gives me deep satisfaction—that there are four parts to a human being: physical, intellectual, spiritual, and creative. If I devote two hours a day to developing each part, then eventually I can become what will later be called "a fully realized being." My creative development, I decide, is taken care of by playing the piano; then, for two hours a day I'll read important books on everything—religion, literature, science; my physical well-being—well, perhaps that can be taken care of by the gym class; and as for spiritual exercises, I don't know what they'll consist of, though I have a vague notion that they should involve contemplation of what is essential in human life. I have every intention of figuring out what that is.

When, by accident, I come across some books on Zen, I feel as though I've found a confirmation of my own resolve. Yes, of course, detachment is the thing to strive for. What do these illusionary experiences I'm going through matter? As I read D. T. Suzuki on a crowded bus, and look around at the faces that seem so bland and inexpressive to me, I feel a sense of triumph. I can overcome all this; I can almost make it go away.

I wish I could tell Marek about these experiments. But there is nobody I can talk to like that; that's why I have to resort to them in the first place. Penny would surely think I'm crazy. "Philosophy is a crutch I'll throw away when I'm happy again," I write in one of the highly unconcrete poems that are beginning to win me prizes in my high school.

Oddly enough, the "philosophy" I am so earnestly improvising bears some very American features; but then, I'm struggling with some very American problems. In Cracow, I'd have been experiencing my youth by going to cellar-cafés and, in the hot intimacy of flushed faces and animated conversation, discussing politics and music and modern poetry. I'd have suffered from close surveillance by vigilantly gossipy friends, and no private place to go with my boyfriend, and the frustration that comes from daily powerlessness. I'd have developed ideas about power and justice, and favorite observations about love and heartbreak. In my lush Western Sahara, I'm confronting a tantalizing abundance that doesn't fill, and a loneliness that carves out a scoop of dizzying emptiness inside. My answer is a kind of spiritual individualism. Since I don't have the ordinary pleasures of sociability, of play, I turn inward with a vengeance. The only self that matters, I decide, is a sort of universal, pure, quintessential self that can hover above all the actual, daily events like a bird suspended in midair. I hover very successfully; the only thing is that I begin to suffer from a kind of high-altitude sickness, and the intensity of my self-suppression transforms itself into a spaced-out, unreal exaltation. There is a thinness in my head, and sometimes I feel faint with the will it takes to rise above myself.

Two decades later, when the Eastern religions vogue hits the counterculture, I think I understand the all-American despair that drives the new converts to chant their mantras in ashrams from San Francisco to Manhattan's Upper West Side. The gospel of detachment is as well suited to a culture of excess as it is to a society of radical poverty. It thrives in circumstances in which one's wants are dangerous because they are surely going to be deprived—or because they are pulled in so many directions that they pose a threat to the integrity, the unity of one's self. Of course, wanting too much, wanting the wrong thing, wanting what you can't have is one definition of the human condition; we all have to learn how to make some livable compromise between the always insatiable self and the always insufficient reality principle. But America is the land of yearning, and perhaps nowhere else are one's desires so wantonly stimulated; nowhere else is the compromise so difficult to achieve. Under the constant assaults of plenitude, it is difficult to agree to being just one person, and in order to achieve that simple identity, one may be driven to extreme paths. One path is to give in completely, to play the game for all it's worth; another is to renounce desire completely—a solution my peers try for a while with such sincere and ineffective zeal. A third is to do both at the same time—to play the game and know that it's maya. This is what many of the same peers try after they fail at material monkishness. Perhaps Money, in America, is a force so extreme as to become a religious force, a confusing deity, which demands either idolatry or a spiritual education.

For a long time, confronting the dangers both of self-division and of deprivation, I cultivate a rigorous renunciation. I suppose it serves me well. Like some visiting Indian swami, I learn to measure myself against no one and to feel at home everywhere. Not envying is the condition of my dignity, and I protect that dignity with my life. In a sense, it is my life—the only base I have to stand on. If I sometimes have to go around with a run in my stockings when I am in college, if I can't afford the long trek home during Christmas recess, it doesn't matter. I have my essential humanity, that essential humanity which I learned to believe in as a Jewish girl in Poland, and which I've now salvaged with the help of withdrawal and indifference. "Sometimes I see you with a steel rod running down the middle of your back," a friend once tells me. He sees more than most.

My detachment would serve me even better if it were entirely genuine. It isn't. Underneath my carefully trained serenity, there is a caldron of seething lost loves and a rage at the loss. And there is—for all that—a longing for a less strenuous way to maintain my identity and my pride. I want to gather experience with both my hands, not only with my soul. Essential humanity is all very well, but we need the colors of our time and the shelter of a specific place. I cannot always be out on the heath—we exist in actual houses, in communities, in clothes—and occasionally, at some garden party amidst meaningless chat, or in my nearly empty dorm during a holiday break, I forget my ascetic techniques, and the desire for the comfort of being a recognizable somebody placed on a recognizable social map breaks in on me with such anguishing force that it scalds my spirit and beats it back into its hiding place.

It is midafternoon on a drizzly spring afternoon, and about a half-dozen cars are parked in the Leitners' driveway. My family has come in our truck, which now joins several long-finned cars parked in front of a classic fifties suburban house; architectural style, nondescript; color, light pink. We approach this structure respectfully. The Leitners are among the pillars of the little Polish-Jewish community in which we've found ourselves, and Mrs. Leitner is one of its leading hostesses. No one cooks as well as she, or serves the food so elegantly. By the time we come in, the living room is filled with guests—all of them familiar from the continuous string of coffees, dinners, and get-togethers that this group produces in carefully revolving order. They stand among the plush wine-colored sofas and deep, velvet-covered chairs, talking somewhat uneasily. Aside from their language—a jigsaw medley of Polish, Yiddish, and English—their provenance, to a casual onlooker, would be very unclear.

The women, having come from their perfectly idle days of shopping and putting their outfits together, now look, in the manner of the period, a bit as though they have had the services of a taxidermist: meticulously made up, sheathed in stiff dresses and totally matching accessories, smiling carefully. The men are wearing suits and ties and are talking, as always, business. After a while, several people go to the den to watch "The Lawrence Welk Show" or "The Ed Sullivan Show" on television—programs to which they bring a sincere appreciation. I sincerely try to appreciate them too. I sit in front of the large set, trying to penetrate the charm of the Andrews Sisters and of Dinah Shore—this group's great favorite—but they seem so eerily low-key that instead of being cheered up, as I know I'm supposed to be, I feel a sort of mopeyness, a lowering of my own pulse, coming upon me in response.

The dining-room table is laden with heaps of cakes, all home-made, delicious, and set out on elaborate platters. This is conspicuous consumption in its most literal form; it says, We, who have either gone hungry or were in danger of it, can now indulge ourselves to our heart's content, and we can do it with some refinement. One of the purposes of these parties is to give the hostess something to do, to gather her skills and activities to some point, and Mrs. Leitner, a small, jolly woman with a humorous twinkle in her eyes, bustles between the kitchen and the living room quite happily. No, she can't give out the recipe for her three-layered torte, it's a secret. As for that delicate French pastry, well, several women in this room have tried to make it, but it didn't come out the same way . . .

This could be mistaken for an ordinary suburban party—but not quite. What is out of sync here? Perhaps it is the contrast between the carefully polite manners and the occasional slap on the back, or a loud laugh that breaks through. The people in this room are behaving properly, as if for someone else's benefit. But who is watching? A Canadian superego, I think—some allegorical notion of what is correct here, and what is vulgar and "green." And so, a layer of boredom falls over the proceedings as people exchange compliments on each other's dresses and comment on the garden and the weather. This is an imitation of Canadian conversation—polite, constrained, bland. It's also conversation without a context. Although this small group is practicing an earnest attempt at assimilation, they have hardly entered into the web of Canadian life. They would all say that they love their adopted country; they've made good here, after all, they have more wealth and peace than they could have dreamed of in Poland. But their love is oddly isolationist: they are not interested in Canadian politics, or the local culture, or even their neighbors, with whom, they'd be the first to say, they have nothing in common.

In fact, while the men go to their businesses, most of the

women in this room have mighty little connection with the world outside their houses. None of them thinks about taking a job; leisure—something different from rest, which comes after labor—is the apotheosis toward which they have always striven, an important sign of having made it, and their husbands' ambitions, not to speak of their own, wouldn't allow them to work for a salary. Their husbands' ambitions, however, do not always extend to making their wives happy, and stories of marital meanness are passed on regularly. One woman's husband specializes in insulting her publicly and apparently does not refrain from hitting her when in private; another is so jealous that he won't let his wife visit her women friends alone, and once, in a fit of truly delusional rage— she hardly goes out of the house—he fires a bullet into her arm and wounds her badly. Neither of these women does anything to defend herself: they're not used to crossing their husbands, and they're hardly surprised by outbursts of male temper. That's how men are, and, of course, they've never even glimpsed ideas of ideological self-reformation or "working on a relationship." Still, in Poland they might have had the pressures of neighborly gossip and censure on their side; here, for all their fancy dresses, they are more helpless, more alone with their troubles. They live too far apart from each other to maintain an unashamed ease of daily intercourse, and without being fully incorporated into a different system of social rules, they do not get the benefit of the local code of civility.

I often find myself with them in the stuffy big bubbles of their cars, crisscrossing Vancouver's relentlessly symmetrical roads, from home to shopping center to an endless round of liquorless parties— women who have gotten everything they have wanted, and who have so little to stave off boredom or private grief, so little to sustain them. They have attained within a few years what it took their Jewish predecessors on the Lower East Side at least two generations to achieve, and on the whole they consider themselves contented, satisfied. But they confuse me, in their perfect propriety. They're a version of what I might become, and even a temptation for what I might want to be: a woman who has the comfort of living within the perfectly knowable orderliness of middle-class convention. "Pretty soon, you should find a nice husband, a smart, talented girl like you," they tell me. Indeed, why should I have the arrogance to have different aspirations? And what, exactly, should my aspirations be? Theirs is an immigrant success story, and that's the story of their own lives that they accept. But perhaps, if they had the words to say just what they feel, something different might pour out, an elusive complaint of an elusive ailment. For insofar as meaning is interhuman and comes from the thickness of human connections and how richly you are known, these successful immigrants have lost some of their meaning. In their separateness and silence, their wisdom—what they used to know in an intimate way, on their skin—is stifled and it dries up a little. Probably, in their phase of immigrant life, full assimilation is impossible, and in trying to take on the trappings of their new environment, they've achieved an almost perfect deracination instead: they move in a weirdly temperate zone, where the valence of cultural vitality is close to neutral. Sitting upright in their cars, in their immaculately pressed dresses, keeping their houses more spotlessly neat than the natives, they say to each other, "I'm fine, everything is fine," and they almost believe that they are.

My sister, who is now eleven, has taken to shaving her legs, surrounding her eyes with large amounts of makeup, and putting on lipstick. When she first shows us her mascaraed eyelashes and depilated calves, my mother cries. What is our Alinka turning into? In our circles in Poland, only loose girls might have done this; in fact, nobody Alinka's age did. I'm also unnerved by my sister's swift metamorphosis. What is she turning into?

Some sort of beatnik, it appears, though in most parts of the continent it's a late day for that. She takes to wearing black clothes and going on the streets barefoot. This last is a blow to the entire family. How can she behave like that?

Altogether, Alinka seems to be striving for a normal American adolescence. The only trouble is that none of us knows what that's supposed to be, and my sister pains us with her capacity for change, with becoming so different from what she was. She is leaving us abruptly, leaving us to find her own pleasures. My mother worries about her younger daughter's friends. Are they proper children, from good families? But the categories don't seem to translate. The kids that Alinka occasionally brings home live in well-appointed houses, and they're certainly respectable. But they aren't like the "better" children we knew in Cracow: these girls are both shy and rowdy, and they observe few rules of mannerliness; when they manage to speak to adults, they hang their heads and revert to defensive monosyllables. They are not children who might sit on the couch, discussing some book they've lately read and shaking hands politely with everyone before leaving. "They're so badly brought up," my mother says wonderingly. "They don't greet anyone, they don't say thank you after they eat. . . . What a strange country."

Alinka is also becoming educated in Jewishness, more rigorously than I ever will be. My parents have sent her to a Hebrew school—ironically, a gesture of assimilation—and for a while she agitates for making our household kosher and debates the merits of letting non-Jews into Vancouver's new Jewish Community Center. My mother has no intention of going back to the kosher kitchen of her girlhood, but I'm not amused by this paradoxical turn of events. I have no knowledge yet of the complex historical arguments that fuel the ideas Alinka has brought home, but her embrace of ethnic exclusivity rubs against the equation I've somehow developed between Jewishness and a kind of secular humanism. To be Jewish, in my mind, is to stand against distinctions, to uphold everyone's equal personhood, pure and simple. "But you're not religious!" I shout at her, quite certain that no sister of mine is going to be born again. "And if you're not, you shouldn't act as if you are! And what do you mean, you shouldn't let non-Jews into the center? That's discrimination! It's supposed to be a community center, don't forget!" "But it's our community center," Alinka answers uncertainly; she is visibly torn between the moral precepts she's been introduced to in a place as respectable as school and the sisterly fury unleashed on her—and suddenly I feel sorry for her and for myself. Everything is getting all mixed up here, and my convictions, of which I've been so certain, can actually hurt my sister.

As for me, I have begun to refuse even the minimal observance of my childhood. This is because Vancouver's conservative synagogue—the house of prayer my parents have judged most appropriate, now that they have a choice of different ways to be Jewish—fills me with a discomfiting sense that a concentrate of feeling, the feeling of mystery, has been diffused and flattened out in its interior. The synagogue is housed in a white, neat building that echoes the perfectly prosy architecture all around it. In the building's basement, there is a hallway and public rooms, which look exactly like my high school's corridors and which, on high holidays, fill up with overdressed children and adolescents. The prayer room is crowded with women who carefully observe each other's hats and suits and men slapping each other affably on the back, much as they do at parties. I know that they have all paid for their seats and that everyone is conscious of who can afford what. But it is the blond wood of the benches and the floors and the daylight streaming freely into the cheery amphitheater that makes this, to me, a secular space.

And so I escape, and my parents don't insist. They don't try to exercise much influence over me anymore. "In Poland, I would have known how to bring you up, I would have known what to do," my mother says wistfully, but here, she has lost her sureness, her authority. She doesn't know how hard to scold Alinka when she comes home at late hours; she can only worry over her daughter's vague evening activities. She has always been gentle with us, and she doesn't want, doesn't know how, to tighten the reins. But familial bonds seem so dangerously loose here!

Truth to tell, I don't want the fabric of loyalty and affection, and even obligation, to unravel either. I don't want my parents to lose us, I don't want to betray our common life. I want to defend our dignity because it is so fragile, so beleaguered. There is only the tiny cluster, the four of us, to know, to preserve whatever fund of human experience we may represent. And so I feel a kind of ferociousness about protecting it. I don't want us to turn into per-petually cheerful suburbanites, with hygienic smiles and equally hygienic feelings. I want to keep even our sadness, the great sadness from which my parents have come.

I adjure my sister to treat my parents well; I don't want her to challenge my mother's authority, because it is so easily challenged. It is they who seem more defenseless to me than Alinka, and I want her to protect them. Alinka fights me like a forest animal in danger of being trapped; she too wants to roam through the thickets and meadows. She too wants to be free.

My mother says I'm becoming "English." This hurts me, because I know she means I'm becoming cold. I'm no colder than I've ever been, but I'm learning to be less demonstrative. I learn this from a teacher who, after contemplating the gesticulations with which I help myself describe the digestive system of a frog, tells me to "sit on my hands and then try talking." I learn my new reserve from people who take a step back when we talk, because I'm standing too close, crowding them. Cultural distances are different, I later learn in a sociology class, but I know it already. I learn restraint from Penny, who looks offended when I shake her by the arm in excite-ment, as if my gesture had been one of aggression instead of friend-liness. I learn it from a girl who pulls away when I hook my arm through hers as we walk down the street—this movement of friendly intimacy is an embarrassment to her.

I learn also that certain kinds of truth are impolite. One shouldn't criticize the person one is with, at least not directly. You shouldn't say, "You are wrong about that"—though you may say, "On the other hand, there is that to consider." You shouldn't say, "This doesn't look good on you," though you may say, "I like you better in that other outfit." I learn to tone down my sharpness, to do a more careful conversational minuet.

Perhaps my mother is right, after all; perhaps I'm becoming colder. After a while, emotion follows action, response grows warmer or cooler according to gesture. I'm more careful about what I say, how loud I laugh, whether I give vent to grief. The storminess of emotion prevailing in our family is in excess of the normal here, and the unwritten rules for the normal have their osmotic effect.

Because I'm not heard, I feel I'm not seen. My words often seem to baffle others. They are inappropriate, or forced, or just plain incomprehensible. People look at me with puzzlement; they mumble something in response—something that doesn't hit home. Anyway, the back and forth of conversation is different here. People often don't answer each other. But the mat look in their eyes as they listen to me cancels my face, flattens my features. The mobility of my face comes from the mobility of the words coming to the surface and the feelings that drive them. Its vividness is sparked by the locking of an answering gaze, by the quickness of understanding. But now I can't feel how my face lights up from inside; I don't receive from others the reflected movement of its expressions, its living speech. People look past me as we speak. What do I look like, here? Imperceptible, I think; impalpable, neutral, faceless.

"When I think of love, I think of running with someone through a sunny meadow, holding hands," Penny says dreamily, rolling over on her bed.

"Sunny?" I say, surprised. "When I think of love, I think of a dark forest that you go into by a narrow path." What I really think about, of course, is Marek, but that's too delicate a matter to talk about with this new friend. Penny and I are lying on two single beds in her pink-and-white bedroom, where I've come for an overnight visit—that luxurious benefit of big houses and private rooms. We're dressed in our nighties, and are talking in that pleasant dozy, irresponsible state in which you can speak slowly and utter your deepest thoughts.

"You know what Larry said to me today?" Penny says, now sounding a little kittenish.

"What?"

"He said, 'Kid, you'd be good on a desert island.' "

"Oh yeah?" I say, interested. "Does that mean that he was giving you a line?"

"Oh God," Penny sighs with mock exasperation. "Sometimes I think you're hopeless. That wasn't a line. I think he likes me."

"Oh," I say humbly. "Do you think you'll go out with him?"

"God, I hope so," Penny sighs, now in earnest. "He's so cute. Don't you think?"

"I guess so," I say uncertainly. The standards for cuteness around here are very different from what I'm used to, and most boys I meet seem to me too round or too gangly, or too splayed in their movements. There are a few at my high school who are hard shaped and as large boned and handsome as cigarette ads, but their faces are impossible to look into, and they usually turn out to be athletes, and those apparently are absolutely off-limits.

I trust Penny to explain some of these things to me. She is a happy, bouncy young person, curly haired and ruddy cheeked, and she is the smart girl in class, the one who always gets the best grades. Penny is a native Vancouverite, and Vancouver, as far as she is concerned, is the best place on earth, though I, of course, know that it is Cracow. We like each other quite well, though I'm not sure that what is between us is "friendship"—a word which in Polish has connotations of strong loyalty and attachment bordering on love. At first, I try to preserve the distinction between "friends" and "acquaintances" scrupulously, because it feels like a small lie to say "friend" when you don't really mean it, but after a while, I give it up. "Friend," in English, is such a good-natured, easygoing sort of term, covering all kinds of territory, and "acquaintance" is something an uptight, snobbish kind of person might say. My parents, however, never divest themselves of the habit, and with an admirable resistance to linguistic looseness, continue to call most people they know "my acquaintance"—or, as they put it early on, "mine acquaintance."

As the word is used here, Penny is certainly a friend, and we spend many hours together, gossiping about our classmates and teachers and futures. And, of course, about dates. Dating, to Penny, is the acme of desire, the focus toward which much of her thought and activity is directed. She spends quite a bit of time applying various brands of makeup to her face, contemplating which one will give her "it"—"it" being, at this time, what every girl wants to have. She analyzes minutely the signs of boys' favor and interest: what does it mean that Tommy looked at her in the hallway, or that Larry kicked her locker?

Dating is an unknown ritual to me, unknown among my Cracow peers, who, aside from lacking certain of its requisite accessories—cars, private rooms, a bit of money—ran around in boy-girl packs and didn't have a ceremonial set of rules for how to act toward the other sex. A date, by contrast, seems to be an occasion whose semiotics are highly standardized and in which every step has a highly determinate meaning and therefore has to be carefully calibrated. I've pored over some articles about it, searching for clues, and have seen some examples on television, and I'm not at all sure that I could pull it off correctly. I know several of the rules: First, you should never let the boy honk for you from the outside; he should come in from his car, so you can introduce him to your parents, with whom he can make small talk for a few minutes. This is the first serious stumble in my imagination. It is very unlikely that I could get my parents to behave with the mixture of white-toothed cheerfulness and offhand casualness that I've seen in American parents on TV, or that they could produce small talk of the "Nice to see you, young man," or "Now be sure to bring my daughter back on time," variety. Then there are the tense moments of getting into the car and negotiating the evening's activity—followed by what is presented as the extremely tricky challenge of making conversation. By this, what is apparently meant is that the girl is supposed to make the boy comfortable enough to get something out of him—an article in *Seventeen* goes so far as to suggest that you bone up on an athletic event, since all of Them are bound to be interested in sports. If there's an uncomfortable silence, you can always break it by reverting to the one unfailing subject—himself.

I don't get the impression from this that an ideal date would be fun for either party. In fact, it seems vaguely scary to me. I never thought that talking to a boy was an enterprise hedged with special difficulty, or requiring special preparation. How can one feel the fresh wind of camaraderie or freedom under such shackled circumstances? On the few occasions when I do go out on a "date," I'm so aware of the many faux pas I might commit, and so little interested in my companion, that in my discomfort I might as well be wearing a tight Victorian corset with high and prickly stays. And the rules and constraints of sexual behavior, as Penny begins to initiate me into them, are even more complicated. I vow to myself never to go through such undignified and "immature" motions. Nevertheless, getting dates is what girls around me seem most to want—especially those Saturday night dates, which are the ultimate proof of a girl's popularity, personality, and presumably her future marriageability. For marriage, of course, is what this is leading up to. Penny's life, in her mind, opens out like a well-kept, sunny road. She will be married; she will have a job of some kind, maybe; she will have children. She will be as cheerful and sensible as she is now—bafflingly cheerful and sensible as far as I'm concerned. Where are her moods, her intensities, the invisible, shadowy part of her personality? I can't penetrate all that transparency; it doesn't give me enough crags and surprises to hook on to.

But that is only because I don't know yet where the surprises in a life such as hers lie, where the painful things are hidden. On one of my overnight visits, our conversation takes an entirely different turn. When the lights are out and I am about to go to sleep, she begins crying softly.

"What is it?" I ask her.

After a long pause, Penny begins to tell me, in a small and pained voice, about her older sister, Janet, who had tried to kill herself, to end her own life.

"But why?" I ask, disbelieving. This comfortable house, this atmosphere of prosy, daily concerns, seems like an utterly incongruous setting for a young girl's attempted suicide.

"Oh," Penny says, "it's my mother. She doesn't really like her. They have fights all the time. Janet has a terrible inferiority complex. I mean, my mother is a good egg, but she is so horrible to Janet . . ."

"That's terrible," I say, utterly at a loss for anything more. A good egg? But she has driven her daughter to this, by not treating her well enough? It doesn't add up, not in my cosmos, and it is only after I come across many more gothic secrets, smoldering in the sensible interiors of these intact suburban households, that I begin to get inklings of what may ail their inhabitants, of the strangled suffering that can be bred within them. For now, I haven't yet learned how to read the surfaces either of Penny's face or of lives like hers well enough to see what's behind them, to discern the paradoxes inherent in their very smoothness.

I'm visiting from New York and sitting on a high, rocky promontory in one of Vancouver's wilder parks. The ocean is beating against the stony shore with white, furiously scattering waves, alternately shadowed by clouds and illumined by the sun. I breathe in this austere beauty deeply and remember how, many years ago, I sat here in a cloud of unhappiness and unknowing, and felt only the terror of this scene and its emptiness. It's enough to make a Berkeleyan of you, this mercurial changeability of all reality under the pressure of the soul. Or a Wittgensteinian, for it is impossible to perceive the meaning of any one thing without knowing the pattern of the surrounding things. Without the color spectrum, there is no yellow or blue, and without seeing its colors, how can one be touched by the beauty of the world?

Vancouver will never be the place I most love, for it was here that I fell out of the net of meaning into the weightlessness of chaos. But now I have eyes to see its flower-filled gardens, and hear small kindnesses under the flat Canadian accents. I discern, in the stories of the people I used to meet at the Leitners' parties, the movements of ordinary struggles and ordinary pleasures. Their lives have the content of change and grief and comfort. I know better now that emptiness is not so easy to achieve, and that assuredly it exists most purely in the soul.

Almost as soon as we come to Vancouver, the search for a music teacher begins. After checking out several pedagogues who strike me as bored, perfunctory, or incompetent, I become convinced that I've indeed found myself in the "cultural desert" that I read about in Cracow's *Cross Section.* It's then that Mrs. Steiner takes me to meet the man who will be my new musical guide. Piotr Ostropov is about seventy when I am introduced to him; he is Russian by origin and accent, and he looks like an Artist—a romantic, nineteenth-century version of one: his head features a large pink bald spot, surrounded by a circle of white hair, sticking impressively upward. His eyes light up with a bright, impish glint, and he strews tobacco from his pipe carelessly all around. I play a Scarlatti sonata for him and a Chopin nocturne, and he confers with Mrs. Steiner animatedly. "More life!" he shouts at me, and I want to shout back that there used to be more life, but I'm much too timid, and anyway, why should he believe me? "Ah, that's very nice," he says at some other point. "You have a nice feeling. Now let me show you what you can do on the piano, even with a simple exercise, mmhm?" And Mr. Ostropov sits down at the piano to demonstrate what he means by "life" with some Czerny exercises. He lowers his large, shapely hands to the keyboard as if he were both a wizard and a snake charmer about to make water spring from a tree branch and transfix his listeners with his power. Then he strikes the rod: he begins with a piece that is nothing more than an arrangement of scales, but as he runs his fingers over the keys, with an insinuating curl to each scale, he makes the rows of notes glitter and shine like some merry brook. His eyes twinkle, and he looks up at me like a magician who has just accomplished the naughtiest, most amusing trick. I give him the best *jeune-fille* smile in my repertory, and our friendship is sealed. "See?" he shouts at me as he gets up, picks up his pipe, and spills some tobacco on my sweater. "See what I mean? Life, life! But you have a nice smile," he adds, looking at me carefully. "You understand a lot, don't you? You're just shy."

It seems that my real friends in Vancouver are fated to be several generations older; but then, in terms of the historical time from which we derive, they are my truer contemporaries. After Mr. Ostropov decides to take me on as a student, we begin a tempestuous musical relationship that borders on purest love. Every week, a large Cadillac arrives in front of our house, and the Ostropovs' chauffeur delivers me at a large Victorian mansion, where Mr. Ostropov meets me at the door and leads me through a succession of beautiful rooms into a studio filled with English antiques, rugs, old paintings, and a handsome baby grand Steinway.

Usually, he cannot resist sitting down at the piano first; he does so on the pretext of demonstrating some new point of technique, or interpretation. He shows me how to move the thumb as if it were a detachable part, or how to get a smooth legato effect by some unusual fingering. Then, he launches into an entire piece—a movement of a Beethoven sonata, or one of his favorite Chopin mazurkas. When he does something that particularly pleases him—an ornament that he accomplishes with a filigree grace, or a sequence of octaves he gets through by sheer bravura (technique and accuracy are not his strong points)—he looks up at me with leprechaun satisfaction and says "Ah? Ah?" and I nod with as much appreciation as one can pack into a shake of the head. Then he jumps up, and shouting "Ah! You see?" indicates that it's my turn. But I barely begin to play when he impatiently stops my hand, saying, "Like this! You have to love every note!" Sometimes he places his hand over mine, guiding and molding it to the swoop or the decline, or the delicate inner oscillations of a lyrical passage. Or he kneads my arm expressively, humming along in an unmelodious, creaky voice to encourage me into more dramatic crescendos, diminuendos, or rubatos.

Although these sessions can last for as long as three hours— Mr. Ostropov is not a watch-compulsive pedagogue—sometimes he calls me during the week to tell me he has just had a "revolutionary" idea that he wants to show me immediately. Then, he comes to our house and takes the living room over. He paces up and down, flails his arms around, shouts, cajoles, spills his pipe. Usually, the revolutionary idea has to do with some new way of distributing the weight of the arm, or positioning your fingers—sometimes very straight, sometimes curved and clawlike. I try to adjust to these epiphanies as best I can, but there is more passion than method to Mr. Ostropov's art.

The quirky journey that landed Mr. Ostropov in Vancouver—an unlikely place for a person of his ilk—was launched by a real revolution, the Russian Revolution of 1905. Sometimes, he tells me a bit about what happened after that event: about giving concerts with his two brothers—together, they formed the Ostropov Trio—throughout the British Empire; about riding in a buggy on muddy roads in Australia; about courting a girl who turned out to be a Canadian nickel heiress in a French lycée; about pianistic giants he knew—Teodor Leszetycki, Ignaz Friedman, Josef Hofmann—and the ease, the "humanness" of their playing.

All of this is interspersed with mini-lectures on the morality of playing and the art of life—which, for Mr. Ostropov, are quite inseparable. Being a great musician is achieved by being human, and being human is . . . Well, actually, Mr. Ostropov is fairly precise about that. "What is a human being?" he asks me rhetorically during one of our lessons, and then, wordlessly, his index finger delicately extended, he points, in a three-beat rhythm, to his head, his heart, and—after the tiniest syncopated pause—his crotch. Then he looks at me impishly. I smile at him demurely and, I hope, knowingly. "Go on," he says, "the Ballade!"

But what being human is really about is having fire, flair, a holy spark of inspiration. That energy, in Mr. Ostropov's view, should instill not only your playing but your every gesture; it should make all your movements forceful, artful, musical. "When you do anything—put a box of matches down, pick it up—you shouldn't just do it. You have to do it with temperament. When you walk into a room, I want you to walk in so that everyone looks up, and is quiet for a moment." He shows me how I should walk to achieve this feat, raising his head and giving his face a gloomy, proud expression. This appeals to every megalomaniacal and romantic vein in my body. If I could only live by inner fire alone! If I could have enough magnetism to stop a conversation dead when I come into a room! I don't quite see, though, where these flights of *polot*—for this is what he is talking about, the *polot* of my childhood—are to take place in Vancouver, or that they would go over very well in Sharon's basement playroom parties.

I only half-tell myself—to me, he is a formidable personality—that Mr. Ostropov's panache is partly bravado, that not all his hopes have been fulfilled. He hasn't entered the pantheon of the greats he so admires, and he is an odd fish to be swimming in Vancouver's ponds. Because he is so out of his natural habitat, and because there aren't others like him around, with whom he could have easy conviviality and shout and exchange sparks of fire late into the night, because he has been dislocated from his center, he has become that recognizable species of an émigré eccentric—a lovable, temperamental, slightly mad Russian artist.

Mr. Ostropov partly accepts this persona, and plays his inventions upon it: he appears at concerts in a dashing velvet jacket, he grabs people by the shoulder and fixes them with his elfish eyes, he drives his car off without noticing that a tray with a tea service is perched on the trunk lid. Still, I don't think he is eccentric, or quaint. His teaching is not systematic or disciplined; nor do his contortions of the hand do much for my technique. But he grapples with the piano as if it were both his demon and his muse; and as I catch some of his obsession, I too want to strike the rod with more beauty and force. "You have to love every note," he says, "love it. The piano is a machine, and that's the only way to make it human." "There are no straight lines in nature," he once tells me, "and there are no straight lines in music." Somehow, I know what he means by this bit of pantheistic mysticism, and I look for the life of music in the arcs, swerves, and tilts of its lines—the parabolas that delineate the rises and falls of our own inner life, and perhaps the drama of yearning of all organic forms.

Although Mr. Ostropov takes me under his wing, and takes me to concerts where he shows me off proudly as his talented student, he doesn't ask me much about how I am, and I don't talk much to him; it's hard to get a word in edgewise, and anyway, he wouldn't exactly listen. But he does listen to me play—carefully—and, in his irrational and sometimes disorderly utterances, I catch messages that resonate like a clear bell. And so, sitting bent over a piano, with this seventy-year-old man who sometimes scares me and sometimes makes me bite my lip with impatience, I nevertheless feel that we are talking a language that really matters. Besides, Mr. Ostropov is one of the few people around who can see through the occlusions of my unhappiness and depression and withdrawal to something he has faith in. "You'll see," he says to Mrs. Steiner, "she'll grow up to be a bombshell! She's beginning to look like Beethoven!" He too thinks I should choose a practical profession, but he keeps something in me awake, alive.

"The synonyms for 'strong' are mighty, vigorous, puissant, stout, hardy," I read. This string of words is followed by sentences from which I can infer the exact shading of these adjectives, and, on another form, different sentences with spaces left blank for the requisite mot juste. I fill them in quickly, and then turn to my history lesson. This requires more concentration, because of the strange names cropping up all the time—Lake Champlain, Frontenac, Diefenbaker—and because tableaux of frontier towns and of western explorations don't have the same pattern of conflict, war, rhetoric, and costume that I used to know as history. Where are the great personages, the grand battles, the patina of age? These tales of skirmishes in small townships, of people making their way across the inimical woods and the freezing northern expanses of the continent, move horizontally across space rather than vertically through time. They summon images of tiny dots on an enormous landscape, huddles of humanity clotting and then making barely visible ink lines across the map, and I find it hard to conceptualize them as events, with a beginning, a middle, and an end.

Right now, though, it is summer, and the sun rays cut right through the clear air down to the blanket in our narrow backyard, where I am doing the correspondence courses I've signed up for so I can get through high school in three years rather than four and catch up with students my own age after being placed a year behind because I am a newcomer.

I don't mind these form lessons or the games they ask me to play, as I don't mind anything that I know I can master easily. But there is another motive driving me as well, an extra edge to my ambition—an edge that wasn't there before, and that comes from a version of the Big Fear. I know how unprotected my family has become; I know I'd better do very well—or else. The "or else" takes many forms in my mind—vague images of helplessness and restriction and always being poor. "The Bowery," I come to call this congeries of anxieties. The Bowery is where I'll end up if I don't do everything exactly right. I have to make myself a steel breastplate of achievement and good grades, so that I'll be able to get out—and get in, so that I can gain entry into the social system from where I stand, on a precarious ledge. I am pervaded by a new knowledge that I have to fend for myself, and it pushes me on with something besides my old curiosity, or even simple competitiveness.

Immigrant energy, admirable name though it has gained for itself, does not seem a wholly joyful phenomenon to me. I understand the desperado drive that fuels it. But I also understand how it happens that so many immigrant Horatio Algers overshoot themselves so unexpectedly as they move on their sped-up trajectories through several strata of society all the way to the top. From the perspective outside, everything inside looks equally impenetrable, from below everything above equally forbidding. It takes the same bullish will to gain a foothold in some modest spot as to insist on entering some sacred inner sanctum, and that insistence, and ignorance, and obliviousness of the rules and social distinctions—not to speak of "your own place"—can land you anywhere at all. As a radically marginal person, you have two choices: to be intimidated by every situation, every social stratum, or to confront all of them with the same leveling vision, the same brash and stubborn spunk.

I too am goaded on by the forked whip of ambition and fear, and I derive a strange strength—a ferocity, a puissance—from the sense of my responsibility, the sense that survival is in my own hands. I don't feel much like a child anymore, and I am both weighted down and concentrated by the seriousness of my—our—situation. I know that I can do anything I have to do. I could jump out of that second-story window the way my father did, or escape out that door. The sense of necessity—that famously ambiguous master—relieves me from small trepidations, the Big Fear supplants small ones of adolescence. I harden myself for whatever battles await me, though it turns out that no battle will ever be as hard as this imaginary one I wage with the dangers in my head. I too suffer from the classic immigrant misconception, and I can't distinguish between the normal and the strenuous road in life, between moderate and high achievement. Becoming a lawyer seems as difficult to me as becoming a chief justice, a teacher of freshman English is as august a personage in my world as a college president. I don't envision that I can get to any of these exalted positions by an ordinary sequence of steps, by putting one foot in front of the other. I have to drive myself, to be constantly on the alert.

The only catch is that I have lost the sense of what, driven as I have become, I am driving toward. The patterns of my life have been so disrupted that I cannot find straight li. es amid the disarray. Gradual change within one context, one diagram, is one thing; scrambling all the coordinates is another. "Being a pianist," for example, means something entirely different in my new cultural matrix. It is no longer the height of glamour or the heart of beauty. "What a nice tune," my friends say when I play a Beethoven sonata for them, but I see that they don't care. Moreover, Mrs. Steiner and others inform me, it's not a solid profession, and it will hardly assure my ability to support myself. "Where are you going to get the money for music lessons in New York?" somebody asks me. "A person in your position has to think practically." "You're too intelligent to become a musician," others tell me. But there is nothing in the world that takes a more incandescent intelligence, the intelligence of your whole being! I want to reply.

Still, I begin to see that my "destiny" is no longer going to pull me toward itself as if I were sitting in a chariot driven by the gods. Even the design and thrust of our passions is in large part written by where and when we happen to live, and mine are not yet molded so firmly that the shape of the wax can't be changed, though they are powerful enough so that the remolding will hurt. The unity, the seemingly organic growth of my desires is becoming fragmented, torn. That wholeness came from the simplicity—perhaps given to us only in childhood—of my wants. But now I don't know what to want, or how to want, any longer. Polish romanticism, in whatever naïve version it has infiltrated my imagination, doesn't superprint easily on the commonsensical pragmatism required of me here. During my solitary walks, I hold long debates with myself about how much I owe to God, and how much to Caesar. Is it right that I should neglect the demands of my emotions, which tell me that music is the medium of my self? No, a voice within me says—but it's a voice I try to silence. It may, by now, be a false siren; purely personal needs, it turns out, are a luxury affordable only by those who have some measure of security, of safety—at least of the internal kind. I'm beginning to respect the force of circumstance—though I am ornery enough that I won't give in to it completely. "Yet all experience is an arch wherethrough gleams that untraveled world . . ." I begin the valedictory speech I've been asked to deliver on graduating from Eric Hamber High School. Plunge into life, I tell my classmates with considerable passion, try to taste as much of it, to understand as much of human nature—experience—as you can. For this moment, I let my desires speak, and I feel a wild, clean urge to take flight.

But where to? I have no map of experience before me, not even the usual adolescent kind. Aside from the endless varieties of apparel, and swimming pools and cars, I don't know what goods this continent has to offer. I don't know what one can love here, what one can take into oneself as home—and later, when the dams of envy burst open again, I am most jealous of those who, in America, have had a sense of place.

I have an absurd fit of envy, for example, when I read *The Education of Henry Adams*—that idiosyncratic work so unlike anything else I've come across in American literature courses. So this is what it means to be a real American! All along, I've been taught about misfits and outsiders, about alienation and transcendence—which, I suspect, really come to the same thing. But for Henry Adams—and for a few others—America has been a fitting habitation for the mind rather than just a complex of ideas, a field for significant action rather than a launching pad for individual ambition, for making it. A fellow student at Harvard—for this is where this mini-epiphany takes place—is understandably incredulous. He points out that I might as well envy the king of Siam; he points out Henry Adams's horrendous sense of failure. It doesn't matter. In Henry Adams, for all the tortuous involutions of his psyche, I encounter a sense of belonging and of natural inheritance. And this, it turns out, from my displacement, is what I long for—the comfort that comes from being cradled by continuity, the freedom from insignificance. The more I come to know about America, the more I have the dizzying sensation that I'm a quantum particle trying to locate myself within a swirl of atoms. How much time and energy I'll have to spend just claiming an ordinary place for myself! And how much more figuring out what that place might be, where on earth I might find a stable spot that feels like it's mine, and from which I can calmly observe the world. "There are no such places anymore," my fellow student informs me. "This is a society in which you are who you think you are. Nobody gives you your identity here, you have to reinvent yourself every day." He is right, I suspect, but I can't figure out how this is done. You just say what you are and everyone believes you? That seems like a confidence trick to me, and not one I think I can pull off. Still, somehow, invent myself I must. But how do I choose from identity options available all around me? I feel, once again, as I did when facing those ten brands of toothpaste—faint from excess, paralyzed by choice.

And later still, when I see that it is through reading and writing that I'll have my adventures, I come to envy those New York Jewish intellectuals, like Alfred Kazin or Norman Podhoretz, who had the slight leg up of being born here, and who were therefore quicker to understand where they wanted to travel, the parabolas of their ambitions. Their journeys from the outer boroughs to Manhattan felt long and arduous to them, but at least they knew where the center was, they felt the compelling lure of its glittering lights. Their dreams were American dreams; their desires were inscribed in the American idiom. My desires, when freed from their protective covering, are forceful, and they are as unchanneled as an infant's id. I'll have to find new rivulets for them. For a long time, I'll thrash around like a fish thrown from sweet into salty ocean waters.

. . .

We're driving to the airport and we are all made serious by the gravity of the occasion. I am going away to college, in Houston, Texas. "You've done so well, you must be so proud, your parents must be so proud of you"—I've heard this often in the last few months. After all, Rice University, which I'm going to attend, is reputed to have very high academic standards—a phrase that at this point strikes awe into my heart—and it has had the kindness to shower me with enough money to make my going there possible. When I begin to receive a succession of letters informing me of the various scholarships I've been awarded, I hold them delicately between my fingers as if they might be pieces of air, or as if my good luck might break under the slightest pressure.

I've looked up Houston on the map, and I see that it's far. Such images of the Wild West as I possess have been overlaid by photographs in *Time* magazine showing tall buildings, oil rigs, and other signs of an economic boom. I've been told it's very hot there.

As I am about to go through the gate to board my first plane ever, my sister embraces me with a fierceness that recalls her silent appeal when she was small and very unhappy—and I feel again that perhaps, in this departure which might take me much further away than the airplane, there is some betrayal. It is hard to pull myself away from Alinka, hard to look at her suddenly pleading face. I try to remember what Mrs. Steiner—who with her daughters has guided me toward this step—said about living my own life. It is not so simple for me to accept this idea, to extricate myself from the mesh of family need and love, to believe in the merits of a separate life. I've hesitated, but there is no resisting this call. I think of vistas of knowledge, steps ascending to the temple of intellect. In my application, I said I wanted to gain genuine understanding of human nature, and I meant it.

On the plane, I strike up a conversation with a tall, tanned man beside me, and an hour or so into the flight he suggests that I descend with him in San Francisco and spend a few days in his house. Being a free woman now, I pretend to consider this proposal carefully, but decide that I shouldn't miss the first days of classes.

The man tries to laugh this off and persuade me that a few days won't make any difference, and he could really show me around San Francisco. He is very handsome, but I remain firm, and with a queenly graciousness decline the offer.

There is, of course, no real decision to make here, and after the man gets off, I start thinking about what lies ahead. I hardly know, but I feel the tingling of anticipation. I am traveling toward Experience.

Among the many immigrant tales I've come across, there is one for which I feel a particular affection. This story was written at the beginning of the century, by a young woman named Mary Antin, and in certain details it so closely resembles my own, that its author seems to be some amusing poltergeist, come to show me that whatever belief in my own singularity I may possess is nothing more than a comical vanity. But this ancestress also makes me see how much, even in my apparent maladaptations, I am a creature of my time—as she, in her adaptations, was a creature of hers.

Mary Antin was born in the 1880s, in a town within the Russian Pale, and came to America with her mother and younger brother—her father had gone ahead some years earlier—when she was fourteen, during one of those enormous movements that washed whole Jewish populations across the ocean on crowded, typhoid-infected ships. The family, once they remet in Boston (why they landed there, rather than anywhere else, is never explained) went through about a decade of grinding, hopeless, near-starvation poverty—poverty of a kind that immigrants in our own, in some ways more benign, times almost never fall into. But Mary had several things going for her—first and foremost, that she was a smart little girl. She had a bit of a talent for language and a curious, lively mind—her writing has an unaffected, sweet freshness, she is an irreverent observer, and her recollections of her childhood are suffused with lyrical detail. In America, she quickly became a star student. She wrote essays and poems, of an inspirational kind, about George Washington's heroism, and the virtues of the American Republic. And she had enough spunk to walk right into the editorial offices of her local newspaper to see if her poems could get published. Soon, she was being singled out and sought by important people; she was invited into their homes, treated kindly, and petted by them. Then, her success as a student took her to Boston Latin High School, and for a while her life was divided between trying to gather some pennies that would enable her family to pay the rent, and mingling with Boston's best.

Ah, how I recognize Mary Antin's youthful chutzpah, her desire to be happy and her troubles, her combination of adolescent shyness and a precocious maturity forced on her by her circumstances! But once she diverges from telling the tale and gives us her views of it, all similarities between us end. For, despite the hardships that leap out from the pages, Mary insists on seeing her life as a fable of pure success: success for herself, for the idea of assimilation, for the great American experiment. She ends her autobiography, entitled *The Promised Land*, as she is about to enter college and pursue her vocation as a natural scientist—and she gives us to understand that everything worked out wondrously well from then on.

There is only one hint that there is another side to the story, and it comes in the preface. "Happening when it did," Mary writes, "the emigration became of the most vital importance to me personally. All the processes of uprooting, transportation, replanting, acclimatization, and development took place in my own soul. I felt the pang, the fear, the wonder, and the joy of it. I can never forget, for I bear the scars. But I want to forget—sometimes I long to forget. . . . It is painful to be consciously of two worlds. The Wandering Jew in me seeks forgetfulness. I am not afraid to live on and on, if only I do not have to remember too much."

Being a close reader of such remarks, I can find volumes of implied meaning in them. But it is exactly the kind of meaning that Mary Antin was not encouraged to expand upon. And so there it is, a trace she never follows up on: a trace of the other story behind the story of triumphant progress.

Perhaps Mary Antin was more genetically predisposed toward optimism than I am, but I doubt it. It's just that she, like I, was affected by the sentiments of her time, and those sentiments made an inveterate positive thinker of her. The America of her time gave her certain categories within which to see herself—a belief in self-improvement, in perfectability of the species, in moral uplift—and those categories led her to foreground certain parts of her own experience, and to throw whole chunks of it into the barely visible background.

And what is the shape of my story, the story my time tells me to tell? Perhaps it is the avoidance of a single shape that tells the tale. A hundred years ago, I might have written a success story, without much self-doubt or equivocation. A hundred years ago, I might have felt the benefits of a steady, self-assured ego, the sturdy energy of forward movement, and the excitement of being swept up into a greater national purpose. But I have come to a different America, and instead of a central ethos, I have been given the blessings and the terrors of multiplicity. Once I step off that airplane in Houston, I step into a culture that splinters, fragments, and re-forms itself as if it were a jigsaw puzzle dancing in a quantum space. If I want to assimilate into my generation, my time, I have to assimilate the multiple perspectives and their constant shifting. Who, among my peers, is sure of what is success and what failure? Who would want to be sure? Who is sure of purposes, meanings, national goals? We slip between definitions with such acrobatic ease that straight narrative becomes impossible. I cannot conceive of my story as one of simple progress, or simple woe. Any confidently thrusting story line would be a sentimentality, an excess, an exaggeration, an untruth. Perhaps it is my intolerance of those, my cherishing of uncertainty as the only truth that is, after all, the best measure of my assimilation; perhaps it is in my misfittings that I fit. Perhaps a successful immigrant is an exaggerated version of the native. From now on, I'll be made, like a mosaic, of fragments—and my consciousness of them. It is only in that observing consciousness that I remain, after all, an immigrant.

Part III

THE
NEW
WORLD

It's April 1979, and I'm standing in a crowded living room on the Upper West Side, sipping wine and surveying the surroundings. The room, modest except for the walls lined with magisterial bookshelves—this is mostly a literary, or at least a writing crowd—is buzzing with the noise of animated group-talk. It's a scene familiar to me in its every detail: the high-ceilinged apartment with the well-buffed parquet floor, the unpretentious furniture with some oak antique items, the pleasant clutter of papers and magazines, the trays of French and Italian cheeses, the sounds of genuine merriment and strained good cheer, the staccato exchanges of witticisms, the voices raised to ride a wave of anecdotal energy, or to dominate the floor.

In the group next to me, the subject of discussion is X, a well-known writer and literary critic whose opinions, in the opinion of this group, are terribly wrong. "The man hasn't had a new thought since Saul Bellow, and we know how long that has been," a short, pudgy man pronounces with languid deliberation.

"And he attacks anyone who has," somebody else offers. "Basically, he can't stand anyone younger than himself horning in on his territory."

"It's called the anxiety of succession. It comes about two minutes after you get over the anxiety of influence," I throw in, and someone kindly giggles at my cattiness.

The daughter of the hosts, six years old and pink with excitement in her Laura Ashley dress, runs by, clearly in heaven, and I flash back to a party about thirty years ago, in a peasant house, and hear the echoing steps of people dancing on the wooden floor, and my mother taking a glass of vodka from my father's hand because he had had too many. He couldn't hold it, she reminded him, she had a stronger head for it.

An editor of a fashionable magazine comes up to me, and we talk about how Y's column on books has gone downhill, but Z has turned out to be surprisingly smart. I must call her and suggest an article, I make a note to myself. Then I listen to a young man talk about the new school of New York writers with such energy of first passion that I promise myself to look at his clippings on Monday when I return to my office at *The New York Times.*

I walk over to the other side of the room, where I see Jiri, who's here from Hungary for a year, to teach at NYU, standing rather shyly on the margin of a little circle. The conversation in this group has turned to Cuba, where one of the men has just spent two weeks.

"The best parties were given by the Russians," he says casually. "The caviar was first-rate."

"They usually bring more than caviar," Jiri says, and everyone stops in an embarrassed silence, as if he'd just made a glaringly obvious faux pas. "It's not that I think Batista was great, or that America should go in there instead," he adds hastily. "I really don't." But the others turn away from him, and Jiri and I studiously avoid looking at each other.

My friend Peter saunters over with his long-legged, deliberately slow gait, and gives me a pat on the cheek and a squeeze on the arm, which he administers as if he were bestowing a favor. He knows he's a prize item in this room—a robust, single, intelligent male—and after making some desultory remarks, he proceeds to look around lazily, like a lion surveying his territory in the knowledge that he's master of it. Lydia comes up to us, as usual humming with effusive excitement, her eyes shining as if there were no tomorrow. "Peter!" she exclaims, "you're just the person I wanted to see! I had a phone call today from a TV station in Germany, and they want to do a show on which I think you should be a consultant. Oh, it would be so wonderful if it worked out! Maybe we could go to Berlin together . . ." The hum continues, a kind of bird song meant to attract males. But she's making too much effort, and anyway, it's the wrong song. Peter looks over her head, puts his hand on her shoulder, and says, "Ah, excuse me, I see somebody I know over there . . ."

America, I think. This goddamn place.

"Hello, silly little Polish person!" It's Miriam, and coming from her, this epithet carries complexities of affection. "So," she says lowering her voice, "are we having fun or is this another glittering occasion we have to suffer through?"

"If things were ever so simple," I say, and we give each other a wry look. "What news?" I ask her—a question that, after some fifteen years of close acquaintance, has the involutions of a many-chambered nautilus.

"Today, I'm on top of the world," she answers. "I got seven hours of uninsomniac sleep last night, Robert agreed to cook twice a week, I wrote two passable pages of my story and the computer didn't eat them up. What more could a woman want?"

"Not much," I agree. "In fact, I can't think of anything at all." We go on to exchange some gossip about the people in the room, knowing that we can catch each other's observations like a bouncing ball, and then other friends come in, and the air in the room thickens with intimacy and the laughter brightens with warmth.

This goddamn place is my home now, and sometimes I'm taken aback by how comfortable I feel in its tart, overheated, insecure, well-meaning, expansive atmosphere. I know all the issues and all the codes here. I'm as alert as a bat to all the subliminal signals sent by word, look, gesture. I know who is likely to think

what about feminism and Nicaragua and psychoanalysis and
Woody Allen. A slight trace of an accent gives me away as somebody not born here, but my friends soon stop noticing it. They
think of me as one of them, even if my opinions are sometimes
slightly askew in relation to the general consensus. When I think
of myself in cultural categories—which I do perhaps too often—I
know that I'm a recognizable example of a species: a professional
New York woman, and a member of a postwar international new
class; somebody who feels at ease in the world, and is getting on
with her career relatively well, and who is as fey and brave and
capable and unsettled as many of the women here—one of a new
breed, born of the jet age and the counterculture, and middle-class
ambitions and American grit.

I fit, and my surroundings fit me. The only thing is that in the
midst of a conversation about the latest clashes between the PLO
and the Christian militia in Lebanon, or the fin de siècle Viennese
revival, or as we lift our wineglasses to each other in a moment of
affirmation and camaraderie, I lift off a little too high, to a point
from which the room becomes only a place in which I happen to
be, where I've found myself by some odd accident. A voice, almost
unconscious, keeps performing an inaudible, perpetual triangulation—that process by which ancient Greeks tried to extrapolate,
from two points of a triangle drawn in the sand, the moon's distance
from the earth. From my removed, abstract promontory, this Upper
West Side apartment looks as surreal as a large foreground object
in a Magritte painting. Weightlessness is upon me; I am here,
feeling the currents of conflict and warmth, but from that other
point in the triangle, this is just one arbitrary version of reality. The
room dematerializes slightly. Nothing here has to be the way it is;
people could behave in a different manner; I could look different,
flirt differently; I could be having entirely different conversations.
Not any specific conversations; the other place in my mind no
longer has any particularity. It's just an awareness that there is
another place—another point at the base of the triangle, which
renders this place relative, which locates me within that relativity
itself.

In the small hours of the morning, I flag down a taxi and drive home through the familiar, empty streets. Broadway: there is the Korean fruit stand where I buy my peaches and pears, there the deli where I get my take-out dinners, there the dry cleaner to whom I've become absurdly loyal over the years without any signs of reciprocity. A spring breeze floats in through the taxi window, and the clock on the Apthorp Building tells me it's too close to when I have to get up. "Had a good time tonight?" the taxi driver asks tentatively, exploring my willingness to get into a conversation. "Pretty good," I say laconically, signaling my preference not to. He understands and turns on the radio. A Madonna song. Suddenly, I'm in this taxi, in this funky rhythm, in this town. In the half-lit streets there'll be, in the morning, sufficient life. This is not a place where I happen to be, this happens to be the place where I am; this is the only place. How could there be anywhere more real? I get out of the cab, and go up to my apartment, and get into bed without turning on the light. How strange, I think, how strange what I've become, and then words cease and, in my drowsiness, I become an animal thing I've always known, only myself.

The Houston air is thick with heat and humidity, which slow everyone's movements to a sluggish, lazy saunter. The humidity is layered with so many smells that I detect a whiff of a Cracow summer among them, and it shoots me through with a sudden nostalgia, as for a love one has almost forgotten to mourn. But not for long, because what's going on right around me is so diverting. The Rice campus has a formal and somewhat stiff aesthetic, with a central quadrangle segmented by impeccably straight hedges and surrounded by Federal brick buildings, some of them with white columns and porticoes. I walk along the well-pruned paths with a sense of pleasurable excitement and confusion: I am in a new country again, and it is as different from Vancouver as Lagado is from Lilliput. This is the real America, I'm convinced, not having any way of knowing that I'm in a particular region of it, at a specific and rather curious time in its history.

Really, of course, I'm in college country, and on first impression, it seems like a friendly and manageable place. My fellow students seem bright and shiny and squeaky clean—the girls in their tartan skirts and bobby socks, the boys with neatly pressed shirts and lively, open faces. "Excuse me," everyone I meet asks politely, "but I notice you have an accent. Do you mind if I ask where it's from?" I don't mind at all, especially since I soon discover that my answer makes a favorable impression. "How interesting," my interlocutors say when I tell them I am from Poland, and some of them proceed to ask me respectful questions, as if this bare fact gave me special stature. I, in turn, listen curiously to the way they speak—in a gamut of southern drawls and Texan twangs, which I find saucy and musical, and which I sincerely long to imitate.

At night, in our dormitory, groups of eager-eyed, fresh-skinned girls gather in their nighties in the common-room area and, to the strumming of someone's guitar, earnestly sing "Swing Low, Sweet Chariot," and "Kumbaya," and "Five Hundred Miles," songs that move some of them nearly to tears, but that seem to me, at first, oddly flat and unemotional; it takes awhile before I become attuned to their foursquare, dignified melodies.

My dormitory room is plain and purely functional—a bed, a closet, a desk—but it fills me with a sense of well-being, because it's a room like everybody else's, an equalizing space. Here, I don't need to be so aware of social distinctions, and neither, perhaps, does anyone else; here, I can be just whoever I am. A few hours after I arrive, I'm joined by Lizzy, who's to be my roommate. She is a tall, bony girl with clear brown eyes and a large, thoughtful mouth. "Where are you from?" she asks immediately, and I tell her. "And you?" I ask, and Lizzy tells me that she comes from Cleveland, and that she is a Lutheran. When I look puzzled, she explains that her ancestors came from Germany, and that American Lutherans were a particularly exacting branch of Protestantism, and that her parents are both people of high principle.

I discover that the social landscape which seems so homogeneous at first is divided into complex configurations that everyone recognizes through subtle signals which are quite lost on me. Lizzy points out to me Baptists from small southern towns who turn out to be mathematical geniuses, scions of old Texan families who are already planning their political futures, smart northern girls with bohemian manners, flirty southern debutantes who like to hide their cleverness, literary sophisticates, and budding religious leaders. And all of them decked out in those tartan checks and bobby socks and the friendliest, white-toothed smiles. Surely, Gulliver had an easier country to understand!

There are, for example, all those customs that nobody told me about—the hazing of freshman boys, the initiations into literary societies, which all the girls want to get into, and the barbecue parties on sunny lawns. Every week that first fall, all the freshmen, wearing extremely unattractive "beanies"—a light-colored version of yarmulkes—march in tandem to the enormous stadium to attend the compulsory football game. There, I witness rituals as arcane as Aztec ceremonies—elaborate choreographies of floodlit cheerleading, collective genuflections to a large stuffed owl, which is the university's mascot, and once a near riot, which starts up when an umpire's decision provokes streams of boys from both warring camps to run down the bleachers with the full intention of attacking each other—only to be stopped dead in their tracks when the Rice band strikes up the national anthem. It is their respect for the law that astonishes me as much as their bloodthirst, but I guess these are university students and good boys. It is at these games that I discover how one can't see the ball without knowing the rules of the game, and I sit through the lengthy events without unraveling the secrets of what goes on down there, in the enormous stadium, where surreally clad men huddle and disperse violently.

There are other phenomena I encounter that I cannot fit on any grid. It happens rather regularly that students whom I barely know stop me in the library or the cafeteria to unburden themselves of some confession. The campus eccentrics gravitate toward me, perhaps because they sense in me a fellow outsider who will not judge them by the mainstream standards. People compliment me on being a "good listener," but they're wrong. I'm more like a naturalist trying to orient myself in an uncharted landscape, and eyeing the flora and fauna around me with a combination of curiosity and detachment. They might be upset if they knew the extent to which I view them as a puzzling species, but instead, they see a sort of egalitarian attentiveness. Since I don't know what's normal and what weird here, I listen with an equally impartial and polite interest to whomever approaches me. In this way, I come to hear the story of a girl who speaks in tongues, and who every weekend submits herself to a leather-strap beating by her religious mentor; I listen to a boy who tells me, his eyes heated and glazed, that the world is foul, cankered, evil—evil with Communism, with sex, with corruption—and who that evening walks off a dormitory roof during a conversation with God. Then there are the three girls who, after swearing me to secrecy, ask me to follow them to the dormitory basement. There, they tell me in breathless whispers that they're preparing for a great enterprise in which they want me to join with them. They have powers of clairvoyance and mental telepathy, they explain, and moreover, they're convinced that I do too, except I'm repressing these abilities because I was brought up under that horrible "system." What they have divined through their clairvoyant vision is that the Russians are going to invade the United States from Cuba. When that happens, they'll be ready: they're going to fight. At this point, they open a large leather trunk for my inspection: in its interior, I see cans of food, powdered milk—and, among these innocuous objects, two large, steely blue revolvers. The three girls plan to conduct guerrilla warfare with these weapons, and they are fully prepared—in fact eager—to die in the Armageddon, because they know what'll follow death as well. They show me poems they've written—lugubrious, gory, and ridiculous—in which, after being wounded and scarred, the heroines have been lifted to another planet, from which they look down on combat cataclysmically spreading to all corners of the earth.

Even I know that this isn't normal, though it isn't crazy in the way I understand that word either. I remember the crazy person on our street in Cracow; from behind the windows of a one-story house, this unseen man howled and screamed with bestial abandon;

that's how one knew he was crazy. Or there was Pani Grodzinska's sister, who was afraid to go out on the street, and shredded newspapers all over her room; that was another example of solid craziness. But this is different; these girls go to their classes and don't scream or wave their guns in public. It's just that they have these Ideas. Each culture breeds its own kind of derangement, I'll later learn, and these American classmates of mine seem to go crazy with a surfeit of moral fervors. But in this, they're not so unlike the apparently very normal man from the Rotary Club who invited me to his large and comfortable house, and showed me his collection of guns, and told me, getting very red in the face, that you can't trust the government, but if the Commies ever come this way, there'll be at least some boys in Texas who will know how to defend their country. "Only in America," I tell myself about such manifestations, meaning that I can't make any sense of them whatsoever.

Even a relatively intelligible person, like Lizzy, poses problems of translation. She—and many others around me—would be as unlikely in Poland as gryphons or unicorns. In her particular mingling of ideas and sensibility, of emotion and self-presentation, she is a distinctively American personality. Is she as smart as Basia? As spunky? As attractive? But the terms don't travel across continents. The human mean is located in a different place here, and qualities like adventurousness, or cleverness, or shyness are measured along a different scale and mapped within a different diagram. You can't transport human meanings whole from one culture to another any more than you can transliterate a text. Nevertheless, Lizzy and I set out to understand each other with a will—and we run into misunderstandings with the rude surprise of rams butting into each other in the middle of a narrow bridge. In the evenings, we spend long hours, sitting on our beds, talking. Lizzy, it turns out, holds beliefs that seem self-evident to her and that run smack counter to truths that seem equally obvious to me. We discuss, of course, the largest questions—whether people are free or determined, and how to fulfill one's potential, and what it means to be happy. Then there are issues that have never crossed my mental horizon but that are central in Lizzy's moral geography—such as the nature of civic responsibility, and how to interpret the American Constitution, and how to achieve the ideal of self-sufficiency.

"You know, I think Barry Goldwater is right," Lizzy declares one evening as we're munching on some cafeteria cookies. "Welfare is a horrible system. Giving people something for nothing destroys their dignity."

"But what if people need help?" I ask. "There are so many rich people in this country. It isn't fair that they should have so much and others nothing." I can't distinguish Barry Goldwater from Adlai Stevenson, but perhaps I've been influenced by ideas of equal distribution drilled into me in elementary school after all, or maybe it's just that the famous American "contrasts" still have the power to upset me.

"Giving people something for nothing destroys their individuality," Lizzy asserts. "You can only have dignity if you're self-sufficient."

"But why shouldn't people help each other?" I ask, really at a loss to understand. There's no common word for "self-sufficiency" in Polish, and it sounds to me like a comfortless condition, a harsh and artificial ideal.

"Because dependence is bad for your character," Lizzy retorts.

"But we're all dependent on each other!" I say, stating what only seems obvious.

"Don't you think it's humiliating to be dependent?" Lizzy asks. She's speaking out of a different sense of the human creature, of where dignity and satisfaction lie, and she's as flummoxed by this disagreement on basic principles as I.

"No, I don't. I mean, what if you get into trouble? What if you lose your job? When there's unemployment, somebody has to lose their job! Do you think that nobody should help you then?"

"People get what they deserve," Lizzy says, her beautiful mouth tightening into a look which suggests that my opinions have something unsavory about them from which she prefers to dissociate herself. "If you have pride, you don't ask for handouts."

But at this, anger compresses itself in my forehead. "Do you think everyone starts out with the same amount of opportunity?" I say furiously, my voice knotting with frustration. "Do you think everyone starts even? And what if people are stupid, or untalented, or sick! Do you just want to throw them to rot, to end up in a ditch?" I have my pride too, and I don't say "And what if you're a new immigrant starting out with nothing?" but of course it's my family I'm defending in this quarrel, and it's the thought of my parents that makes my temperature rise so high.

"If you have enough character, you can always pull yourself out," Lizzy says, iron in her voice. "That's what this country is all about, and that's the philosophy that made it what it is."

"Then it's a mean and cruel philosophy!" I shout.

"I think your philosophy is pinko!" Lizzy hurls at me, looking hurt, and runs out of the room, slamming the door behind her. I'm left badly jangled by the exchange, and Lizzy, it turns out, runs up to the dormitory roof, where she cries tears of frustration and rage. But the next day, we start up again, talking about how we want to experience everything, and what kinds of adults we want to become. On this subject too it turns out that our mental pictures are quite at odds. Lizzy thinks maturity is a condition to be avoided at all costs. "Everyone keeps saying you should be well adjusted," she says. "But well adjusted to what?" The condition of adulthood, in her mind, stands for her mother's repetitive days, rows of suburban houses in which nothing new or exciting ever happens, and a conventionality that keeps you from being curious and alive. Maturity, in this system of associations, is the opposite of experience: it is a kind of shrinking of the soul. Her mother, Lizzy tells me, does not understand what it's like to be very happy or very unhappy, or to want to have adventures; it's as though she belonged to an entirely other, not fully human species, and Lizzy is genuinely afraid of turning into somebody like her, or other grown-ups she has known. Since I yearn for maturity with every fiber of my soul, I try to convey to Lizzy the mastery, and the self-possession, and the wherewithal to express myself fully that I keep hoping for. I try to paint the image, so potent in my mind, of Pani Witeszczak playing the piano with tenderness and control. I tell her that my mother is not some straw woman whom I've never seen suffer, or storm, or cry. "We're all human," I say, echoing my mother's line. I want to explain how maturity means entering into the great stream of experience, coming to know what people have always known. Lizzy looks at me thoughtfully, but she, literally, doesn't see it; her mind has been stocked with different images, and just as I can't see the pictures of her childhood, she can't leap outside them, can't imagine what's not in her head. Growing up will prove painfully difficult for her, as difficult as for most of her, and my, generation.

In between these earnest conversations, Lizzy teaches me how to apply tactful makeup to my eyes, and tells me I should buy some loafers and Villager dresses so I'll look more with it. When I tell her I haven't got the money, she looks upset.

"But you look fine in whatever you wear," she assures me, and I'm grateful. "Do you know Mary, the senior who looks so feminine?" she continues. "Yes?" I say, "What about her?" "Well," Lizzy hesitates, "you know, they say she sleeps with her boyfriend. She's so feminine. I wonder how you get to be that way." The vexing question of femininity continues to come up on many occasions. At late-night get-togethers in dormitory rooms, girls try to sort out just what you should do on the first date, and whether it's any fun anyway, and how Rachel doesn't get dates because she's too tall and masculine, and Moselle because she's too beautiful and therefore boys are afraid of her. I never thought you had to do anything special to be feminine—surely, it's enough to be a woman, isn't it?—but this belief, which seems a given to me, strikes my college-mates as very sophisticated.

The boys who take me out think I'm very sophisticated too. At this point I'm not inhibited by a real knowledge of sexuality or the indigenous rules of intersexual behavior, and with the insouciance of perfect innocence, I tell my companions about my plans to have three affairs before I get married, and my resolve not to engage in anything as adolescent as necking, which, I say, strikes me as a "Puritan custom." And really, I find the sight of serious Lizzy, coming back from her dates with chapped lips and raw chin and glazed eyes, incongruous, and I turn my head away from the couples kissing each other furiously in the cars parked in the perfectly public parking lot. It seems far less embarrassing to me to go to bed with somebody than to enter into the coy collusion of this messy struggle. But for now, nobody is proposing anything so daring, though there's a brisk succession of boys who ask me to go to rowdy beer parties with them, or for walks on a tree-lined street surrounding the campus, during which they shyly hold my hand and talk to me about literature and the beauties of math and the difficulties of love. They are curious about what I have to say, and fascinated by the fact that I'm a "European," which in their minds guarantees some mysterious and profounder knowledge.

I must admit that I do nothing to dispel this impression. Instead of being an uncomfortable glitch in the smooth texture of adolescent existence, I've now gained the status of an exotic stranger, and this brings high color to my cheeks and sharpens my opinions. I'm excited by my own otherness, which surrounds me like a bright, somewhat inflated bubble. After a while, this will become a treacherous condition, for it will be difficult to break out of my difference and reclaim a state of ordinariness in which, after all, we want to live. But I'm still a visitor here, not deeply implicated in what goes on around me, and for now, I thrive on the pleasures of being "interesting." In the middle of the year, my music teacher arranges for me to give a concert in the Rice auditorium, and at the end, my youthful audience rises and claps for a long time. Afterward, several boys approach me, their eyes enthusiastic with appreciation, and tell me courteously that my playing sounded great, and I looked real pretty up there on the stage in that long green dress. In the exhilaration of the moment, I feel that life is once again as it should be.

> Labour is blossoming or dancing where
> The body is not bruised to pleasure soul,
> Nor beauty born out of its own despair,
> Nor blear-eyed wisdom out of midnight oil.
> O chestnut-tree, great-rooted blossomer,
> Are you the leaf, the blossom or the bole?

O body swayed to music, O brightening glance,
How can we know the dancer from the dance?

I'm sitting in a bracingly uncomfortable chair in the Rice University library, reading slowly, laboriously. The chestnut tree in the stanza summons my private chestnut tree, and the last line moves me all on its own, because that's what it's like to play the piano, in those moments when I can no longer tell whether I'm playing the music or the music is playing me. But what does "bole" mean, or "blear-eyed," or "midnight oil"? I have only the vaguest idea, and by the time I look up these words in a dictionary and accomplish the translation from the sounds to their definition, it's hard to reinsert them into the flow of the lines, the seamless sequence of musical meaning. I concentrate intensely, too intensely, and the lines come out straight and square, though I intuit a beauty that's only an inflection away. And so I struggle harder to enter the stanza, like a frustrated lover whose hunger is fed by the inaccessible proximity of her object.

Much of what I read is lost on me, lost in the wash and surf of inexactly understood words. And yet, chagrined though I am by this, I soon find that I can do very well in my courses. I believe this happens not only despite but also because of my handicap: because I have so little language. Like any disability, this one has produced its own compensatory mechanisms, and my mind, relatively deprived of words, has become a deft instrument of abstraction. In my head, there is no ongoing, daily monologue to distract me, no layers of verbal filigree to peel away before the skeleton of an argument can become clear. Without this sensuous texturing, the geometries of my own perceptions have become as naked to me as the exposed girders of a building before the actual building hides them. When I'm presented with an object of study—a problem or a book—it's easier for me to penetrate to the architectural plan than to appreciate the details of the exterior.

It's precisely because I know how thinned out the air of abstraction can be that I'll develop great respect for the significance of the surface and the concrete detail. But for now, it so happens that my accidental predisposition is perfectly fitted to the educational premises of the period. The education I receive at Rice is almost entirely formalistic, and the things we're required to do with what we read are just what I can do best in my verbally deprived condition. In a philosophy survey that introduces us to medieval religious thinkers and French existentialists, we're not asked whether arguments about God or the absurd seem true but how arguments about truth are constructed. In a history course on the Renaissance, we don't need to remember what sequence of events led up to the Reformation; instead, we're asked to contemplate the nature of retrospective knowledge, or whether an accurate interpretation of the past is possible. This I can do by arranging blocks of abstract ideas into a logical pattern, without stumbling on the treacherous shoals of specificity.

It takes me awhile to discover that this is a valuable talent. At first, I'm reluctant to study at all, lest I prove a miserable failure. Then in a philosophy class, a professor discussing the Platonic qualities of "largeness" and "smallness" asks whether we want to talk about a large or a small orange, and when I cheekily suggest "How about medium?" he throws a piece of chalk at me in the most friendly way. In my English class, my paper on a John Donne sonnet is singled out to be read aloud, and I decide that it might be worthwhile to make an effort after all.

Not that my efforts ever become very disciplined. Studying too systematically or too hard would violate my Polish code of honor—that one should, in any system whatsoever, break as many rules as one can—and would take the flash and flair out of the grand game of getting away with it. But I perceive that there is another game going on here—of an intellectual kind—that I can play very well. I soak in the academic vocabulary of the time with an almost suspicious facility; for me, this is an elementary rather than an advanced language, a language I learn while I'm still in my English childhood. It does not have to make its way through layers of other vocabulary, and I can juggle it with resistless ease, as if it had no weight.

Even in literature, that most sensuously textured of expressions, my abstracting bent turns out to be useful. The Rice English Department in the mid-sixties is firmly in the grip of New Criticism—that laboratory method which concerns itself with neither writers' lives nor their worlds—and whether I'm reading Chaucer, or Jacobean tragedy, or *The Sound and the Fury*. I'm asked to parse pieces of text as if they were grammatical constructions. "Form is content," at this time, is taken to mean that there is no such thing as content.

Luckily for me, there is no world outside the text; luckily, for I know so little of the world to which the literature I read refers. My task, when I read a poem or a novel, is to find repeated symbols, patterns of words, recurring motifs, and motifs that pull against each other. These last are particularly prized because they have the honorific status of "irony" and "paradox." These are exercises I can perform with ease. The local details, from which most readers get their most immediate, primary pleasure, don't obstruct my way. The clothes people wear in novels, the places where they live, their characteristic gestures and turns of speech have, for me, no mimetic resonances in English; Daisy in *The Great Gatsby* does not summon in my mind a spoiled, Waspish girl of a certain type, as she might for other readers; she is for me a formal entity, the symbol that Gatsby, another symbolic construction, craves. They are symbols clashing on the pages, until they resolve into their neat denouement, symbolic of American tragedies, of America itself.

I become an expert on this business of symbolic patterns. They seem to come in several varieties. There is, in American literature, individualism and the frontier, and there is society versus nature, and self versus society—and there is, first and foremost in those days, alienation. I become an expert in alienation too. I notice that it comes up in American literature more than elsewhere, and has a particularly American flavor. People are often lonely in American novels, and can't easily talk to each other; they flub human contacts horribly, and tend to find themselves in seedy rooms, alone, or out on the frontier, grimly questing. As for men and women, they either speak to each other with great sentimentality, as in *For Whom the Bell Tolls,* or find each other truly disgusting, as in *Miss Lonely-hearts.*

Being an alien myself in the midst of all this alienation turns out to be no disadvantage. For one thing, New Criticism is an alienated way of reading meant for people who are aliens in the country of literature. It prizes detachment, objectivity, and the critical rather than the sympathetic faculties. It is a very cool criterion, but also an egalitarian one, for it requires no privileged acquaintance with culture, no aristocratic, proprietorial intimacies of connoisseurship.

But my particular kind of alienness serves me well too, for I soon discover that triangulation is a more useful tool in literary criticism than it is in life. As I read, I triangulate to my private criteria and my private passions, and from the oblique angle of my estrangement, I notice what's often invisible to my fellow students. When I read *The Catcher in the Rye,* it's Holden Caulfield's immaturity that strikes me, and I write a paper upbraiding him for his false and coy naïveté—my old, Polish terms of opprobrium. Reading *The Ambassadors* requires a torture of concentration, but a glimpse of Strether coming ashore in France and registering the ever-so-minute changes of light and smell and facial expressions and angle of objects delivers a thrill of recognition: that's just what it's like to land on a foreign shore, and I want to write Henry James a thank-you note for capturing the ineffable with such exactitude. In Malamud's *The Assistant,* it's not the religious parable that fixes my attention but the dingy, dark little store in which the Jewish shopkeeper ekes out his hopeless living; I'm grateful again, that someone has made literature of such a condition.

Some kind of intellectual passion—or perhaps a passion for the work of the intellect—is being stoked in the midst of these placid exegeses. For one thing, I've learned that in a democratic educational system, in a democratic ideology of reading, I am never made to feel that I'm an outsider poaching on others' property. In this country of learning, I'm welcomed on equal terms, and it's through the democratizing power of literature that I begin to feel at home in America, even before I understand the literature or America, or the relationship between them, very well.

That relationship, as I find out firsthand, is confoundingly indirect. A visitor coming to the United States armed with the knowledge of Melville, and Hemingway and Faulkner and John Updike and Harold Robbins and Stephen King, would still be almost entirely unprepared for the broad and the intimate spectacle of the actual country confronting him. Driving on Interstate 1 would still be an immense surprise, and coping with the New York subway a sui generis experience; attending a party in a San Francisco home, or a wedding on Long Island, would be as strange as witnessing the rites in a Japanese novel; and while the Statue of Liberty might be recognizable from a book-jacket picture, an ordinary conversation in an ordinary living room would be full of those odd angles and slants of light and eruptions of the unfamiliar that Henry James registered so uncannily. It is only after a longer while that such a visitor might start putting together the living culture and the literature to which it has given rise: the crazed holy-talk of a street-corner preacher in Times Square might cross with a flash of Hazel Motes; the staccato aggressiveness of a New York intellectual elaborating some unlikely political proposition might synchronize with the rhythms of Norman Mailer's prose; during a long cross-country drive in the vastnesses of unpopulated wilderness, Thoreau's obsessions might become clear. Mimesis, it seems, works smoothly in only one direction, and life refuses conveniently to mirror the art in which it's seemingly mirrored.

At this point in my education, I can't translate backward. Literature doesn't yet give me America in its particulars—though as I read Emerson and Thoreau and Walker Percy, I feel the breath of a general spirit: the spirit, precisely, of alienness, of a continent and a culture still new and still uncozy, and a vision that turns philosophical or tortured from confronting an unworded world.

At the end of my freshman year, I take the bus back to Vancouver. It's a long trip—fifty-two hours in all—and for a seemingly interminable time, the bus moves through the stony moonscape of the

Texas panhandle. Next to me on the bus sits a pasty-faced young woman, her blond hair in curlers. She got on at one of the panhandle stops, in a place that seems a no place, and as we approach the Rocky Mountains, she begins praying and holding my hand, for she has never seen mountains and she's afraid that they'll fall down on her. From time to time, we stop at dismal bus-stop cafeterias, where I can't bring myself to eat the damp sandwiches or the runny cherry pies. After a sleepless night, I arrive at the Vancouver Greyhound Terminal, where I'm greeted by my parents, whom I have not seen since September. They tell me that one of their acquaintances has arranged a summer job for me as a clerk in a dry-cleaning establishment. I'm glad to have it, but I hate the low-ceilinged, overheated room in which I work, and the lunchtime conversations about astrology or the latest airplane disasters, and the endless slips of paper on which I log in clean and dirty laundry. I hate it more than I can admit: quitting, or other forms of rebellion, are not an option, and so I slip again into the befogged indifference that's becoming my form of protest. The best relief, that summer, is talking with Alinka, who has turned thoughtful and philosophical, and who now reads Sartre and Simone de Beauvoir when she skips classes. She tends to stay out late at night with unapproved companions, and to be seen with men of various ages. I too begin to feel maternal worry and lecture her on how she should be careful: within our family divisions, I'm allowed the adventurousness of a son; but Alinka, the little one, the girl, must be protected. It's clear, though, that my sister is readier than I to defy family rules and plunge fullheartedly into whatever she finds here.

It's a confusing return home; none of us knows very well what's to become of us. One afternoon, when I come back from my job, my mother hands me a letter. It is from one of my literature professors, who has written to tell me that I'm really very good in his subject. He would have no hesitation, he writes, in sending me to graduate school right now. I should consider going on in English. I look at the short, exhilarating note for a long time. At the moment, the clear, easy world of ideas and literary exercises seems like a most welcome antidote to the sad messiness of daily reality—

to the oppressiveness of my dreary office, and my reluctant return home each afternoon. Besides, I am as susceptible to flattery as anyone. I form the resolve to become a literature major.

But it's not until many years later, not until I've finished graduate school successfully, and have begun to teach literature to others, that I crack the last barrier between myself and the language—the barrier I sensed but couldn't get through, as I read "Among School Children." It happens as I read "The Love Song of J. Alfred Prufrock," which I'm to explicate to a class of freshmen at the University of New Hampshire the next morning. "Let us go then, you and I," I read, "When the evening is spread out against the sky / Like a patient etherised upon a table; / Let us go, through certain half-deserted streets, / The muttering retreats . . ."

My eye moves over these lines in its accustomed dry silence; and then—as if an aural door had opened of its own accord—I hear their modulations and their quiet undertones. Over the years, I've read so many explications of these stanzas that I can analyze them in half a dozen ingenious ways. But now, suddenly I'm attuned, through some mysterious faculty of the mental ear, to their inner sense; I hear the understated melancholy of that refrain, the civilized restraint of the rhythms reining back the more hilly swells of emotion, the self-reflective, moody resignation of the melody. "And I have known the eyes already, known them all—/The eyes that fix you in a formulated phrase . . ." I read, tasting the sounds on the tongue, hearing the phrases somewhere between tongue and mind. Bingo, I think, this is it, the extra, the attribute of language over and above function and criticism. I'm back within the music of the language, and Eliot's words descend on me with a sort of grace. Words become, as they were in childhood, beautiful things—except this is better, because they're now crosshatched with a complexity of meaning, with the sonorities of felt, sensuous thought.

How do you talk to an alien? Very carefully. When I fall in love with my first American, I also fall in love with otherness, with the far spaces between us and the distances we have to travel to meet at the source of our attraction. My fair-haired Texan is tall and blue eyed and has a sweet smile meant to be well liked. I watch his loose, graceful movements raptly; this is a new kind of male beauty, and I am all the more fascinated because I have seen it on posters and in the movies, and I can't quite believe he's made of warm, vulnerable flesh. Drinking bottles of acrid wine in his apartment, or eating hamburgers in a neighborhood restaurant that features an enormous plaster cow on its roof, I listen to him with such intentness that my face flushes and my head begins to throb from the strain. What does he tell me about? Emptiness. There is a great emptiness, a vacuum within him and there's nothing with which to fill it up. He started out as a golden boy, president of his senior class in high school and captain of the debating team—one of those headed to become a leader in his community, or a powerful executive in an oil company. But then he realized that he has never experienced anything, that he's afraid. He was afraid to love the one girl he did love, he tells me sadly; he's afraid to love me. He went off to New York in search of . . . something. There, he hid out in an unheated, cockroach-infested apartment. He was trying, trying to get hold of Experience, something real. He is trying still.

"You have to make a leap of faith," he tells me, a pained intensity lighting up his eyes. "You have to give up everything you have, everything you want. You have to let go. Then everything will come to you. You can't hold on to things too tight."

My head pounds with the effort of understanding. The words my Texan speaks come out from some unknown place; I can't tell what burden of feeling infuses them, what has led up to this pass, to this youthful extremity. Maybe if I could imagine his childhood, and the loneliness, and great nothingness he speaks of, I would know the meaning of his words to him. But when he describes his neo-Colonial house, and his father, who always tinkers in the basement, and his mother, who was too much alone, and who told him to make love pure, the pictures he draws are stark and melodramatic in my mind, because I don't know the stuff of the lives that fill them.

"I want to love you," my Texan tells me, looking anguished, "but I'm afraid to take the responsibility for you."

"But why do you need to take responsibility?" I ask, genuinely surprised at a concept so staunch and moral in the field of love. "When people love each other, it's out of pleasure, isn't it?"

"I'm afraid to hurt you," he says.

"If you hurt me, I'll tell you," I say reasonably enough. "You shouldn't worry about me so much. I'm pretty strong, you know." I say these things with a perfect lack of self-consciousness. Later, I'll come to recognize words like "responsibility" and "hurt" as a telltale buzz emitted by the men of my generation to signal that they don't really want to get involved. Once I do, my own freedom will be lost, and I'll begin to engage in those contorted maneuvers by which the women in the same generation try to conceal their desires so as not to scare the men off. But, for now, I see that my fair-haired Texan is genuinely wrenched by these dilemmas, burdened by a sense of sin and weighted down by a terrible urge to lift himself out of his body. Most of all, he's afraid to sleep with me. "But there's nothing impure about sex," I tell him, when he says he doesn't want to violate my purity.

Much later, I find out that his parents weren't exactly happy about his involvement with a foreigner, and a Jewess to boot. I'm hardly the kind of girl this former golden boy should have as a companion, and I suppose he too must have moments in which the sense of fortuitousness that attends all relationships—how has this stranger come to be in my life?—is compounded by the extreme unlikeliness of this coupling. We're young enough and infatuated enough to try to jump across the rifts. But our ideas of love are so different—and being in love is so different from what I had imagined it to be. This is all intensity and anguish, without a letup. Once I fall into sex as well as love, I find that I only want to be around my Texan; when I see him, I want to rush toward him; I want us to say everything to each other, in the freedom of our camaraderie. But I know that he's afraid, and I begin to restrain my gestures. I compose my walk and my face when I see him; I assure him that he can have all the independence he wants.

The question of femininity is becoming vexing to me as well. How am I to become a woman in an American vein, how am I to fit the contours of my Texan's soul? The allegory of gender is different here, and it unfolds around different typologies and different themes. I can't become a "Pani" of any sort: not like the authoritative Pani Orlovska, or the vampy, practical Pani Dombarska, or the flirty, romantic woman writer I once met. None of these modes of femininity makes sense here, none of them would find corresponding counterparts in the men I know.

In the middle of my junior year, I hear from my mother that Marek, in remote Israel, got married. I've forgotten to think about him for a while, but nevertheless the news sends me into a muted repetition of that earlier grief: so I must lose even the fantasy of running on the shore toward him; I must let it go and become a young woman here.

But I'm not sure how to transpose myself into a new erotic valence. The flattering sobriquets I heard as a young girl have no American equivalents: "She's a maddening woman," people would say about X, meaning that she had great quantities of classiness and brains and beauty. Or, "she's a fabulous woman"—implying some favored combination of whimsicality and wit and a touch of ruthlessness. I should become a more earnest sort of creature, learn more sensible melodies in my bones. The structure of personality is shaped at least as deeply by culture as it is by gender—or rather, each culture shapes both genders to be recognizable to each other in their difference. From within our alien structures, my Texan and I can't play in counterpoint; we miss the pitch of each other's erotic inventions, can't get to the heart of each other. We keep trying to travel the spaces between us. We keep talking strenuously, attentively, hoping that we can translate ourselves for each other, and a tenderness grows up between us in the very effort of the enterprise. He struggles with me mightily, as if I were an important task sent to him by a mystifying fate. He'd like to break through to me, break through his own involutions. But the strangeness remains— and it's not just the strangeness of discovering another person's ineradicable separateness. It is, ironically, in the smallest, quietest phrases, when we're nearest those soft and vulnerable crevices where intimacy is lodged, that my Texan and I know most poignantly that we don't speak exactly the same language. "I love you, Eva," he says in his mellow and terribly intense voice, and it's an oddly disembodied phrase I hear. It's an ethereal, sacred love he wants; a meeting of the spirits. I'm touched by his striving, but I miss the vigor and ease of friendship. We talk and talk to fill in those tiny, enormous lacunae between us. We explain ourselves like texts. We learn to read each other as one learns to decipher hieroglyphs. But we never meet in that quick flash of recognition, the intuitive click which comes from knowing the play and surfaces of each other's personalities. I come to know all the big and trivial things about him: about the time he hit his sister and his mother didn't punish him enough, and about his father's rages and why he loves Frank Capra. He knows about all the touchstones of my biography. Stereotypes fall away, become irrelevant. It no longer matters that he is a Texan, an American, or that his house boasts a collection of antique guns. He is just himself, this specific form of strangeness. He becomes familiar, only increasing the wonderment that the familiar should be so unfamiliar, the close so far away.

During my freshman year, Kennedy is assassinated. It happens so close by that it's as if the shot had been fired in the neighborhood. People mourn en masse, and some are scared: perhaps this was done by some vigilante group, and perhaps a wider violence is about to erupt. A boy I've been dating worked side by side with Oswald in the Dallas Book Depository. He's shocked to have known him, shocked that he had normal conversations with him. Lizzy's eyes grow big with thought, and after the service for Kennedy, she comes back to our room and cries; whatever her political persuasion, this is a horrible blow to her American faith. I understand the tragedy of what has happened, but not the full significance: it's too early in my American political education for me to know what has been lost, and what an earthquake such a political assassination constitutes. So it is with many things: because I don't know the background, I don't always grasp the meaning of the foreground.

In the middle of my sophomore year, my philosophy professor pastes up a sign on his door that proclaims THE STONES ARE THE HAIRY MEN OF ROCK. THE BEATLES ARE THE SMOOTH MEN. Hairy and smooth men at Rice begin to grow their hair well below the neckline. My English professor is frequently seen locked in ostentatious kisses with lovely young women. In a special Sunday class for selected initiates, Dr. O'Rourke, a medieval scholar, introduces us to Marshall McLuhan and R. D. Laing. At parties, the atmosphere becomes aerated with generalized affection; everyone in the room is good; everyone is one of us. We all share a secret together; we're all acolytes in a secret cult. Timothy Leary visits the campus and tells us that brain cells begin degenerating after you turn thirty, news which I find terrifying, but which the overflow audience in the large auditorium greets with approving glee. By the end of my sophomore year, the philosophy professor has written an article on transcendence in St. Thomas Aquinas and the Jefferson Airplane. The counterculture has hit the campus.

Ironically enough, just as I'm trying to fill myself with the material of language, my fellow students begin to cultivate willed inarticulateness, as if strings of complete sentences showed a questionable investment in a sick civilization. "Hey," people say when they run into each other, and they look meaningfully into each other's eyes, and proceed to laugh and mutter and sway in earnest and prolonged hugs, in a frantic simulation of spontaneous sincerity that seems as stylized to me as Marie Antoinette's attempts to play the naïve and sentimental milkmaid.

At parties, the atmosphere becomes honey thick with the pulsing rhythms of Aretha Franklin and the Stones and Janis Joplin, and I abandon myself with the others to the new motions this music awakes in my body. This part of what's happening is unequivocally good. About the rest I'm less sure.

Everywhere around me is heard the buzz of the new, and as if on cue my fellow students begin to undergo startling transformations. There is, for example, Janice, a shy, unprepossessing girl whose shapelessly cut brown hair and wire-rimmed glasses proclaim that she doesn't think she's pretty and doesn't want anyone to look

LOST IN TRANSLATION

at her too closely. Janice comes from a fundamentalist family, in which, she tells me wryly, "sex was supposed to be kept in the church." Her mother cried bitter tears when Janice decided to go to Rice, this dangerous Babylon, this seat of secular heresies. For a while, Janice gobbles up the heresies with an almost religious fervor. Then, other things begin to happen.

After our sophomore year, Janice spends the whole summer following Sviatoslav Richter. She goes to Europe on a scholarship to study French, but then she hears Richter in a concert and feels something like a call. So she learns Richter's tour itinerary and begins following it by train or by bus. Wherever the pianist gives a concert—Aix-en-Provence, Marseilles, Milan, Düsseldorf—she is there. Finally, someone in Richter's entourage notices her, and Janice has her reward: she is taken backstage and introduced to the object of her devotion. After she tells him what she has done, Richter is impressed, or moved enough, to kiss her hand.

Janice recounts her adventures with her eyes shining fiercely behind her glasses, and I don't know, as I sit listening to her, whether I should admire her recklessness, so surprising and seemingly out of character, or be disturbed by its irreality.

By our junior year, Janice's appearance begins to change rather dramatically. The glasses come off, to be replaced by contact lenses; the dowdy straight skirts are supplanted by colorful, perilously short dresses and overbright bell-bottom trousers, in which she moves with an earnest stiffness, as if the clothes were a duty she is determined to fulfill. Then, she tells me momentous news: she has fallen in love with her geology professor, and they are having an affair. The professor, unfortunately, is married, but Janice isn't bothered by that. She's going to talk to his wife and move in with them. "Love should be freely given," she says, her face gloomy with conviction. "There's enough of it to go around." I'm amazed by her plans, but the power of faith seems to triumph, and Janice has her way. She moves in with the geology professor and his wife, and for a while, she goes around with the dreamy and self-contained expression of a woman in love and a new convert. Then she learns she is pregnant, and the arrange-

192

ment falls apart. The lawfully married couple want Janice out of the house; the professor offers to arrange an abortion, and that's what she decides to do; but afterward, she begins acting oddly. "God didn't want it to be," she tells me, her eyes now opaque and turned inward. "The world is divided into the rose and the thorn, and I'm one of the thorns. I'm unworthy. I don't know why I thought anyone should love me."

I protest that this is not the end of everything, but Janice looks at me stonily: clearly, she thinks it is. Shortly thereafter, a local counterculture guru decides to give Janice mescaline in order to wean her from her mistaken ideas about the world. The guru has long hair, he wears old army uniforms, and he has adopted the mannerism of inarticulateness, though he continues to write papers that are often judged brilliant. "Don't worry about her," he tells me. "She'll see things differently after this. She'll see that she can accept everything."

"And what if she gets confused? What if she has a nervous breakdown?" I ask, distraught by his confidence and by what seems to me like a terrible risk.

"Take it easy, don't upset yourself," he says with a coolness that makes my distress faintly ridiculous. "She'll be all right. That's her only hope, anyway."

I am left chagrined by this encounter, on my own behalf as much as Janice's. Years later, while traveling in Jerusalem, I get lost in the Old City's Arab quarter; while I wander through the maze of winding white streets, consulting a map and getting more and more confused, I pass by women in chador, moving with quick steps and downcast eyes, and young boys throwing down buttons on the sidewalk in some unknown game, and groups of men, arms linked, who look at me with fierce eyes. It's all profoundly strange and fascinating, but also frightening in a particular way. During the hour or so it takes me to find my way out, I feel—rightly or wrongly, I don't know—that if I were taken for an unwanted intruder here, I would not have even the most fundamental means of appeal; it would be useless to signal with my eyes that I mean no harm; such signals would meet no response from the eyes of the men I see in these streets; their faces seem to hide and reveal a different emotional world; I doubt that I could find a meeting place.

That's the slippage, the elision I feel as the figure in army fatigues walks away with a rather swaggering step. My appeal ran off him like water, and he seems to me cold with conviction, and as inaccessible as those Arab men—as though we were enclosed by different reality principles.

Is there a reality principle in Texas? Or has it diffused itself over the state's vast spaces? It is a curious amorphousness I feel as I cozy up with others, in group-grope intimacy, at our New Cult gatherings. We light up joints at these events, and sit in a transport of togetherness and altered perceptions. The Real Thing at last. The music sounds so much more clear; we can make out the raga-like bass line in a Beatles song, and the three separate strands of a Bach fugue. Occasionally, someone makes an observation, and occasionally, everyone breaks into a harmonica of infectious laughter. I remain too sober by half. Oh, I am fascinated by all this, by the colorfulness of these new happenings. I like the bright new clothes and the gritty rhythms of the music; I argue with R. D. Laing in my head, and once I take mescaline. My private cult of Experience prescribes it, and indeed, under the stimulus of the substance, an Experience does take place, and my mind manufactures a series of phantasmagorically beautiful and disturbing images. But I cannot convert this single Experience into experience—something that can be incorporated into the stuff of my identity, that can be felt in the bones. For my companions in the marijuana-fragrant rooms, though, the impetus for the adventure is just the opposite: it seems to me that they would like to leap out of themselves, to become, in one transforming moment, something they are not. I want to live within language and to be held within the frame of culture; they want to break out of the constraints of both language and culture. Perhaps those constraints have been too severe; perhaps that is the root cause of this revolution. But their oppressions have not been mine, and therefore their fight—against the established terms of a middle-class, American reality—cannot be mine either. The lines of conflict and of defiance are different for me; it's different idols that

I need to fight. I miss the solidarity of a youthful rebellion; but from within my otherness, this seems too much a High Mass and a masque. And so, while my companions are trying to achieve some interesting metamorphosis, I try to hold on to some ordinary points of reference. I'm having enough trouble remaining myself as it is. Perhaps because I've been bombarded with so much change, I have to distinguish carefully between true additions to my knowledge and spurious voyages of discovery. I'm fearful of trickling beyond my boundaries, fearful of metamorphosing into false selves. What counts for me is not how much I can get out of myself but how much I can truly take in.

As I sit in a darkened room among friends, I'm a secret traitor to the spirit of the occasion. I don't want to be a Fifth Columnist; I'd rather be with it, with the others, right here. But the "here" we start from is located in a different place, and so our departures are different too. Perhaps because I don't quite know where my peers come from, I don't know where they're coming from. I'm pulled into the common circle; I genuinely like many of the people here and feel their friendliness and warmth. Then, to retain my ground, my grounding, I pull away. And then, pulling away too far, an astronaut floating in an enormously lonely outer space, I know that I cannot sustain my sense of a separate reality forever, for after all, the only reality is a shared reality, situated within a common ground.

I've heard American expatriates and other immigrants to Western Europe complain that the societies of England or France are strati-fied, closed, and impregnable from the outside. When I begin the process of my Americanization, I find myself in the least snobbish of societies and the most fluid of generations. It's that very mobil-ity—upward, horizontal, and of some topological varieties not de-scribed in classical symmetry—that makes assimilation an almost outmoded idea.

The startling transformations that I begin to see at Rice con-tinue in the next decade to take their by now familiar patterns. Lizzy—who has never done things halfway—launches on an odyssey that's so extreme as to be archetypal. Within ten or so years after graduation, she will marry, become a union organizer, take up women lovers for a while, try to commit suicide, get a Ph.D. in political science, write a very scholarly and somewhat overobedient structuralist critique of working-class movements in late-eighteenth-century England, and get tenure at one of the country's more respectable universities. Eventually, she remarries, has a child, buys a nice suburban house; eventually, her life begins to bear—in its outward form, at least—some surprising resemblances to the lives of her parents.

I wonder at the extremity of these changes, and the extremity that must drive Lizzy in her quests. Allen Tate, anticipating Milan Kundera, uses the term "angelism" to describe the dark side of the transcendent impulse in American literature, and sometimes it seems to me that my peers suffer from a form of angelism—a desire to become more immaculate beings, avatars of pure ideas. They want to be sexually liberated, emotionally cleansed, politically correct angels—and so they ricochet from one vision of Utopia to another, from a hope for transcendence to disillusionment to the next hope for a more ultimate transcendence.

I sometimes feel betrayed by this combination of rigid opinion and Protean changeability, for it makes my peers elusive; in the nebulae of proclamations and argument, it's difficult for me to disentangle fashionable views from true belief, passionate conviction from defensive dogma. What do they think, feel, hold dear? It's harder for an outsider to make these distinctions anyway, and particularly important to make them—for it's only when you can identify where a person stands that you can establish genuine trust. But insofar as I'm an outsider wishing to be taken in, I've come at the wrong moment, for in the midst of all this swirling and fragmenting movement, the very notion of outside and inside is as quaint as the Neoplatonic model of the universe. I do not experience the pain of earlier immigrants, who were kept out of exclusive clubs or decent neighborhoods. Within the limits of my abilities and ambitions, I can go anywhere at all, and be accepted there. The only joke is that there's no there there.

In a splintered society, what does one assimilate to? Perhaps the very splintering itself. Once I enter college, the rivulet of my story does join up with the stream of my generation's larger saga, and the events of my life begin to resemble those of my peers. Marriage, divorce, career indecisions, moving from city to city, ambivalences about love and work and every fundamental fact of human activity. I share with my American generation an acute sense of dislocation and the equally acute challenge of having to invent a place and an identity for myself without the traditional supports. It could be said that the generation I belong to has been characterized by its prolonged refusal to assimilate—and it is in my very uprootedness that I'm its member. It could indeed be said that exile is the archetypal condition of contemporary lives.

Ironically enough, one of the ways in which I continue to know that I'm not completely assimilated is through my residual nostalgia—which many of my friends find a bit unseemly, as if I were admitting to a shameful weakness—for the more stable, less strenuous conditions of anchoring, of home.

I wish I could breathe a Nabokovian air. I wish I could have the Olympian freedom of sensibility that disdains, in his autobiography, to give the Russian Revolution more than a passing mention, as if such common events did not have the power to wreak fundamental changes in his own life, or as if it were vulgar, tactless, to dwell on something so brutishly, so crudely collective. I wish I could define myself—as Nabokov defines both himself and his characters—by the telling detail, a preference for mints over lozenges, an awkwardness at cricket, a tendency to lose gloves or umbrellas. I wish I could live in a world of prismatic refractions, carefully distinguished colors of sunsets and English scarves, synesthetic repetitions and reiterative surprises—a world in which even a reddened nostril can be rendered as a delicious hue rather than a symptom of a discomfiting common cold. I wish I could attain such a world because in part that is our most real, and most loved world—the world of utterly individual sensibility, untrampled by history, or horrid intrusions of social circumstance. Oh yes, I think the Nabokovian world is lighted, lightened, and enlightened by the most precise affection. Such affection is unsentimental because it is free and because it attaches to free objects. It can notice what is adorable (or odious, for that matter), rather than what is formed and deformed by larger forces. Characters, in Nabokov's fiction, being perfectly themselves, attain the graced amorality of aesthetic objects.

How trite and tedious, in contrast, to see oneself as a creature formed by historic events and defined by sociological categories. I am a Jew, an immigrant, half-Pole, half-American. . . . I suffer from certain syndromes because I was fed on stories of the war. . . . At a party given by some old-moneyed Bostonians, I feel that their gracious smiles mask a perfect condescension. . . . I haven't escaped my past or my circumstances; they constrain me like a corset, making me stiffer, smaller. I haven't bloomed to that fullness of human condition in which only my particular traits—the good mold of my neck, say, or the crispness of my ironies—matter. Nabokov repaid America's generosity with *Pnin* and *Lolita,* with amusement never soured by anger. Of all the responses to the condition of exile, his is surely the most triumphant, the least marred by rage, or inferiority, or aspiration. His observations are those of an entirely free man; but perhaps such aristocratic freedom to rise above confining categories and merely material conditions can spring only from a specific circumstance, the circumstance of aristocratic privilege. Perhaps it's not possible to transcend our circumstances entirely after all.

We're driving, my Texan and I, in his clunky old Chevrolet, from Houston to Austin, where we'll visit some friends. The highway is nearly empty and very hot. By the roadside, there are clumps of tall, pale green weeds, with occasional patches of sagebrush and lavender. Otherwise, there is nothing but us and the speed of the car and the endlessly receding horizon. Freedom. We talk little, breathing in the utter comfort of our solitude. Occasionally, like a blessing, a bonus from God, a hill. No matter what happens to me, I think, there will always be this. There will always be landscapes, and I'll always have the liberty to breathe them in, the wherewithal to contemplate them. I'll always have the freedom of my insignificance. Even this empty road throbs with the silence of my own experience. I need not be so afraid.

Should you marry him? the question comes in English.
 Yes.
 Should you marry him? the question echoes in Polish.
 No.
 But I love him; I'm in love with him.
 Really? Really? Do you love him as you understand love? As you loved Marek?
 Forget Marek. He is another person. He's handsome and kind and good.
 You don't feel creaturely warmth. You're imagining him. You're imagining your emotions. You're forcing it.
 So you're going to keep me from marrying him? You realize this is an important decision.
 Yes. That's why you must listen to me.
 Why should I listen to you? You don't necessarily know the truth about me just because you speak in that language. Just because you seem to come from deeper within.
 This is not the moment to lie to yourself.
 I'm not lying. I'm just not a child any longer. My emotions have become more complicated. I have ambivalences.
 When you get married you have to assent to someone with your whole self.
 A romantic illusion.
 If you don't satisfy me, you'll always be dissatisfied.
 Go away. You're becoming a succubus.
 I won't be so easy to get rid of.
 I don't need you anymore. I want you to be silent. Shuddup.

Should you become a pianist? the question comes in English.
 No, you mustn't. You can't.
 Should you become a pianist? the question echoes in Polish.
 Yes, you must. At all costs.
 The costs will be too high.

The costs don't matter. Music is what you're meant to do.

Don't be so dramatic. I can play for myself. For pleasure.

Don't kid yourself. You want to play for others. You want to hear the applause.

That's a shallow ideal.

It's those eyes when people have heard you play . . .

I'm going to end up giving concerts in small towns and colleges. There are too many pianists in the world going over the same tired repertory. What can I add to all those recordings of the Chopin études?

Reasons, reasons . . . You're passionate about it. . . . You have a duty to yourself.

I live here now. I can't just close my eyes and follow my passions, I have to figure out how to live my life.

Oh God, I don't know. I don't know what you should do anymore.

I like literature a lot. I'm good at it. Perhaps someday I can write. Sometimes, I almost get the same high . . .

Not the same. Nothing else expresses as much. . . . What else will you love like that?

I'll love other things. I'll love people. I promise.

Remember how you felt . . .

No. I don't want to remember.

What do you want? What do you want?

I want . . . I want not to have to change so much. But I have to. I have to catch up to myself. It's not just a question of music, you know.

Yes, I know. But it's going to hurt, giving it up.

Yes, it's going to hurt.

But we'll get along somehow.

Yes, we'll get along.

■ ■ ■

It's April 1969, and I'm walking, idly, across Harvard Yard. My first year at Harvard is coming to an end, I've just come out of a class on Victorian aesthetics, and I'm about to meet some friends in the cafeteria, where we'll exchange bits of literary gossip and personal analysis. Like so many events in my patchwork American existence, my being here is a sort of accident. In the middle of a year I spent at the Yale Music School—a year I gave myself to solve the music question—a friend drove me to Boston, and the city's hilly narrow streets, its brownstones rosy in the wintry light, an apothecary store with gleaming wooden fixtures, and a sudden, premature dusk so answered some deep desire in me that when I decided to follow the academic trail after all, I knew this was the place where I wanted to do it.

I get into Harvard itself on the last blaze of immigrant bravura. I had spent the previous summer in a paralysis of conflict about what to do next, so it's only in the early fall that I walk into the English Department office and tell the chairman that he must let me in. At this point, I'm decorated with enough honors and fellowships not to be an impostor, but the chairman, a gruff, affable man who looks at me with some interest once I present him with my clearly unreasonable request, tells me that even if John Donne himself showed up at this point, he couldn't do anything for him—or in any case, "they" wouldn't. "Who are they?" I ask, and the chairman informs me that they are the admissions office, which would surely refuse to process an application at this late date. "And if they agree to do it?" I say with a conspiratorial smile, and the chairman waves me out of the office with a gesture of mock exasperation. Once he gives me the opening, it's child's play, and I use the pressure of my need and my best Polish wiles to persuade all the parties concerned that they want to do their part; after a few days, I'm in.

After this outburst of willfulness, the last blaze of Polish *polot*, I go into a moping, glassy-eyed despondency. At this moment, when I should feel the muscular pleasure of success, my will deflates as if from overuse; just when I've gotten myself where I supposedly want to be, I feel as disoriented as a homing pigeon that has been blindfolded and turned around too many times, and now doesn't know the direction of home. "I'm Eva, I live in Cambridge, Mass.,

I go to Harvard University," I keep repeating to myself. I've been confounded by being too long a stranger.

And so, after I emerge from this hiatus, I begin walking around the crooked, cobblestoned streets of Cambridge as if I were tentatively trying on a new home. I'm pleased by its low wooden buildings, the ramshackle comfiness, the coffeehouses where I spend too many hours gossiping with friends, and the bursting bookstores—even though they also induce a kind of anxiety of plenitude in me, because so much has been already written, and so much needs to be known; I'm pleased by the New England modesty of Harvard Yard, and the wood-paneled rooms in which the English Department conducts its endless sherry parties, and the tweed-jacketed professors with their dry faces and perfectly professorial airs.

My friends assure me that, having come to the republic's eastern shore, I've landed in the real America at last. "Being American means that you feel like you're the norm," one of my friends tells me, "and the Northeast is the norm that sets the norm." An ironically timed statement, since we've entered a period during which these very friends of mine will try to unwrap, unravel, and demolish every norm passed on to them from their parents and the culture at large; for a while, they will use their inheritance and their sense of entitlement for that most luxurious of rights, the right to turn down one's privileges; for a while at least, they will refuse to inherit the earth.

As for me, I want to figure out, more urgently than before, where I belong in this America that's made up of so many sub-Americas. I want, somehow, to give up the condition of being a foreigner. I no longer want to tell people quaint stories from the Old Country, I don't want to be told that "exotic is erotic," or that I have Eastern European intensity, or brooding Galician eyes. I no longer want to be propelled by immigrant chutzpah or desperado energy or usurper's ambition. I no longer want to have the prickly, unrelenting consciousness that I'm living in the medium of a specific culture. It's time to roll down the scrim and see the world directly, as the world. I want to reenter, through whatever Looking Glass will take me there, a state of ordinary reality.

And that's when I begin fighting with my friends.

Although I've always thought of myself as a pliable, all-too-accommodating sort of person, I now get into fights all the time. Sitting with a friend over an afternoon coffee at the Pamplona, or walking with another along one of the more bucolic Cambridge streets, I suddenly find myself in the middle of an argument whose ferocity surprises us both. Anything can start it, any conversational route can suddenly take a swerve that'll lead us down a warpath. We fight about the most standard and the most unlikely subjects: the value of exercise and the proper diet, the implications of China's Cultural Revolution, whether photography is a form of violence, and whether all families are intrinsically repressive. In the conversation of my friends, I sniff out cultural clichés like a hound on the scent of hostile quarry. An innocent remark like "Well, I don't know what to tell you, it really depends on how you feel" provokes in me the most bitter reflections on American individualism, and how a laissez-faire tolerance can mask a callous indifference. Behind the phrase "You've got to stay in control," thrown in as a conversational filler, I vengefully detect an ironical repression on the part of those who hate repression most. In the counternorms my peers profess, I perceive the structure of the norms they ostensibly reject, inverted like an underwater reflection, but still recognizable.

Much of the time, I'm in a rage. Immigrant rage, I call it, and it can erupt at any moment, and at seemingly minuscule provocation. It's directed with equal force at "the Culture"—that weird artifice I'm imprisoned in—and at my closest friends. Or rather, it's directed at the culture-in-my-friends. My misfortune is to see the grid of general assumptions drawn all over particular personalities, to notice the subjection to collective ideology where I should only see the free play of subjectivity. In the most ordinary, interstitial gestures—secretiveness about money, or a reluctance to let sadness show—I sense the tyranny of subliminal conventions. Where my friends suppose they're voicing their deepest beliefs, I whiff the dogma of intellectual fashion; in the midst of a discussion, I cease seeing the face of one person, and start throwing myself against the wall of an invisible, impregnable, collective force.

In Peter Schneider's novel, *The Wall Jumper,* the West German narrator has an East German girlfriend named Lena. Lena has chosen to live on the Western side of the Berlin Wall, but she's severe about what she sees there. When her boyfriend happens to glance at a cover of *Playboy,* she accuses him of decadence, and when he cracks jokes with friends in a bar, she scowls at their triviality. She thinks the West Germans' politics are frivolous, and their pleasures vapid. Her boyfriend sees how much she suffers from this hypersensitivity; for a while, he admires her severity; but finally, it drives him away.

I know what I'm supposed to think of Lena, but I identify with her. I think she's in the right. I want more severe standards of seriousness to obtain. In other words, I'm a scourge.

I think I also know the cause of Lena's defensiveness and seeming arrogance: It's that her version of things is automatically under suspicion and at a discount. That's the real subtext of my fights, the piercing provocation behind the trivial ones. My sense of reality, powerful and vulnerable, is in danger of coming under native domination. My interlocutors in these collisions stare at me with incredulity or dismay; what am I getting so worked up about? They, after all, are only having a conversation. They don't want to question every sentence they speak, and they don't need to; the mass of shared conviction is so thick as to constitute an absoluteness, a reality of a kind. They explain politely and firmly where I'm wrong. Or they become goaded to anger themselves. At parties, my demurrals are often greeted with plain silence, as if they didn't need to be entertained. This increases my frustration, my ire, still more. Censorship in the living room, I mutter to myself bitterly, and after a while begin to censor myself.

"If you've never eaten a real tomato, you'll think that the plastic tomato is the real thing, and moreover, you'll be perfectly satisfied with it," I tell my friends. "It's only when you've tasted them both that you know there's a difference, even though it's almost impossible to describe." This turns out to be the most persuasive argument I have. My friends are moved by the parable of the plastic tomato. But when I try to apply it, by analogy, to the internal realm, they balk. Surely, inside our heads and souls things are more universal, the ocean of reality one and indivisible. No, I shout in every one of our arguments, no! There's a world out there; there are worlds. There are shapes of sensibility incommensurate with each other, topographies of experience one cannot guess from within one's own limited experience.

I think my friends often suspect me of a perverse refusal to play along, an unaccountable desire to provoke and disturb their comfortable consensus. I suspect that the consensus is trying to colonize me and rob me of my distinctive shape and flavor. Still, I have to come to terms with it somehow. Now that I'm no longer a visitor, I can no longer ignore the terms of reality prevailing here, or sit on the margins observing the curious habits of the natives. I have to learn how to live with them, find a common ground. It is my fear that I have to yield too much of my own ground that fills me with such a passionate energy of rage.

My American Friend: What did you think about that Hungarian movie last week?

I: I thought it was quite powerful.

M.A.F.: Me too. It was a very smart comment on how all of us can get co-opted by institutions.

I: But it wasn't about all of us. It was about the Communist party in Hungary circa 1948.

M.A.F.: Collaboration isn't the monopoly of the Communist party, you know. You can be bought and co-opted by Time, Inc., quite successfully.

I: I think there may be just the tiniest difference between those two organizations.

M.A.F.: You with your liberal quibbles. I don't think your eyes have been opened about this country.

I: For heaven's sake, don't you understand what went on over there? That people got imprisoned, tortured, hanged?

M.A.F.: Don't get so upset, this was a Hungarian movie. You don't have to be loyal to all of Eastern Europe.

I: I'm loyal to some notion of accuracy, which is more than I can say for you! The world isn't just a projection screen for your ideas, highly correct though they may be.

M.A.F. I'm allowed to have my interpretation of the world. That's called theory, for your information.

I: That's called not thinking, as far as I can see. You're not allowed to let theory blind you to all distinctions.

M.A.F.: Spare me your sarcasm. Just because awful things happened over there doesn't mean that awful things don't happen here. You like to exaggerate these distinctions, as if you wanted to keep yourself apart.

I: This is not a psychological issue!

M.A.F.: On some level, everything is.

I: This makes me want to emigrate.

M.A.F.: Feel free.

I: How are things going with Doug?

M.A.F.: Terrible. We fuck each other blind, and then he won't tell his wife that we're involved.

I: I imagine that'd be hard to do.

M.A.F.: Why?

I: Why! Haven't you ever heard of possessiveness? Jealousy?

M.A.F.: Yes, I've heard about them. I just don't think they're natural instincts that we're supposed to accept as sacred. They may have served some purpose in the Paleozoic era, but we aren't running around being hunters and gatherers anymore, if you've noticed.

I: Yes, I've noticed. I've also noticed that we continue to be possessive and jealous.

M.A.F.: You know, you're becoming a perfect bourgeois.

I: And you're turning into a Stalinist of everyday life. You're not supposed to be jealous, you're not supposed to be guilty, you're supposed to get in touch with your anger. . . . What is this, some kind of internal morality squad?

M.A.F.: I'm beginning to suspect that you're threatened because I fuck a lot.

I: As far as I'm concerned, you're welcome to have as many affairs as you like.

M.A.F.: You see, you can't even say fuck.

I: I can say fuck very well, thank you.

M.A.F.: Why are you getting so hostile?

I: Because I believe you're attacking me.

M.A.F.: *I'm* attacking *you*?

I: I don't like being on trial for my vocabulary.

M.A.F.: You've been dripping disdain during this whole conversation. You've got me pegged as some naïve American country bumpkin.

I: I think you pretend to innocence. Some things are perfectly self-explanatory, you know.

M.A.F.: Nothing is, unless you're a reactionary.

I: I can't stand this!

M.A.F.: Believe me, the feeling is mutual.

The dialogues don't end, though, with our going off in a huff, or with whatever tentative resolutions we're willing to settle for. Afterward, as I walk down the street hardly conscious of my surroundings, or at night as I toss on my bed, the furious conflicts continue to rage within my own head. The opposing voices become mine, and each of them is ready to lacerate the other. In one of them, I'm ready to dismiss all of American Culture as a misconceived experiment. Scornfully, I think there's too much reinventing of the wheel going on around here. The wheel has already been invented, why bother again? There's too much surprise at the fact that the earth is round, and too much insistence the sun may be moving around us after all. My American Friends think privileged thoughts, I think bitterly, thoughts that cost nothing and that weren't produced by the labor of their own experience. Surplus thoughts that do not have to be paid for in consequences either. Do they, in their own private triangulations, in their night accountings with themselves, believe that a marital squabble has causes too deep for analysis, or that jealousy can be eliminated by ideological fiat, or that the revolution is just around the corner? It is in my incapacity to imagine my friends' private thoughts that the gap between us continues to exist. I can't enter sufficiently into their souls to know where conviction stops and self-presentation begins. Certainly, my American Friends do not deliberately say things they believe to be untrue in order to make themselves look better or somebody else look worse. Hypocrisy, that old-fashioned and un-American vice, requires a public ideal of virtue to pretend to; it also needs the certainty of ego to do the pretending effectively. For all their many certainties, my friends don't seem to have that toughness, or hiddenness, which would enable them to pay lip service to the proper pieties while keeping their true opinions to themselves. The dance of personality happens differently here, and the ideal of personal sincerity—supplanting common virtues, perhaps—is deeply ingrained. My friends want, sincerely, to believe what they would like to believe. But I wonder how much leeway that leaves for a willful self-deception—that subtle falseness that the self only half-knows. "We French lie to others. Americans lie to themselves," a Frenchman I know once remarks, and sometimes I think that my friends' desire to possess only the best ideas prevents them from knowing which ideas are really theirs.

But when the full force of my disapproval is spent, the dialogue with myself takes a U-turn, and I remember that my rage is an immigrant's rage, my suspiciousness the undignified, blinding suspiciousness of an outsider. Then I try, fairly, to think from the other point of view, to stand on the other end of the triangle's base. What's going on here, I think, is a new version of the grand Emersonian experiment, the perennial American experiment, which consists precisely of reinventing the wheel, of taking nothing for granted and beholding human nature with a primeval curiosity, as though nothing has ever been observed or thought before. This is the spirit that invented the cotton gin and Whitman's free verse, and the open marriage. My American Friends are just running a few theoretical experiments on themselves—but why should they do otherwise, since so little in their condition is given, and so little is forbidden either? They live in a culture which is still young, and in which the codes and conventions are still up for grabs. Since there are no rules for how to be a lover, they need to figure out the dynamics of an affair as if it were a complicated problem in physics, and their minds grow new muscles in the process. My American Friends have gained insights about the human mechanism they may never have come by if they had not needed to ask the most rudimentary questions about love and anger and sex. Their explorations are a road to a new, instead of an ancestral, wisdom—a wisdom that may be awkward and ungainly, as youthful wisdom is, but that is required in a world whose social, if not physical, frontiers are still fluid and open and incompletely charted.

Theodor Adorno, that most vitriolic of America's foreign critics, once warned his fellow refugees that if they lost their alienation, they'd lose their souls. A bracingly uncompromising idea of integrity: but I doubt that Adorno could have maintained it over a lifetime without the hope of returning home—without having a friendly audience back there for his dialectical satires. The soul can shrivel from an excess of critical distance, and if I don't want to remain in arid internal exile for the rest of my life, I have to find a way to lose my alienation without losing my self. But how does one bend toward another culture without falling over, how does one strike an elastic balance between rigidity and self-effacement? How does one stop reading the exterior signs of a foreign tribe and step into the inwardness, the viscera of their meanings? Every anthropologist understands the difficulty of such a feat; and so does every immigrant.

It is no wonder—in our time of mass migrations and culture collisions and easy jet travel, when the whole world lies below us every time we rise into the skies, when whole countries move by like bits of checkerboard, ours to play on—it's no wonder that in this time we've developed whole philosophies of cultural relativity, and learned to look at whole literatures, histories, and cultural formations as if they were toy blocks, ours to construct and deconstruct. It's no wonder, also, that we have devised a whole metaphysics for the subjects of difference and otherness. But for all our sophisticated deftness at cross-cultural encounters, fundamental difference, when it's staring at you across the table from within the close-up face of a fellow human being, always contains an element of violation. My American Friends and I find it an offense to our respective identities to touch within each other something alien, unfamiliar, in the very woof and warp of our inner lives. I suppose we could—following one kind of philosophy—adopt an attitude of benevolent openness to each other, and declare our differences interesting and beautiful; but such mellow tolerance is easier to maintain with, say, an Indian swami, who remains safely exotic, and doesn't intend to become our personal friend. Or, adhering to a later, and more skeptical philosophical fashion, we could accept each other's irreducible otherness and give up on our nettlesome and painful back and forth. We could declare each other products of different cultures—as we, of course, are—and leave it, respectfully, at that. But that would leave us separate and impermeable—something that is easier to accept with impersonal entities like class, or gender, or country than with a fellow human being clamoring to be understood.

My American Friends and I are forced to engage in an experiment that is relatively rare; we want to enter into the very textures, the motions and flavors of each other's vastly different subjectivities—and that requires feats of sympathy and even imagination in excess of either benign indifference or a remote respect.

Of course, in these entanglements, our positions are not exactly symmetrical. In the politics of daily perception, I'm at a distinct disadvantage. My American Friends are so many, and they share so many assumptions that are quite invisible to them, precisely because they're shared. These are assumptions about the most fundamental human transactions, subcutaneous beliefs, which lie just below the stratum of political opinion or overt ideology: about how much "space," physical or psychological, we need to give each other, about how much "control" is desirable, about what is private and what public, about how much interest in another person's affairs is sympathy and how much interference, about what's a pretty face or a handsome body, about what we're allowed to poke fun at and what we have to revere, about how much we need to hide in order to reveal ourselves. To remain outside such common agreements is to remain outside reality itself—and if I'm not to risk a mild cultural schizophrenia, I have to make a shift in the innermost ways. I have to translate myself. But if I'm to achieve this without becoming assimilated—that is, absorbed—by my new world, the translation has to be careful, the turns of the psyche unforced. To mouth foreign terms without incorporating their meanings is to risk becoming bowdlerized. A true translation proceeds by the motions of understanding and sympathy; it happens by slow increments, sentence by sentence, phrase by phrase.

Does it still matter, in these triangulations, that my version of reality was formed in Eastern Europe? It is well known that the System over there, by specializing in deceit, has bred in its citizens an avid hunger for what they still quaintly call the truth. Of course, the truth is easier to identify when it's simply the opposite of a lie. So much Eastern European thinking moves along the axis of bipolar ideas, still untouched by the peculiar edginess and fluidity created by a more decentered world. Perhaps I'm not quite equal to the challenge of postmodern uncertainty. But as I wrestle with the American Friend in my head, I am haunted not by a longing for certainty but by the idea, almost palpable, of the normal. The normal, in my mental ideogram, is associated with a face: Pani Ruta's face, perhaps, or Piotr Ostropov's. It's not an innocent, or a particularly cheerful face; it bespeaks, instead, both a quick perspicacity and an unforced seriousness. *"C'est normale,"* the expression on this face says. *"N'exagères pas."* It's a face that has seen a lot, and is not easily astonished. It knows, in its cultural memory, the limits of human ideals, and the limitations of human passions. Foibles, in its steady gaze, are just that: foibles. It's not apt to work itself up into moral heat or analytic anguish. It has a stored knowledge, passed on through generations, of the devious traceries of the human heart, and it has learned where the mean lies in the soul, and what's excess. The normal is derived not from a conventional norm but from this knowledge of proportion. The face expresses a skepticism that is a hair's breadth away from cynicism, but is also adjacent to an acceptance of things as they are, and not as they should be or might be in a more ideal, a nonhuman world.

I think if I could enter the subjectivity of that face, then I could encompass both myself and my American Friend within it. I could then see our polarities within some larger, more capacious terms, and resolve our antitheses within a wiser synthesis. I could see that we're both—as the phrase echoes from my childhood—just human. It's that face that I keep as a beacon in my furious mono-dialogues and my triangulations. I want a language that will express what that face knows, a calm and simple language that will subsume the clangor of specialized jargons and of partial visions, a language old enough to plow under the superficial differences between signs, to the deeper strata of significance.

My Japanese friend gets angry at different things than I; it's bank clerks and salespeople in department stores who ignite his rage. They are so rude, he says, they mumble and ignore you, and since he is very polite and doesn't like to put himself forward, he just stands there, waiting to be noticed. Inside, though, he's seething.

My Japanese friend loves America. He came here because he felt innately mismatched with the Japanese weltanschauung. "You know how the Japanese control their emotions," he says. "Well, I was always very good at expressing myself. I think that much control is weird." But then, he finds himself getting angry at salespeople and bank clerks, and particularly, when they violate one of his rules of decorum, at his friends. "And then I hate myself," he tells me with a kind of perplexity.

I don't understand why it's rude salespeople who set my Japanese friend off. Most people around here seem quite polite to me. What's he getting so worked up about? I try to triangulate in an entirely different direction, somewhere to the far east of my usual points of reference. I know that to him, I'm often a puzzle, and that in his mind, all of Eastern Europe is a small abstract cluster somewhere to the west of his imagination. Suddenly, I see us both as figures in a burlesque, running about and waving our hands on a stage grown too circumscribed and crowded for anyone on it to take himself very seriously. The drama of intercultural clash, repeated often enough, becomes a farce. Perhaps a computer species would be more appropriate to our overpopulated world. Computer people wouldn't have so much ego, which might have been suitable to a midsized country but loses all persuasiveness in a global village. In our new situation, they would comport themselves with less fuss and more innate dignity.

How far this is from Cracow, from the time when shadows moving across the ceiling sufficed for the world, because I was without question its absolute center. We're called upon to travel so far beyond our borders, but neither my Japanese friend nor I can divest ourselves of those irrational, instinctive reactions that we take to be our personalities, our selves. To do so would be to jump outside the borders of our skin. How, with this bifocal vision, does one keep one's center? And what center should one try to keep? The cherishing of our particularity seems as outmoded as the wearing of many skirts. And yet, so long as we are not computer species, we cannot give up on our subjectivity, our ability to experience. Sometimes I see what I need: an objective subjectivity, a laser beam that concentrates my energy, and uses the collected light to illuminate and reflect the world.

It's a beautiful spring day, and I'm in a car with several friends heading out to Lincoln for a picnic. My second year at Harvard is coming to an end. The gorgeous exurban countryside speeds by, offering the perfectly lucid New England sky, delicate foliage, clumps of daffodils, and a few cows in a grassy field for extra picturesqueness. We're all of us, the foursome in the car, full of youthful sap, exorbitant hopes, and exorbitant fears. "Bloomsbury or Bumsbury," is how we jokingly describe our alternatives for the future. In the dilatory way of our generation, we're as reluctant to plunge into adulthood as we are eager to be seized by its privileges, and I include myself among our common presumptions and common trepidations. In the car, everyone is in high good humor suited to the end of the semester and the beautiful weather. I'm wearing a red miniskirt I'm very pleased with, because after years of parsimoniously limiting myself to gray and navy blue and black, I'm learning how to dress in colors. "Is that comfortable?" my mother asked me about this extremely short item. "Sure," I lied, because actually, bending over in it presents some logistical problems. "Besides, it's a sort of test for men. If they don't see you as a sex object in this, then you know they're really advanced." It's the kind of joke I know she enjoys.

Somebody in the front seat begins to sing "I'm Walking in the Rain," and everyone joins in, then eliding into "Poetry in Motion" and a Little Richard song. I hum along without the words. There are certain gaps in my American education I'll, sadly enough, never make up. Then there are reminiscences about old segments of "I Love Lucy"—TV madeleines, *recherche du temps perdu*. I'm always slightly uncomfortable about these rituals of regression, because I can't regress to the same place, and I compensate for my unease by saying that the show was "before my time."

The conversation in the car, like the young women's fresh, unmadeup faces and the long hair on both sexes, bears all the hallmarks of the period, though of course now it seems like talk for all time—or rather, talk for a new time, for a new world.

"Actually, Lucy is a perfect example of false consciousness," Paul, a slim, handsome young man with wild bushy hair, interjects in his habitually nonchalant tone. "A show about working-class people made for television. I mean, what a way to defuse political energies."

"Surely, people can't devote themselves to politics full-time," I say, almost in spite of myself. I don't know what imp of the perverse insists that I provide my friends with these corrective views.

"If people in this country weren't fed all that pabulum, they could figure out what their real interests are," Paul answers with just a touch of threat in his voice. He's the firebrand radical in this group, and he's warning me not to go on with my line.

"It may be pabulum, but you enjoy watching it," I say. "Why shouldn't others, even if they are working class?"

"Listen," Beth says from the front seat, impassioned. "This country offers false rewards. It blinds people with its promises."

Now it's me against them. A soldering heat travels up my spine. "I agree," I say. "I couldn't agree more. But some people can't afford to give those rewards up so easily. Why should they? I don't see you giving up your trust fund . . ."

It's out. I've said too much.

"Hey guys, cool it"—Don, a psychology student who hates fights, jumps in. "This is a theoretical discussion."

"Someday you'll have to forgive us for having been better off," Miriam, turning to me, says after a pause. Her voice is soft, but quite unflinching.

"I think you're right," I answer in a small voice, because she has hit the nail on the head. She is right, and I'm grateful that she has the confidence in me to say it.

"Speaking of false consciousness," Don says casually, "did you guys see Peterson's article? Or I should say zombie consciousness, I mean the guy is half man, half book, and who knows which half is which . . ."

"Well, of course, anyone who thinks that Bulwer-Lytton is the greatest writer who ever lived has a lot to answer for," I say, and we are off on safer ground, relieved that the tension has been defused. Then we come to the lovely grounds of the DeCordova Museum, and we decide that we'll picnic by the lake. We walk companionably through the woods, and then take out our wine bottles and bread and delicious concoctions made out of the Julia Child cookbook, which is de rigueur these days for all of us, bohemians, rebels, and revolutionaries.

"What's that?" Miriam asks me in a severe tone, pointing at a school of ducks making its way across the lake.

"Ducks, a school of," I say with exaggerated pride.

"Ah, I see you know something, silly little Polish person," she says in a mock-pedagogical voice, and then we all sit staring at the lake for a while. Tomorrow, Paul and Beth and I will meet to talk about a screenplay on which we're collaborating in our bid to become Bloomsbury rather than Bumsbury. We begin to fantasize about what will happen if; Paul's eyes get quite dreamy, and he squeezes my arm. "We'll go far together, kid," he croons, "you'll

see, we'll go far." "Right now, I don't want to go anywhere,"
Miriam says, and really, I agree. Paul and Don get up and lazily
throw a Frisbee back and forth. I relax into the shadows of the late
afternoon, the cooling breeze, and the familiarity that encloses us.
I look at my friends fondly; I know them so well. Still, shards of the
silly fight remain lodged in my flesh, occasionally inflicting a small,
acute stab. Why can't I just take things lightly, in the spirit in which
they're probably intended? Why do I have to be a Savonarola of
daily life? It's odd that these conflicts have become sharper just as
I've gotten closer to the people around me, as if illuminated by the
merciless headlights of a border patrol, which show the choices in
stark relief—there's one side, there the other—to a person trying
to get across. But of course, that's the moment when the stakes
become high. It would be easy enough to shrug off these disagreements if the people with whom I'm having this picnic didn't matter
to me. But if I'm to live here—if I'm to know where and with whom
I belong—then I have to take my friends with that full seriousness
one grants only to those with whom one shares a world. Of course,
one of the shards sticking in my ribs suggests that maybe I'll never
belong comfortably anyplace, that my sensibilities and opinions will
always be stuck in some betwixt and between place. But as I smile
and joke and look up at the sky—out of my Savonarola mode and
back into spring fecklessness—I know that I can allow these brush-
fires to erupt, because they're contained in a larger territory of
affection. I know these friends won't like me any less despite the
discomfort of my opinions. Perhaps these skirmishes are border
engagements, a sign that a crossing has begun.

I've become obsessed with words. I gather them, put them away
like a squirrel saving nuts for winter, swallow them and hunger for
more. If I take in enough, then maybe I can incorporate the language, make it part of my psyche and my body. I will not leave an
image unworded, will not let anything cross my mind till I find the
right phrase to pin the shadow down. Each week, as I drive a route
of leafy New England roads to teach a class at the University of
New Hampshire, my head heats up as if the circuitry were over-

loaded. "Beveled, chiseled, sculpted, ribbed," I think as a wooden lampstand I liked flashes through my mind. I see myself, speeding in my orange VW, a comical figure, mouthing a litany of adjectives like some overeager freshman. But this stream of hypertrophied consciousness is not something I can stop. I search for the right shade of a pearly pinkish shell I found on the beach as if my life depended on it, and to some extent it does. I can't live forever in a windy, unfurnished imagination; I have to make a comfortable habitation there, fill it with a few household things, some comfy, everyday objects, maybe a beveled lamp. I have to add a bottom to the language that I learned from the top.

The thought that there are parts of the language I'm missing can induce a small panic in me, as if such gaps were missing parts of the world or my mind—as if the totality of the world and mind were coeval with the totality of language. Or rather, as if language were an enormous, fine net in which reality is contained—and if there are holes in it, then a bit of reality can escape, cease to exist. When I write, I want to use every word in the lexicon, to accumulate a thickness and weight of words so that they yield the specific gravity of things. I want to re-create, from the discrete particles of words, that wholeness of a childhood language that had no words.

I pounce on bits of colloquial idiom, those slivers of Americana in which the cultural sensibility is most vivid, as if they could give me America itself. "Hair of the dog that bit me," I repeat to myself with relish; "pork-barreling"; "I'm from Missouri, show me"; "He swallowed it hook, line, and sinker." When I speak, I'm awkward in using such homely familiarities; I still feel the presumption in it. But in writing, I claim every territorial prerogative. Perhaps if I cast my net wide enough, it will cover the whole continent.

My voice is still a highly unreliable instrument. At the oddest moments, it betrays me, buckles, rasps, refuses to go on. It plays only in flat, shallow registers, and sometimes I literally cannot find it. Sometimes it seems to be lost in an echoing well; or else it shifts location to someplace high within my throat, from where it emerges tight and choked. In a Cambridge coffeehouse, where I sit at my ease, gossiping or listening to a friend, it begins to do its tricks.

"So there I was"—Tom launches into one of his stories—"in this Indian village in the middle of the Punjab, I mean I hardly know how I got there except there was this guru-type I was following, an American, but he had been there for a while so he set himself up as a guide to us eager beavers, so there I am, early in the morning, nothing is moving, nothing I tell you, except this mangy mutt comes out, this was no Brahman mutt, I mean the animal can't even make a sound it's so famished, and there's this dusty road through the middle of the village, and it's so quiet you think maybe it's time for Krishna to put in an appearance, I mean he has this tendency to show up in unlikely places—and then all of a sudden, I tell you, I don't know why, but it was significant, it was a eutectic point, I realized, it just came to me, bingo, just like that: this wasn't on television! This was the real thing! Then this woman comes out of a clay hut, I think it was made of clay, and she's wearing this gorgeous sari, you know how lush they look, you can hardly believe they're not in *Semiramide* or something, but she rubbed her eyes because she'd just woken up, and she looked sort of pissed off, and she was real too! So then I knew something had happened, and that's the end of the story, kid, but nothing since has been the same, I mean, even my parents' goddamn house in Westchester, I mean how much more unreal can you get—even that's real, well, sort of . . ."

This is one of Tom's solos, his riff—that all-American form, the shape that language takes when it's not held down by codes of class, or rules of mannerliness, or a common repertory of inherited phrases. A riff is a story that spins itself out of itself, propelled by nothing but the imagination—a story that can go anyplace and take off into the stratosphere without anyone minding . . . Tom invents himself with every phrase, for every phrase is a surprise to himself; he swerves into digressions that go on forever, conducts whole jam sessions with himself, sparks off metaphors as if they were encoded in his chromosomes. Language takes off like a sudden gust of swallows, observations collide unexpectedly and procreate a joke, words jump around like fireflies, so that there's no telling what's up or down, what ground and what outer space, no telling where the always frail connection between words and reality breaks off and pure performance takes over. It makes me dizzy, this hurling of antic verbal balls in the pure air; with my earthbound sensibility, I want to touch ground, want to know what, where is the real thing. But who can tell and who cares: this is America, where anything is possible, and this slip-and-slide speech, like jazz, or action painting, is the insertion of the self into the space of borderless possibility.

I listen breathlessly as Tom talks, catching his every syncopation, every stress, every maverick rush over a mental hurdle. Then, as I try to respond with equal spontaneity, I reach frantically for the requisite tone, the requisite accent. A Texas drawl crosses a New England clip, a groovy half-sentence competes with an elegantly satirical comment. I want to speak some kind of American, but which kind to hit? "Gee," I say, "what a trip, in every sense of the word."

Tom is perfectly satisfied with this response. I sound natural enough, I sound like anybody else. But I can hear the artifice, and for a moment, I clutch. My throat tightens. Paralysis threatens. Speechlessness used to be one of the common symptoms of classic hysteria. I feel as though in me, hysteria is brought on by tongue-tied speechlessness.

When I fall in love, I am seduced by language. When I get married, I am seduced by language. My husband too is a master of the riff, and when I listen to him improvise about Whitman's poetry, or his Jewish aunts and uncles, or a Wasp Connecticut wedding, I think, maybe this bebop speech can carry me right into the heart of America. . . . It's a tricky contract, and I get confused between my husband and his eloquence, distracted as by shadows and shimmers thrown on a white screen by a camera obscura, but I want to catch the wordplay, ride the energy of the nervy bounds and rebounds, give myself over to the insouciant leaps . . .

All around me, the Babel of American voices, hardy midwestern voices, sassy New York voices, quick youthful voices, voices arching under the pressure of various crosscurrents. I've become a skilled diagnostician of voices, and of their neuroses. I know how people feel, how they are, not from what they say but from how they sound. I can hear the snags and broken rhythms of nervousness, the jumps of pitch that happen when someone is uncomfortable, the tensing of the vocal cords in disapproval. I can also hear the sounds of good health—the even tones of self-assurance, the deepening melodiousness in consent to deep feeling, the canter of clean enthusiasm.

Since I lack a voice of my own, the voices of others invade me as if I were a silent ventriloquist. They ricochet within me, carrying on conversations, lending me their modulations, intonations, rhythms. I do not yet possess them; they possess me. But some of them satisfy a need; some of them stick to my ribs. I could take on that stylish, ironic elongation which is X's mark of perpetual amusement; it fits something in my temperament, I could learn to speak a part of myself through it. And that curtailed, deliberate dryness that Y uses as an antidote to sentiment opens a door into a certain New England sensibility whose richness I would never otherwise understand. Eventually, the voices enter me; by assuming them, I gradually make them mine. I am being remade, fragment by fragment, like a patchwork quilt; there are more colors in the world than I ever knew.

Like a tourist in a new city, who has no particular neighborhood and who therefore is always confronting "the city" as a whole, I, an incompletely assimilated immigrant, am always confronting "the Culture." In this too it turns out that I am like my American friends, though perhaps a little more so. "The Culture," in America, has become a curious monster, a thing that throbs and vibrates out there and bellows. Everyone I know measures the Culture, gauges it, diagnoses it all the time, because, after all, the monster might enter the living room, and so it's important to be on the lookout. The Culture is becoming more conservative, more progressive, more celebrity obsessed, more materialistic, more sentimental. Each shift is carefully observed; the beast may, after all, lurch or bite, or co-opt us, make us more like itself, a graceless, lumpish, philistine thing. The Culture is a dangerous seducer; one must resist its pull.

I'm a vigilant Culture watcher, like everyone else. And undoubtedly, like everyone else, I've ingested parts of the Culture even while I've prudishly pulled my skirts around me. I see this paradox in my friends clearly enough, culture turning into counterculture and counterculture into culture despite everyone's best intentions, the organization man giving way to the dropout and the dropout to a new technocrat, loneliness to love-ins and then loneliness again, as if any set of cultural terms necessarily determines the terms of the subsequent rebellion, and the rejections carry in them the seeds of what is rejected. It is always difficult to know how a culture flows through our veins, and by now I've lost track of how much America flows through mine. Fragments of Janis Joplin songs and the Rolling Stones surface in my mind as I walk down the street; the landscape of Amagansett, where I've spent several summers, is just under my retina, to be retrieved whenever I think vacation, time off; films about New York are films about my hometown; "Gimme a break," I say, when a street vendor gets pushy, and the issues I debate—how to conduct one's career without losing one's sanity, what to eat without becoming contaminated, how to deal with passive-aggressive lovers—are American conversations, dictated by "the Culture" as much as this season's fashions. And I never, never say "It's only psychological" anymore. Maybe, behind my back and while I wasn't looking, I've acquired a second unconscious, an American one, made up of diverse cultural matter. Like any unconscious, this one is hard to pin down. I only know that the hybrid creature I've become is made up of two parts Americana, that the pastiche has lots of local color. Despite my resistance, or perhaps through its very act, I've become a partial American, a sort of resident alien.

■ ■ ■

My private illustration of how small the world is begins at a chamber music concert I casually walk into at Harvard. When I look at the program, I see that the first violinist of the quartet performing that evening is named Zofia Ciesin. "I used to know a person by that name in Cracow," I tell my husband, who's sitting beside me. "I wonder if it could be the same one."

It is, unmistakably. I recognize Zofia's strong, bony face and her pouty mouth as soon as she walks out, even though we were both ten years old when we last saw each other, and she's now a very tall, beautiful woman with an impressive mane of curly black hair. She plays the violin like a dervish; during intermission, I go up to introduce myself, and remind her that some eighteen years ago, our families used to know each other, and her brother studied with Pani Witeszczak, my piano teacher. "Oh my God," Zofia says—the only response possible in such situations—and we look at each other with a sort of primitive astonishment. We're neither of us used to such recurrences, which must happen to other people more often. After the concert, she comes to our apartment, where, to our further astonishment, I unearth a photograph of the two of us and Alinka taken some twenty years ago. In this picture, three little girls are standing on a riverbank holding hands and showing off the daisy wreaths on their heads. I remember the day when this picture was taken quite distinctly—the excursion on the Vistula during which we disembarked for a picnic, and how the three of us looked for flowers to weave those wreaths, something little girls in Poland did in those days. But as Zofia and I look back and forth from the photograph to each other, we feel the madeleine's sweet cheat: "Oh my God," Zofia keeps saying, in mixed delight and befuddlement. We can't jump over such a large time canyon. The image won't quite come together with this moment. It's probably my husband, looking on affectionately, who's getting the full satisfaction from this scene—a classic tableau of two women scrutinizing a photograph intently, trying to recapture the past.

Zofia and I go on to give some concerts together, and I come out of them exhilarated. In the timelessness of music, nothing is ever lost, and there's the extra kick of the coincidence to throw these occasions into a high gear. Sometimes during our rehearsals we stop and talk; usually our conversation turns to a sort of wondering recounting of our families' patchwork paths. Zofia's brother, whom Arthur Rubinstein once praised and endorsed, has gone on to become a high school teacher somewhere in Arizona; her mother has become a Mormon, seduced by the only people who paid assiduous attention to her when she was very lonely in her first years in Queens. Zofia herself has been married, divorced, married again. She is successful, though something stops her from the full unfolding of her career. She suffers from deep and unaccountable depressions. "Of course, in my family it was my brother who was supposed to be famous," she muses, "and my shrink tells me I have a sort of taboo about overtaking him. But sometimes I wonder if it's that . . . well, that I can't put it all together."

The contemporary world, by the sheer thickness of events and the incessant movement of people over the globe, multiplies coincidence. A few months after meeting Zofia, at the end of my last year at Harvard, I pick up the telephone and hear a man's voice speaking in Polish.

"Ewa?" the voice says. It's my first name, so it can't be somebody from the Polish consulate, where I recently called to inquire about getting a visa to Poland; other than that, I know no one outside my family who says my name like that. No, implausible though it seems, I'm quite sure who this is.

"Good heavens," I say.

"Why?" He laughs. "Why good heavens?"

"Marek," I say. "Right?"

"Well, yes, yes, it's me," he laughs again.

"Where are you?" I ask.

"In New York," he says, "in some awful apartment. They tell me it's on the bottom of the city."

"You mean downtown," I say.

"Yes, yes, that's what I mean. Can you come and see me? Today?"

The calculations in my head are very quick. It so happens—in a dizzy piling up of serendipities, as if fate wanted to tell me that this is a Significant Moment—that Marek has called a few days before I'm to get my doctorate, and my parents are arriving from

Vancouver this afternoon. It's their first visit to Boston, to the East Coast. It's almost unthinkable that I should just leave on such an afternoon. And there is, of course, my husband to consider. I'm usually highly conscientious about such things, and poor at making impulsive decisions, not to speak of ones that might have emotional consequences. It turns out that none of it matters.

"Yes," I say, "I'll get there on the next shuttle."

A few hours later I'm standing in front of the Time-Life Building, where we've arranged to meet. As with Zofia, I recognize the man who is walking toward me with no trouble. For one thing, he stands out on this street—he's darkly tanned, and his casual khaki suit is too trimly cut, too deliberately stylish, by the local standards of good taste. But also, I know those resolute movements, and something about the face: maybe the olive skin, maybe the concentration in the eyes. We hold each other in focus as he approaches me; we look at each other straight on, with full seriousness; and then we don't quite know what to do.

"Well, what shall we do, where do you want to go, and how did you get my phone number, by the way?" I say, and Marek laughs again.

"I asked my mother to get it from your mother," he says, "and maybe we can get something to eat. The fridge in that goddamn apartment is completely empty."

And so, after a seventeen-year interruption, we're sitting across the table from each other in a comfortable New York restaurant, for all the world as if we were two acquaintances meeting for dinner after work. Nothing could be more incongruous. We look at each other with some disbelief. This vigorous, handsome man is somebody I don't know at all, but he carries within himself a person whom I once knew completely.

And so we begin talking with the double sense that we need to start from the very beginning, and that everything can be said, without the usual preliminaries. The last time I heard news of Marek was when he got married. Now he tells me about that marriage, which is not happy, and his two children, whom he hardly knows. He fought in the war of '68 and then again in the Yom

Kippur War; he was badly wounded in the first, his body torn by shrapnel in so many places that it had to be reconstructed through several operations; his odds of surviving were slim. He got his degree in engineering from the University of Haifa—I didn't even know that much!—and now owns a small factory producing electronic devices for which the Israeli army is one of his customers. He's in New York on business, to look at some high-tech equipment he might want to buy.

"You know"—Marek suddenly looks hesitant—"when we first got to Israel, and we kept being transported from one small town to another—they were no more than outposts in the desert, and I never wanted to move—they kept telling me you'd be in the next place to stop me from screaming and kicking. I believed them every time."

A door has opened. "You know," I say, trying to sound sensible, "for a year after you left, I went by to look at your house, at 8 Sobieska Street, every week."

"Do you remember," he says, "what happened by the railroad tracks, when we got into a fight with the village kids in Biały Dunajec?"

"That wasn't by the railroad tracks, that was in the wheat field," I correct him.

"Yes, but the railroad tracks were nearby," he says, and consulting my mind's eye, I can see that he's right, can see the railroad tracks back of the wheat field where we're wrestling with a bunch of village scamps.

The vigorous, handsome man across the table from me is Marek, and we're enclosed in a sort of bright dream space in which everything is hyperreal: the large watch face on his bony wrist, the quick, competent flick of his fingers as he snaps the cigarette lighter shut. After all, we are the only two people in the world for whom an excursion to a small waterfall in the Tatry foothills has the luminosity of an epiphanous moment. Marek's memory is rich: he remembers episodes in our favorite childhood novel, *In the Desert and the Jungle,* which I can no longer bring up from the recesses of my mind even with his aid; he recites whole verses of Polish poetry;

he remembers the date of my birthday. We keep bringing up those childhood tidbits as if we were kids gorging on candy. But oddly enough, there's nothing sentimental about this exercise: Marek talks eagerly, memory after memory tumbling out: to whom else, could he talk about this? For this, we're each other's ideal, the only listener. I had held on to these memories in such solitude, and then had put them in such deep storage, that after a while I was no longer certain whether I hadn't made it all up. But I hadn't; Marek is here to confirm that it all happened. Here before me, unbelievably enough, is the evidence. It's as if he had given me a hand and helped me walk through the Looking Glass, back, to a place where the past regains a plausible reality.

A few days later, Marek comes to Cambridge. "But you're a man!" my father cries delightedly when he's told that the person standing in front of him is Marek. Marek spends long hours talking to my parents; he's still a member of the family, it turns out, and they have a language in common.

After the doctoral ceremonies, the masters of the Harvard house where my husband and I have lived as graduate tutors give a small party. Like characters in the climactic scene of a comic opera summoned to deliver a furiously paced summation, the main figures of my personal mythology have all gathered in one place at the very point when, in effect, I receive the certificate of full Americanization. Through the haze of the inevitable sherry, I feel the reassuring blur of a reconciliation. Everything comes together, everything I love, as in the fantasies of my childhood; I am the sum of my parts. It's all turned out all right; a wave of gratitude sweeps over me. I've been the recipient of so much generosity. Harvard has been accepting of me, the American educational system as hospitable and democratic as advertised. Respected men of letters have taken my literary opinions seriously, and I've gained enough confidence to resolve that I want to write. I've seen more clearly how useful my bicultural triangulations are in this enterprise. "Where did you learn how to be a critic?" an editor of a magazine for which I've written an article has asked me, while treating me to lunch in a chic midtown Manhattan restaurant. "At Harvard, I guess," I answered.

"No," he said, "there's something else." "I suppose it's that I'm an immigrant," I said. "Ah yes," he said. "That must be it."

It's all turned out so well, but in the next moment, I'm gripped by fear, and it's only the cracks between the parts I can perceive. My parents are standing with slightly guarded dignity in the book-lined, deliberately unostentatious room. My husband is carrying on a conversation with our hosts, light, erudite conversation at which he's so good, and at which I've acquired some skill as well. I married him partly for this, for the gift of language, and I listen to him with admiring pleasure. But as I join him in a snappy exchange about the communal impulse in Thoreau and the difficulties of getting tenure and the merits of the celery remoulade in a new French restaurant, I feel my parents' eyes looking at me with pride: look how far she's come, their eyes seem to say, look how well she's learned to behave here—and I want to stop, pained at their approval. Who is this that's behaving this way, anyhow?

And who is this husband of mine, carrying on in this foreign language? I'm touched by his niceness, which exhibits itself in this energy of sociability, but I know that though I'm captivated by his eloquence, I still can't read the language of his feelings. As with my Texan, I keep missing some essential knowledge between us, and I'm keenly aware at this moment how much I keep hurting him by my distance.

Marek circles the room impatiently, as if he wanted to bolt; he's not used to the restrained civilities of this quietly elegant living room. I give him a reassuring look; it'll be over soon, I'll come for a walk with you. The points of my mental triangle have externalized themselves so neatly that I can't make a move without bad faith. We're not done with you yet, they seem to be saying. At this moment, every one of my complicities is a small betrayal.

Marek stays in Boston for a few days, and we're happiest when we're off by ourselves, in my VW, striking out for the open road. Then we fall into a sort of suspension, in which we almost glide again through a magical seamlessness, that childhood wholeness in which there are no obstacles, no friction, no disunion. Almost, because we can't quite slough off the burden of our adulthood. We look at each other in wonder from time to time. "Who are you?" Marek says, examining my face. "Sometimes you seem a woman, sometimes a little girl . . ." I return to his gestures, his movements, as to the most uncannily familiar dream, though I see that his face carries within it experience of which I have no knowledge.

I drive him around Boston, show him the surrounding countryside. "So much green," Marek says. "So many trees. It reminds me of Poland. Israel is so small. As soon as you turn around, you come to the end of it. This country goes on forever." But he moves even within these big spaces restlessly, impatiently, as if his energy itself were imprisoned. "Sometimes . . . I feel such a sadness," he says, placing his hand on his heart in the unconscious gesture inherited from our parents. Perhaps if he left his wife . . . But he can't, she would be destroyed, she would have no means of fending for herself. "Maybe you're being unfair to her, maybe she would learn, develop a truer life of her own," I say, imparting some of my American wisdom, but Marek stops me with a wave of his hand and a look of pity on his face. Once, we take out an atlas, and, as when we were kids, we look at maps of faraway places, and Marek says the talismanic words: Tahiti; Patagonia; Madagascar. Once, he happens on a book about Auschwitz, and looks at some of the awful photographs; then he shuts it angrily, saying "Never mind, never mind . . ."

He tells me about some of the kids we used to know in Cracow. Henry, whose hand I held in the awe of first beholding the ocean, has turned into a petty thief, and is in and out of prison, to his parents' great shame. And Ludwig, one of the Filiponki twins—the one who once threw all his toys out of a third-story window to annoy his parents—was killed in the Yom Kippur War. He died an ironically unheroic death—run over by an Israeli tank when he forgetfully put himself in the line of a maneuver because he was absorbed in one of his beloved mathematical puzzles. "That was a terrible war," Marek says. "The generals got fat on it. But in those early days, we were all in it together, I think you would have loved it . . ."

Sometimes, as if we were still seven years old and trying to outrun each other in the park, we have spurts of competitiveness: Marek goes to some lengths to prove to me that my salary isn't larger than his, and when we jump in for a swim in Walden Pond, we break into a race; I must be driven by powerful adrenaline, because we finish quite close. Then, we're once again half siblings, half lovers. Marek recites Polish poetry to me, and he says, "Your skin, your smile; it's home. Home." And though these words emerge as though from the center of my desire, and though, miraculously, for a moment we're almost the children tousling on a red carpet in a Cracow apartment, in love with each other's smooth limbs—we cannot, after all, get further than the vividness of our remembering, cannot beat our way back through the wall of accumulated time.

As Marek leaves, he places his hand on his heart and looks at me as though he has just realized that this parting has some pain in it. I hardly know how much I regret it this time. The fulfillment of a fantasy *is* different from the fantasy of fulfillment. Or perhaps a fantasy can literally never be fulfilled, since only another fantasy could supply its proper apotheosis. Actuality operates by more gritty and friction-filled laws.

Of course, I would have wanted to marry my fantasy lover, but Marek isn't the figment of my imagination anymore. He has grown more substantial, more mysterious, more himself. Really, I no longer know who he is. He has escaped me. We moved, for those few days in Boston, in refracted time, neither quite in the past nor fully in the present, and he has remained veiled by the haze of memories. Now, as I watch him get his ticket and his boarding pass, I want to hold him back, to hold on; to find out what he likes and dislikes, where we agree and disagree, what prompts him to anger or compassion. . . . I want to force us quickly, at this late moment, into the brisker reality of the current day.

For a while after he returns to Israel, we occasionally write to each other. Marek often sounds like a creature penned in, circling around problems he cannot solve; maybe he'll come to America again, he writes in one of his letters, but he never does.

And then, on a drizzly day in Vancouver, on one of my visits home, my parents tell me that he is dead. He has taken his own life, and there's no known cause. My parents show me the letter from Pani Ruta that conveys this news. There's little to garner from it. Marek had been visiting one of his Bedouin customers—he liked that, he told me, liked the rituals of hospitality in the Bedouin tents—and after finishing the business transaction, he drove out into the desert, and in that complete solitude, put a bullet through his head. There was no note, and no foreshadowing. The tone of Pani Ruta's letter is grim, but the handwriting is even, and there's no piety in it, no extra tears. It's a tone that says, one must go on; one does go on.

I leave the park bench where I'm sitting with my parents, and I want, urgently, to talk to Marek. I want him to tell me what happened; I want him to tell me why he couldn't go on. I want us to explain many things to each other, many things we didn't talk about. I'm ashamed that in my illusion of knowing him so well, I failed to know him better. Really, I have so little information to go on. But sometimes, I think of him and Zofia and myself, and others like us I know, as part of the same story—the story of children who came from the war, and who couldn't make sufficient sense of the several worlds they grew up in, and didn't know by what lights to act. I think, sometimes, that we were children too overshadowed by our parents' stories, and without enough sympathy for ourselves, for the serious dilemmas of our own lives, and who thereby couldn't live up to our parents' desire—amazing in its strength—to create new life and to bestow on us a new world. And who found it hard to learn that in this new world too one must learn all over again, each time from the beginning, the trick of going on.

Over there, you wouldn't even be thinking about getting divorced. You'd be staying married, happily or unhappily, it wouldn't matter much.

Oh, wouldn't it? Think hard. Wouldn't your unhappiness be just the same as here?

No, it wouldn't. It would exist within the claustrophobia of no choice, rather than the agoraphobia of open options. It would have different dimensions, different weight.

But surely an incompatible marriage is unacceptable.

An American notion.

A universal notion. Women in Bengal rebel against bad marriages, for God's sake.

Women in Bengal don't rebel against emotional incompatibility. They wouldn't understand what you mean.

But I'm not in Bengal!

If you were in Poland, you'd be making a sensible accommodation to your situation. You've seen people live perfectly happily within their less than perfect unions. They just have affairs, they don't go around blowing their lives apart.

It's dishonest to live in a state of emotional compromise.

You're becoming a sentimentalist of the emotions. At least don't pretend you believe something you don't.

I believe I believe this.

Aha.

I've acquired new ideals, do you mind?

You're an immigrant, you can't afford ideals.

I'm trying to live as if I were free. At least I can have that dignity.

Free. You're playing a dangerous game. A charade.

Leave me alone. It's you who's playing the charade now. Your kind of knowledge doesn't apply to my condition.

I'll never leave you quite alone . . .

But I don't have to listen to you any longer. I am as real as you now. I'm the real one.

I remember Cracow, literally, from my dreams. Usually in those dreams, I have been baffled in my desire to get where I want to go—an elusive homing place just beyond the edge of sleep. Now, in actual Cracow, it turns out that the dreams, repeated so often over the years, enable me to find my way. I move from street to street not by map or rational plan but because I've memorized them in my night wanderings. I come upon spots and buildings and streets which I recognize without knowing that they've been encoded in some region of my memory: a coffeehouse in a cellar filled with famous caricatures, a statue in a park, a nameless patch of grass. It's both eerie and fulfilling, this appearance of seemingly forgotten things, as eerie and fulfilling as if one woke up to find one's dream materialized.

I was literally baffled in my desire to go to Poland once before, in 1968. An unfortunate year to choose for going there, a year when most of the Jews remaining in the country were being forced to emigrate by a campaign of official and officially stimulated anti-Semitism. I spent most of that summer visiting a succession of Polish consulates—in London, Paris, Vienna, Prague—and being refused a visa for reasons that the embassy apparatchiks did not care to explain. "Why does Madame want to go there, anyway?" the one in Prague asked, looking at me from behind his dark glasses, and in a voice so full of familiar, sinuous innuendo, that I thought—well, perhaps I don't.

"Why do you want to go, what's dragging you there?" my parents ask disapprovingly. Maybe to be done with it, I say. To see how the story might have turned out. When I try again, in 1977, it's easy to get a visa—the rules, in Poland, change more often than anything else—but there are signs of another kind of trouble as soon as I arrive. In a taxi on the way from the Warsaw airport, the driver announces, "They've killed a student. In Cracow." He says this with an offhand unceremoniousness, which simultaneously expresses the rudeness of this event and his own rude feelings toward "them."

I have arrived in Poland at another of those moments when the pressures of the political situation have begun to simmer, threatening to blow the lid off. The student killed by "them" was a participant in one of the demonstrations that have been becoming more frequent lately, and the building where he lived has overnight become a sort of shrine, with flowers piling up on the staircase and the sidewalk in front of it. Phone lines between Cracow and Warsaw have been cut, the taxi driver further informs me; trains and planes have been canceled. Instantaneously, I recognize an old, instinctive response: a focusing of attention, an almost exciting alertness to every word. And in the next few days in Warsaw, I come upon that old mood, of people pulling together, mother and son and lady and servant, of lowered voices and rooms thick with cigarette smoke and vodka and conversations that last late into the night, of incessant speculation and analysis. There's a whiff of danger in the air, and the undoubted, pleasurable frisson of risk.

The trip was planned at the last moment, and I haven't contacted anyone beforehand. I worry about how I'll find my old friends in Cracow. But it turns out to be easy. The Cracow phone book has grown thicker than I remember it, but the addresses of the Dombarskis and the Orlovskis and Pani Witeszczak tally with the ones I have recorded in a crumbling little notebook in childish handwriting. After standing in an interminable queue in the crowded and damp train station in Warsaw, I board an evening train. It speeds through the pitch-black countryside with a more rattling noise than Amtrak; in my compartment, two men and a woman with briefcases, in very badly cut clothes, discuss a conference they have just attended. "If those Swedes would sell the hubcaps cheap to those Germans, then we could talk," one of them says, but soon they take out a piece of dried sausage and vodka and a deck of cards, and the men proceed to flirt with the buxom woman over rummy bridge. Ah yes, I'm in Poland, and the arrangement of this scene, the men bending toward the woman, their voices, with an edge of sarcasm and provocation, the knife slicing into the sausage—all of this will be forever more natural, more uncannily natural to me than the immaculate commuters folding *The Wall Street Journal* neatly in half on the Long Island train.

The Cracow station is badly lit, but a cluster of people approaches me as soon as I step off the train. Perhaps it's the wide-belted cotton dress and natural leather sandals—casual clothes made of good materials—that mark me as foreign. Anyway, the small group picks me out without hesitation. Somebody hands me a bouquet of flowers; somebody says, "Our Ewa." I recognize Pani Orlovska at once; her hair has grown quite white, but her beautiful face is strong and clear and her bearing upright. I pause in front of a spreading, middle-aged person with stringy blond hair. "Krysia," she identifies herself shyly, and we hug. A lanky, tall man in blue jeans and a T-shirt, which says University of Nebraska on it, informs me that he is Jacek, Danuta's younger brother. "How is Alinka?" he asks laughingly, because they used to have a childish flirtation going, "is she married yet?" and I tell him no, she's not married, and she's getting her doctorate in psychology and is very pretty and hardly speaks Polish anymore.

We all pack ourselves into Jacek's Polish Fiat, of which he is intensely proud, and a few minutes later, Pani Dombarska opens the door on the third-floor landing at 72 Kazimierza Wielkiego, the building right next to ours. I am immediately enveloped by an acrid, sweetish smell of cigarettes mixed with perfume and bales of fabric, which in my girlhood was the atmosphere of female eroticism. Pani Dombarska exhales the smoke of her cigarette, looks me over appraisingly—she still bears a slight resemblance to Marlene Dietrich; her lips are still outlined with sharp red lipstick and her eyebrows are a pencil-thin arc—and she ushers me into her apartment. "So this is how we live," she says, extending her arm in a gesture of self-explanatory resignation. "Nothing ever changes."

Indeed, except for a television standing on the sewing-machine table, the apartment is just as it was eighteen years ago: a living room doubling as a bedroom, a tiny foyer, a small kitchen. The sofa beds and the oak chifforobe and the gas stove in the bathroom, and the dust visible in the air under the overhead light, all have the plainness of things to which one is long accustomed, as if I have lived around them all this time. Only Danuta isn't here; to my disappointment, she's at a conference in Breslau, and I'll have to wait until tomorrow to see her.

We sit at a table laden with plates of cheeses and herring and ham—I don't yet sufficiently appreciate how much effort has gone into acquiring these rarities—and raising glasses of vodka, we speak in disconnected questions and phrases. "How are Mother and Father?" Pani Dombarska wants to know, and I explain that they live on the other end of the continent from me, and I don't see them all that often, though once a week we talk on the telephone. "How terrible," Pani Dombarska says, shaking her head. "It must be terrible for them." Jacek is fascinated by the fact that I've traveled a little; he has a shortwave radio and he prizes the messages he picks up from the West—the fabulous, unattainable, terrifying West. Actually, he has been abroad—in West Germany, as a guest worker. But he hardly saw anything; he was trying to make as much money as possible in a short time, so he could buy his Fiat.

"Is it true that the post office in America is mostly run by Negroes?" Pani Orlovska asks, and I wonder where she acquired this extremely curious bit of information. "I hear that the level of education over there is very low," Krysia's husband says a bit officiously. "That's too bad. As you know, the Russians really pay attention to their education. It'll give them an advantage, unless the Americans do something about it." I launch into a desperate attempt to explain the complexities of the American educational system, the Ivy League universities and the community colleges, the enormous disparities, the social stratifications, and then I give up and say, "It's a complicated country. It's very big," and everyone nods sagely, gratified to have a cliché we can all hang on to.

Krysia has been quiet during most of the conversation, observing me diffidently from her pale blue eyes, but on the way out, as we hug again, she asks me in a private voice, "Are you married?" "Separated," I say. "I'm probably going to get divorced," and she winces as if I'd told her about a painful accident. "I think it's the right decision," I say to her quickly, resorting to my standard American formula, but the puzzlement on her honest face tells me that this is not the right phrase, not the way to reassure her that everything is just fine.

"Ach, darling, you see now it is with us," Pani Dombarska, a little drunk, sings out after everyone has left. "There's no hope for tomorrow, so we live for today." "It's all right, Mummy," Jacek murmurs and kisses her hand. The three of us—Pani Dombarska, Jacek, and I—are all to sleep in the living room, Jacek in a reclining chair he has dragged in from a next-door neighbor. They assure me that they do this often, but I've gotten unused to such communal proximity, and I toss and turn through much of the night.

The next day Danuta returns from her conference and comes over to her mother's place. "Let me see you, let me see you," she chirps. "Did you turn into a real American?" She inspects me carefully. "Half and half," she diagnoses, and smiles mischievously. "I, as you will soon see," she announces with energy, "have turned into a regular house hen." But that's not how she seems to me: she is sexily plump and bouncy, her eyes are dramatically outlined with kohl, and her neck is draped in several strands of big wooden beads. From a pious, cheerful girl, she has grown into a cheerful, irreverent woman. Her face has a mercurial changeableness, registering every passing mood. If she sees Americanness in me, it's partly because my face has become more composed, more controlled than the faces of the women around me. I move in a more "American" way too—with looser, more resolute strides. I've allowed my body a certain straightforward assertiveness; but I've inhibited the capricious, impulsive mobility of expression that's the sign of the feminine here. Danuta's features and mine carry within them different ideologies of femininity, different loci of restraint and expression.

I move into Danuta's apartment for the next few days. "Do you like it?" she asks happily, as she shows me around, and I say, "It's capital," quite sincerely, although a few days ago it would have seemed fairly ordinary. My standards are undergoing a quick readjustment, and now I see the separate bedroom for her twelve-year-old daughter, the dishwasher in the kitchen, the old velvet-covered sofa, and the folk art on the walls for the signs of luxury and charm they're supposed to be.

"Mesdames, messieurs, à table!" Danuta's voice rings out each evening about eight o'clock, and at this signal, her husband rouses himself from his newspaper and her daughter, Marysia, emerges from her room. "So how do you like it, Olek?" Danuta asks about a salad she managed to concoct by dint of spending several hours in queues, in the morning, and after work. Danuta teaches biology in a high school, and she usually pores over student exercises till

late at night. Olek usually approves of the salad, and he kisses Danuta's hand affectionately. He's a tall man with perpetually mussed hair, and an absentminded expression on his face, which occasionally breaks out into an unexpected, unguarded smile.

"Imagine what that bastard Spiwak did today," he says to Danuta as we sit down to supper. "In the middle of our research meeting, he made an allusion—you can just imagine how subtle it was—to the fact that Janek skipped the afternoon last Thursday, to attend that demonstration, of course. I tell you, I felt blood in my head. D'you mind getting me another cup of coffee?"

"Well you know, you always knew he was a bastard," Danuta says, getting up. "It's just that until now, people like him didn't have to show their true colors. That has been the characteristic of the Gierek period," she explains for my benefit, "that various swine and bastards could keep their camouflage. This will be a hard time for them, poor swine."

"What's going to happen, Mummy?" Marysia asks, and Danuta assures her that it'll probably be nothing much, more's the pity. "Well then, excuse me, can I go now to play with Adam?" Marysia says, and after Danuta tells her not to get mixed up with "elements"—a half-joking word for people who're not quite of one's class—Marysia says "Thank you" politely and goes off to change into her beloved jeans and a T-shirt. "Victim of a liberal upbringing," Danuta comments as her daughter wafts out the door, but Marysia seems as well behaved to me, as much in fundamental agreement with her parents' values, as if she'd never heard of a generation gap.

For the next few days, I pursue my *recherche du temps perdu* with mixed results. The central city square is no longer a gathering place for pigeons; instead, it has burst with dozens of flower stands, selling shockingly expensive carnations and roses. Sukiennice still gives the square its Renaissance decorum, but I know that, like other ancient buildings in Cracow, it is being eaten away by a very contemporary disease—pollution. This blight comes, mostly, from Nowa Huta, an enormous steel plant built on the outskirts of Cracow as one of the monuments to socialism. There are almost no controls on industrial emissions in Poland, I'm told, and people working in Nowa Huta come down with horrible diseases in large numbers.

That's the kind of contemporary irony we're used to dealing with, but I'm aggrieved nevertheless: pollution, here, seems like a violation of innocence. My Cracow, ancient, fixed, crumbling from this invisible worm! Still, to the naked eye, the city, even at a moment of political turbulence, remains remarkably unchanged. In coffeehouses, elderly gentlemen peruse literary journals at their leisure; in Park Krakowski, mothers sit on benches rocking their prams, and children skip on one leg through squares drawn in the sand. At the Slowacki Theater, decorated in plush Rococo style, an audience dressed with slightly dated elegance gathers to see a spirited performance of a satiric play by an exiled author.

At Pani Witeszczak's apartment, the piano still stands in the corner against the window; the lovely miniature portrait I used to stare at between pieces still hangs on the wall above it. Pani Witeszczak now spends her days on the living-room sofa, which used to be occupied by her mother, covered by a puffy goose-down quilt. She looks frail reclining against the large pillows, but her eyes are strong and unclouded. Her son and daughter-in-law move around the apartment in their slippers, smiling softly, bringing her cups of tea. "So you didn't go on with the piano," Pani Witeszczak says, looking at me very directly. "You were a talented child, but I'm sure it's for the best. You're talented in other ways too; you're going to write something interesting. Do you remember Lydia Sulik? Older than you, also very talented? Well, she just wrote some interesting stories, a bit surreal, based on her experiences in England." Ah, the absolution of it! So I was simply one talented child among many; I didn't destroy a golden apple, I didn't betray a sacred trust. Perhaps only Pani Witeszczak, with her few simple words, could untie the complex tangles twisting up my choices; perhaps only she—the original keeper of the golden apple—could release me from its thrall.

I walk along the *Planty* slowly, and when I come to a spreading chestnut tree, I pause. It is here, under its protective branches, that

I once sat cupped in the heart of childhood knowledge. No, that knowledge cannot be recaptured by any tricks or mnemonic aids; and yet, like a pinpoint pulsar of light, it emits an intermittent glow.

In the courtyard of the synagogue, as tiny as the one in which Baba Yaga once stooped over, three old men sit on a bench. "Boris Wydra," one of them says. "Yes, I think I remember. We're all old here now. Our children are all in America or in Sweden." The Jews have become exotic in Poland, an almost extinct species; they're an object of friendly jokes and nostalgia and superstition. Some of the younger people growing up in Poland have never met actual Jews. Peasants in the countryside go to old Jewish cemeteries, where some wise old wizards are reported to be buried, to ask for good luck and to cast spells. I've known all this from newspaper statistics and magazine articles, and as I go inside the synagogue and sit in what used to be the men's section—no one bothers about such niceties by now—I find myself reciting numbers: there were 40,000 Jews in Poland until 1968, now there are about 5,000, although there are many more people of mixed descent . . . The numbers march through my head, as if I needed to interpose their cold factuality between myself and the deeper chill of this stone-walled interior.

I don't tell Danuta about this particular part of my memory researches. Whenever the subject of Jewishness comes up, people look embarrassed or fall into a compensatory volubility. This is the rift, the gap from which all the larger rupturings have proceeded. And yet, like all rifts, it's almost impossible to grasp. That I'm Jewish; what does it, after all, mean, at this moment, here? Perhaps only this silence between Danuta and me, this awkward space that inserts itself between us.

After I complete these private pilgrimages, I fall ill with a semihallucinatory high fever. Cracow air often does that to tourists, the doctor whom Danuta summons tells me. There's no fruit juice or Kleenex to be gotten anywhere, and on alternate days, the hot water, the gas, and the electricity break down in Danuta's deluxe apartment. But the doctor comes every day, and Danuta tends to me solicitously. Familiar discomforts, familiar comforts.

"Do you ever regret that you didn't stay here?" Danuta asks me one day, as she checks the thermometer she's taken out of my mouth. Now that the question is asked out loud, its meaning seems to dissolve. How can I possibly answer? I no longer know who would have lived the life I might have lived here. It is easy enough to reconstruct the basic blocks of a hypothetical history: if we'd stayed, I would have become a pianist, possibly achieved a measure of success; I would have married and had fights Polish-style, and gone on winter vacations to Zakopane. All of these events would have seemed to follow from one another, in an intelligible sequence. The ratio of change to stability would have been different: the stable elements—Pani Witeszczak's apartment, and the *Planty,* and the particular sleet of Cracow winters—would have formed the quiet ostinato of the known against which the modulations of change might have seemed milder and more harmonious. I would have got involved in student politics, and would have felt deeply about the issues as one does about matters one has grown up with. I would have gained the invigorating moral clarity that comes from knowing which side is in the right and which in the wrong, what is the truth, and what a lie—that clarity which gives Polish conversation and thinking such robustness and wit. The frame of culture is stronger here, and it holds the individual personality more firmly in place. These are things I know, but I no longer know how it is to live within them. In 1968, and in the wake of the anti-Semitic purges that followed student riots, I would probably have been forced to emigrate, as were most of the Jews who were still in Poland then. I would have left regretfully, perhaps heartbrokenly, but consciously: a different kind of departure from a despairing and blind adolescent uprooting. Where would I have gone? Israel, America, West Germany, Sweden? Here, the speculations become more attenuated, for I don't know the person who would have made that decision: I don't know how her daily life felt until then, how successful or frustrated she was, how adventurous or timid. I don't know the quality of her sensations, or what her yearnings were, or how she satisfied them. I don't know the accidents that left little scars on her skin, or the accretions of sorrow and pleasure on her soul. No, one can't create a real out of a conditional history; in the light of the simple declarative statement of actual existence, "would have been" or "as if " loses its ontological status. In a way, it doesn't count, though without it, we would have no imagination: we would be truly prisoners of our selves. But the shadow that this conjectural history casts over my real one is not a shadow of regret but of the knowledge—to which we all must reconcile ourselves—that one is given only one life, even though so many others might have been.

"So much has happened since then," I finally answer Danuta's question.

"Of course, your life is so much more interesting there," she says.

"No, that's not it," I say, and truly, I don't know how to compare the interest of our lives. "It's just that it happens to be the life I happen to have lived."

"Ach, darling," Danuta says ruefully. Of course, she understands—the poignancy, and the inevitability of having only one, peculiar version of a life, and living it within the confines of the first-person singular.

"Send some Bayer aspirin," she asks me when it comes time to part. "And maybe cocoa. Sometimes I dream about good cocoa."

Jacek drives me to Warsaw, where he has some business to transact, in his Fiat, and that's the first time I catch glimpses of the countryside. Bales of hay, old wooden houses, and some ugly one-story cement structures among them; peasant women, in long skirts, unbend from their labors and stare at the speeding car impassively. My illness has taken up the time I'd allotted for visiting villages. Next time. Poland is only a long plane ride away from the East Coast. That distended, uncrossable, otherworldly distance I had created had been the immeasurable length of loss and longing: a distance of the imagination.

It is strange, in spite of all we know about such transactions, that the Looking Glass through which I step into the past releases me to go on into the present. Perhaps now I can get the different blocks of my story into the right proportions. As every writer

knows, it's only when you come to a certain point in your manu-
script that it becomes clear how the beginning should go, and what
importance it has within the whole. And it's usually after revising
backward from the middle that one can begin to go on with the rest.
To some extent, one has to rewrite the past in order to understand
it. I have to see Cracow in the dimensions it has to my adult eye
in order to perceive that my story has been only a story, that none
of its events has been so big or so scary. It is the price of emigration,
as of any radical discontinuity, that it makes such reviews and re-
readings difficult; being cut off from one part of one's own story is
apt to veil it in the haze of nostalgia, which is an ineffectual relationship to the past, and the haze of alienation, which is an ineffectual
relationship to the present.

On the plane to Paris, I take out some preparatory notes for
an article I'm going to write on a current cultural epiphenomenon
in France. I look at my notebook with anticipatory excitement: I
remember how much I enjoy these quick forays into different mini-
worlds, how much I've come to relish my freedom to hop around
the world without special difficulty or restraint. But as I look at the
notations I'd made to myself, I fall into the kind of musing that
comes upon one in the netherspace of airplanes, and images of the
journey I've just made rise in my mind. Gradually, they cohere into
a single image, of a glass sphere within a sphere: in the inner circle
is the real Cracow, with the smokestacks of Nowa Huta forming
vertical lines, next to Danuta's apartment and the miniature arches
of the Sukiennice; in the outer sphere is a dream Cracow, with
images folding into one another, luminous and somnolent and
heavy with the promise of revelation. Then the inner and the outer
sphere exchange places, and the real Cracow is on the outside,
palpable and vivid, curving around the inner, milky sphere of the
dream.

Back in New York, I dream one night of a faraway place. I think
it's China, because of a calligraphic mountain in the background,
and a flat, nonmelodic line of music emanating from a flute.

In the dream, there is also a foursquare cottage, such as children everywhere draw when they draw home. The cottage has an earthen floor, and underneath this floor, there is a furnace, or another powerful source of warmth. A voice in the dream says,

> *The Cottage is the Heart of Desire; it's the Sun itself that stokes the Fire.*

When I wake up, I understand that words which I would never make up in the daytime, words compressed into metaphor and rhyme, were manufactured somewhere within my sleep. Having lived in a psychological culture, I can run several rings of interpretation around this dream: I can see its Jungian implications, and the Freudian ones, its sexual symbolism and its archetypal allusions. But this is the most important thing: that it was in English, and that English spoke to me in a language that comes from below consciousness, a language as simple and mysterious as a medieval ballad, a gnostic speech that precedes and supersedes our analytic complexities.

I've had English words in my dreams for a long time. But now they break up, de-form, and re-form as if they were bits of chromosomal substance trying to rearrange itself. When I study the poetry of Dryden, I have a dream about a town called "Dry Den," which, of course, suffers from a shortage of water. Sometimes, my unconscious does me proud by coming up with bilingual puns—as in a dream about the fear of time, in which the word *chronos* and the Polish *chronić,* which means to protect, are elaborately interwoven. Perhaps I've read, written, eaten enough words so that English now flows in my bloodstream. But once this mutation takes place, once the language starts speaking itself to me from my cells, I stop being so stuck on it. Words are no longer spiky bits of hard matter, which refer only to themselves. They become, more and more, a transparent medium in which I live and which lives in me—a medium through which I can once again get to myself and to the world.

It's when language stops traveling on its own frantic, disconnected circuits that I begin to regain the integrity of a more real courage, rather than my compensatory, counterphobic immigrant bravado. I will not go on to become an academic, but my Harvard degree has found excellent uses: it has given me the wherewithal to know that I can negotiate my way in this society and the time to learn some of the rules. My confidence is still a wavering thing; sometimes, I'm convinced that no one will ever give me a job because of my lack of "typological fitness"—a term which disguises my fear that no one will ever recognize me as one of their own. But on one occasion, I tell a sympathetic friend, though I say this sotto voce and with a consciousness of making a somewhat embarrassing confession, that really, I'd like to be a "New York intellectual"; by this I mean that I want to use whatever spunk and talent I may possess not to burrow in the layers of the canonical tradition but to throw myself into the living issues of the day. He tells me that New York intellectuals are a rather exclusive club, and not many new members are admitted, but what the hell, why not try?

Well, who knows, I may try. I may go to New York, I may knock on editors' doors. I have no methodical plan. But sometimes, a fresh wind of curiosity and energy reminds me how much I once wanted to live and act in the middle of the world. Perhaps I've gathered enough safety to take some risks again, to stop keeping myself to this frightened regimen of playing it safe. After all, even to set out on explorations one needs a place of departure and return, and I may have figured out just enough where I am to look about me with an open-eyed interest. Or perhaps the pragmatism-by-necessity that has governed my choices is cracking apart from internal contradictions. It hasn't exactly worked.

"You know," my husband said as we were sitting in our dismantled living room, in one of those moments of heightened closeness that comes over people just before they're about to separate, "right now we could've been looking for an apartment in New York; we could've been planning a vacation in France. But instead we've got to be happy." Then we both smiled wryly at our mutual understanding. Happy! That will-o'-the-wisp.

The phrase echoes my parents' old injunction: "Try to be happy." Oh, how well I've learned what a difficult precept this is to follow. But I've also learned, in my practical and self-protective efforts, that one cannot go against the grain of one's temperament forever. No, it's time again to rediscover the springs of my desires and love and appetite, to live from the place from which music flows. It will be a complicated task, trying to break the carapace of fear and will, but by now, I know that if I don't set out to do it, I run the true peril of living an alien life.

"I love you," I murmur to the man beside me in the nearly inaudible voice in which these most private utterances are made. These words are meant only for my lover; they are said in that space in which there's almost no space between us, in which they're almost the palpable filament of breath.

For a long time, it was difficult to speak these most intimate phrases, hard to make English—that language of will and abstraction—shape itself into the tonalities of love. In Polish, the words for "boy" and "girl" embodied within them the wind and crackle of boyishness, the breeze and grace of girlhood: the words summoned that evanescent movement and melody and musk that are the interior inflections of gender itself. In English, "man" and "woman" were empty signs; terms of endearment came out as formal and foursquare as other words. In that neutral and neutered speech, words were neither masculine nor feminine; they did not arise out of erotic substance, out of sex. How could I say "darling," or "sweetheart," when the words had no fleshly fullness, when they were as dry as sticks?

But now the language has entered my body, has incorporated iself in the softest tissue of my being. "Darling," I say to my lover, "my dear," and the words are filled and brimming with the motions of my desire; they curve themselves within my mouth to the complex music of tenderness.

Perhaps you cannot love one person when you don't love the world surrounding him, the common sensibility that somehow expresses itself in each one of us. It has taken me awhile to recognize sexuality in the American grain, to see what is to be trusted within it. I can read the lineaments of decency and a sort of ardent honesty in the face of this man beside me. I trust the will that drives him hard to make sense of things without games or camouflage—that modest American forthrightness that is the best part of innocence. His passion flows from that honesty, and it propels me to speak with that ease in which everything can be said. We speak, my lover and I, until words tumble out without obstacle, until they deliquesce into pure flow, until they become the air we breathe, until they merge with our flesh.

At the Vancouver airport, my parents and my sister are waiting for me. I see the little group as I come out of customs: three people made smaller by the sturdy, tall, western crowd all around them, two of them marked by a fragility of age and an unmistakable foreignness. My father, thinner now than he used to be, and with a very upright bearing; my mother, tiny, with a scarf on her head; my sister, looking strong and vigorous—a stylishly dressed woman with long earrings set off against her short dark hair. My father hugs me briskly, man to man; my mother places her cheek against mine with a sort of imploring shyness; my sister gives me an unexpectedly sweet smile, which softens her sharply etched features.

"Guess what," Alinka tells me, "I got that job I wanted. And I'm going on a talk show next week, as an expert in the psychology of sexual perversions. Pretty good, eh?"

"You see what famous daughters I have," my mother says, not without a touch of mockery. Fame, TV talk shows, research on male sexual fantasies, articles in *The New York Times:* these are not unimportant, but they are at a remove from the heart of things—from happiness, from family intimacies, from what really matters.

Vancouver looks lovely on this summer afternoon; there are flowers everywhere, and the air has that delicate, pellucid quality that comes in the Northwest after a fresh rain. My father drives his Buick, of midsixties vintage, carefully. His vision has gotten worse, and he worries about this car, the only one he has ever bought in Canada. Then we walk into the modest stucco structure to which my sister and I refer as "parents' house." I've never lived in it long enough to think of it as mine, and it is only over the years that I have gotten used to its being really theirs. Some incongruity remains in the house, furnished so much in the local manner. We sit down around the Formica-topped kitchen table, and my mother heats up the mushroom-barley soup—my favorite—and presses some honey cake on me. Here I am, in my shtetl-on-the-Pacific.

"You look tired, you're working very hard," my mother says as she always does when I arrive. "You'll get a good rest here."

"I'm not working so hard. I like working hard," I answer with the irritability of someone trying too hard to make a point.

"Tell me, do you ever regret that you got divorced?" my father asks me, as if this question had never come up before. In fact it has, almost every time we've seen each other. When I told my parents that my husband and I were going to split up, my father sent me a consolation note: "Dear Eva," he wrote. "What happened is not your fault. You're the victim of your environment and the psychosis of your times." But the reason the question recurs is that he can't come up with anything like a satisfactory explanation. My mother tactfully refrains from saying anything, because she knows there are some new rules of privacy I observe, but I see in her eyes that she's waiting for my answer too. "No, I don't," I answer, too flatly. "I don't regret it. We just didn't make each other happy. I know it was the right decision."

"Well, then, that's good," my mother says, but in this matter, she doesn't quite believe me, and faced with my parents' puzzlement, I'm shaken in my belief as well. My explanation is as close to the truth as I know how to come, but from this vantage point, it seems like a very recherché sort of truth. What did I give up my modest order for? What do I want in exchange?

"Tell me, do you have a certificate saying that you've worked at *The New York Times?*" my father inquires, and I try to explain why I don't need such a document.

"Do you have a warm winter coat?" my mother asks. Yes, Mother, I mentally answer, I have a new Geoffrey Beene coat, and a pair of Charles Jourdan shoes . . . I can buy myself such things now, though I still, if you must know, feel as though I've gone on an indecent binge when I do.

"Do you know that there are twenty million people on welfare in the United States?" my father informs me, as a way of commenting on my desire to go off on my own and write for a while. These conversations always come like that, thick with fundamentals. My parents don't much believe in lighthearted banter, or discreet restraint in approaching problematic issues.

"For heaven's sake, I can always get a job. I have developed a bit of a professional reputation by now," I say, feigning self-assurance, but my stomach tightens. It's such a thin ledge onto which I'm holding, it's so easy to slip . . . I think about how much I got paid for an article I recently wrote, and the tension twists into a knot. Within hours of arrival here, I'm no longer a hybrid but an oxymoron. My professional, self-confident, American identity recedes like an insubstantial mirage. Why does anyone think they should pay me so much for articles, how have I pulled the wool over their eyes? Next time, I'll be more humble, I'll thank the editor more gratefully. It's wondrous enough that I'm allowed to write at all, and that actually existing American publications want to print my words. . . . I'm afraid that somebody from my work life might call me while I'm here; if they did, my tone would be all wrong: supplicating, intimidated, pleading.

When my sister first starts living with a man, my father writes me that she is "committing a tragic mistake whose consequences will haunt her during her entire life." The notion of a Mistake looms large in my father's mind. It is, I suspect, the inverse of that trust in instinct that got him through the war, the dark side of the belief in the saving or the damning gesture, the crucial moment on which your whole life hangs, in which you can turn your fate in your favor, or forever against you. He anguishes about the mistakes he's made in his life; he fears the mistakes my sister and I are likely to make. I shrug off such fears impatiently. There are no such things as fatal mistakes anymore, I say to my father in my mind, no irreversible choices, or irrevocable consequences. We live in a post-tragic condition. If you marry the wrong man, you can get divorced; if you start out on a wrong career, you can retrack and start another one; in this country, you can pick yourself up from bankruptcy, and a stint in jail; and you can always, of course, pick up stakes and head out, if not for another frontier, then at least for another town. There is no ultimate failure here, no undying shame—only new branchings, new beginnings, new game plans. Go to X; if that doesn't work, veer off to Y; and so on, and so on. That's what freedom is about, and we live in a free country, understand, Father?

I hold on to this view as gingerly, as delicately, as if it were a rope that might snap if I tug at it too hard. My father's fatalism, I explain to myself carefully, was perfectly suited to his conditions. But in my less threatening world, I need to develop the art of optimism and of benign expectations. Think positive, an assertiveness-training voice in my head exhorts me. Think of the book review you have to write when you get back, of the dinner engagement at the Café des Artistes. You have a place in the world now, friends who can help you. There's no need to be sucked back into the vortex of these atavistic anxieties; they're misplaced and will only harm you; this Pavlovian pessimism will prevent you from rational planning, and from showing a cheerful, confident face, which is what you need, what your world requires.

The next day, my sister and I walk along Kitsilano Beach. It's a brisk, grayish day, and Alinka's dog romps ahead of us. "How do you think they are?" Alinka asks, and as usual, we worry the question of our parents' condition for a while. Then we go on to discuss her recent marriage and my current boyfriend, and her scuba diving and my upcoming trip. "Look at how well you've arranged your life," I tell her. "You know, I think your life is really OK," she tells me. We need to reassure each other like this from time to time, need to get a fix on our just slightly anomalous condition. And we need each other for these periodic summaries: I trust Alinka's appraisal of me: for all of our divergences, there's some common standard of measurement we have. We situate "the normal" in a similar place; we feel the pull of the ground's gravity a bit more strongly than most of our American peers.

"Come and sit by me," my mother says when I get back, a note of appeal in her voice. "You never sit quietly anymore." I make myself slow my internal speedometer down, carve out a scoop of time in which I don't feel the need to run to something else. "It all somehow goes by so fast," my mother says.

We sit on the sofa in the den, and my mother gives me the shtetl-on-the-Pacific gossip. She wants to ask me about how I really am, but it's difficult for her to know just what to ask, and it's difficult for me to know where to start explaining.

"Does your writing give you pleasure?" she asks, and I wonder why I don't pose this simple question more often. "It feels worthwhile," I say after a pause. "I like it best when it's done. Besides"—I swerve to another track—"it's fun to work on the computer."

"When I think what I've lived to see," my mother says, and goes on to reminisce about the first radio that came to Zalosce when she was a girl. In the evenings, people gathered around the house with the radio in it, and stood outside, listening with their faces glued against the windows. Then there was the first film she saw, in a larger town near Zalosce; it was something about New York, and she still vividly remembers the sound of breaking dishes that magically came from the screen.

"You must think that Alinka and I are some kind of monsters," I say. Through this time telescope, I see my sister and me as sci-fi creatures, with shiny, hard carapaces, living in a sci-fi world. We've grown such high-gloss, competent personae.

"No, I don't think of you as any kind of monsters," my mother says quite seriously. "Don't forget that I've come some way from Zalosce too."

But the crossing of the ocean has bollixed up the time distances between us. We've been catapulted across so many generational divides, backward and forward at the same time, that it's hard to know how to count them. Sometimes I measure the distance between us by how much I travel. My mother, through all of her uprootings, has retained the habits of a small-town life. Going downtown is a considerable outing for her. She has never learned how to drive a car, and once, when she sees Alinka break into a sprint, she says regretfully, "I've never done that. I've never run."

Such rapid and independent movement surely did not belong to the female side of the equation among the traditional Jews of Zalosce, and my mother has never swum, or skied or skated, or taken a trip entirely on her own.

Alinka and I move around on our own as if the globe were a large toy to play with. Alinka tends to take off on risky excursions, and to get into close encounters with grizzly bears and flash floods. I've acquired the assurance, which seems second nature to me but is relatively new for a person of my gender, that I can land in any city and within hours figure out how to get around it, use the metro, and find a good neighborhood restaurant and a decent midpriced hotel. Of course, it has helped in nurturing this confidence that I live in an imperial center whose currency is the international standard and whose language the Esperanto of the modern world.

In all of this, I've developed a certain kind of worldly knowledge, and a public self to go with it. That self is the most American thing about me; after all, I acquired it here. "Don't let them spit in your kasha," my mother advises me defiantly, meaning, roughly, "Don't let the bastards grind you down." In an American way, I don't: I've learned how to tough it out and stand my ground, cut my losses and choose my fights and talk back to tall men. I've learned how to size people up; stepping into a room crowded with strangers, I can figure out quickly what species—public species, that is—the people in it belong to; I recognize that self-assured young man who peppers his international technocratic career with a few progressive ideas, that British academic who mutters hilarious remarks without bothering to change the pitch of his voice, that young poet whose posture is stiff with the strain of his sacrifice, that cosmopolitan Indian woman who has made the transition to modernity with evident grace. I've learned to read the signs and symbols governing the typology of the contemporary world.

I take great pleasure in these skills, and the sense of mastery they give me. But how fragile they seem as I step back into that first, most private kind of knowledge.

On the third day of the visit, my mother and I are preparing lunch while my father reads the newspaper. "They're writing here about a Jew who was a Kapo in a concentration camp," my father says. "They're threatening him with deportation." No, I think, not another moral quandary from hell to consider over lunch. Why are the goddamn newspapers so obsessed with these things, anyway? "After forty years," my father says. "And in the meantime, they have hundreds of Germans, Ukrainians."

"If they start going after Jews who cooperated with Germans, it'll be a horrible mess," I say, unable to keep away from the subject after all. "There were so many of them, and how can you judge them? It was that or virtual suicide."

"Ah, yes, yes," my mother says. "But there were plenty of Jews who worked for them willingly. They tried to get these jobs. They thought they could save themselves and their families that way." She smiles with her bottomless skepticism. "You know," she continues, "that your father's sister was given away by one of them." No, I shake my head, I didn't know. And I don't know any longer how we can talk about these things in such normal tones in this well-lit room. "Yes," my mother continues, "he brought the Germans to the place where she was hiding with her little son. The Jews knew about the hiding places, of course. Your father's brother was hiding with her, and he was on the other side of the wall. He heard the Jew say to the German, 'I work well for you, don't I?' Your father's sister was saved that time," my mother goes on, "because she promised to pay them. But by the time she got back with the gold, the child was dead, of course."

I see that my father has gone slightly pale. "Let's not talk about these things," he says, lowering his head, and I want to stop too, right now. All this time I've done my father the injustice of not knowing this story, and now I can hardly bear to hear it. This is no longer a frightening fairy tale, as it would have been in childhood. I have a flash of my sister and my little niece in that room, and I shut it out as if even a flicker of such an image were indecent. Indecent to imagine, indecent not to imagine. Indecent not to say anything to my parents, indecent to say anything at all: pity is too small for this. We stop, and go on to talk about something else, in normal tones. Later, in the upstairs bedroom with the powder pink wallpaper, I see the scene after all, and thinking of its weight on my father's soul, I allow myself to cry.

There's no way to get this part of the story in proportion. It could overshadow everything else, put the light of the world right out. I need seven-league boots to travel from this to where I live. And yet, this is what I must do. A writer of my parents' generation who was himself in a concentration camp once told me that the Holocaust is the standard by which we should judge the world. But I think that the paradoxical task of my generation, caught within this awful story, is to get adjusted to the ordinary world in which we actually live, to acknowledge the reality given to us. While my American friends, after undergoing the normal disillusionments of adult life, gradually temper their optimism, I try to slough off the excess darkness that is false to my condition. Paradoxically, it's not an easy adjustment to make; our first knowledge is the most powerful, and the shadows cast by it upon the imagination can be more potent than the solid evidence of our own experience.

My visit, by my parents' standards, is brief. They haven't gotten quite accustomed to the idea of bicoastal mobility. "Try," my father says at the airport, making his old gesture of closing his fist, "try to be happy." "This will be a good year, I can feel it," my mother says. They so much want happiness for us; it must be hidden somewhere just nearby, and they would unlock it with a magic formula if they could. In the no-man's space between the check-in counter and the airplane, I go through the automatic motions: customs, metal-detector check, cup of coffee. The plane takes off, and I watch Vancouver change to a toy city, and then to a geometric shape jutting into the ocean. A small lick of departure anxiety: not fear of flying, but only the more obscure sense that I may never see Vancouver again, that my job has disappeared in New York, that everything can vanish so easily . . . But as the plane lifts above the cloud line, there is the heady pleasure that repeats itself every time I travel. The whole world lies below me, waiting for articles to be written about it. There is the great ocean below, and the great sky above, and nothing between me and pure possibility.

. . .

My Polish friends are eating smoked eel and drinking vodka around a simple wooden table in a Lower East Side apartment, and they are talking about the war. That war, of course, the war that defines history, the war that's still felt, like an avalanche in a downstream flow, in the course and currents of these people's lives. Elka, a robust blond woman in her fifties, spent the war years in England; her father was a parachutist courier between the Polish army in the West and the resistance forces within Poland. Jurek's parents were both in the resistance; his mother, aside from acting as a contact person for the delivery of arms, organized poetry readings in a Warsaw apartment. Yes, there were poetry readings during the war in Warsaw; there were theater performances and cabarets; there were stipends for promising young writers. This was not my parents' war; theirs was the other stream within Polish history. Stasiek, an older man and usually the resident raconteur, doesn't say much during this conversation. His position during the war—judging retrospectively, that is—was ambiguous. He fought in the Communist underground and happily joined the new Communist government when it came into power after the war. He was one of the young true believers who thought that from the ashes and the ruins would rise the phoenix of an utterly new Poland: a seductive, understandable dream, especially given the horror he had lived through. In the name of the new Poland and the New Man, Stasiek became the scourge of the unbelievers; at this table, there are relatives of people who spent years in prison because of his diktats.

But when the conversation turns to Poland's present situation, Stasiek leaps into it with the same impassioned abandon as everyone else. He has long ago left the Party. And anyway, there are vectors of force around this table that bind these people even across the lines of tension. There are arcs of history that pursue them even to this room on the Lower East Side. "The Question of Poland"—of what Poland should be, of its oppression, of the small room for personal maneuver—is a central one in all of their minds, as central as the numerous sexual liaisons they carry on. Or rather, more central: the sexual liaisons are the free, relatively unproblematic part of life. The Question of Poland is the perpetual knot, the great conundrum: it's where the moral fervor lies, the issue around which ideologies and philosophies evolve. It's a question of identity.

The Poles have begun arriving in New York around 1981, courtesy of General Jaruzelski, and yet another turnabout—the declaration of martial law—in the perpetual drama of Polish events. They have swept into New York on great gusts of energy, desperado drive, wit, and malice. The people drinking vodka with each other at this table have maligned each other indefatigably, and with acerbic zest. They've transported their habits of gossip and intrigue—delicious in small, closely knit societies where everybody knows everything about everybody, and everyone will stay friends anyway—to the more indifferent and inchoate stage of Manhattan. What was analysis there, here becomes overinterpretation—but to the Poles, merciless and clever scrutiny of their neighbors' doings and hypocrisies is a grand and absorbing game, a form of stimulus and exercise, as necessary to their mental vigor as the sun is to their health.

"So tell us how things look right now," Joanna, a stylishly dressed brunette, asks a newly arrived dissident journalist, who's here on a visit.

"Well, you know, it's hopeless," the journalist says, with gusto. "The economy is producing almost nothing—it's worse, I tell you, than when you were there—and how they're going to pay all those debts to the West nobody knows. The apathy is terminal. People get used to living in their own mess. Poland is a country strangling on principles it never accepted."

"Paranoia," a large, bearded man with glowing eyes says, expressing the general absurdity of the situation.

"But it can't be hopeless," I say. "There must be some way out. Surely, Gorbachev's loosening of the reins will have some consequences."

"Gorbachev will be out, or dead, within two years," the visiting journalist says with a well-practiced pessimism.

"I can't accept a no-exit situation," I say, as my mind busily tries to find tracks leading out of the cul-de-sac described to me.

"Well, you know, you don't have to accept it, but the situation exists nevertheless," the journalist tells me with elegant sarcasm. Obviously, my urge to look for solutions has no appeal at all.

"Leave her alone, she's American," Marysia, a feline-looking, sharp-spoken woman says, looking at me protectively. "She's not as cynical as you," and I reflect that it's not often I'm accused of an overly positive attitude.

"Listen"—Felek, a compact, sandy-haired fellow addresses me—"today I saw my editor, and he told me that my book needs more local references for an American audience. What's that supposed to mean? You think that Ramski got to him first? After all, we know what he's capable of." Ramski is Felek's sworn enemy, and they've both spent many entertaining hours telling character assassination stories about each other.

"No, it means he thinks that your book needs more references for an American audience," I answer.

"Aren't you being just a bit naïve?" he asks, in a gratifying echo of childhood. Some values never change.

"Editors are busy people," I say, "they don't generally listen to tales of skulduggery and intrigue poured into their ears at parties by itinerant Poles. Or at least they don't make their commercial decisions on that basis. They tend to pay attention to . . . how would you say this in Polish? To the bottom line."

"Bottom line?" Marysia asks sharply.

"Money, basically," I say.

"You are a little naïve," Felek concludes, and I sigh in mock exasperation. Explaining that things are sometimes exactly what they seem is an ungrateful job.

"Why does everything take so long to do in America, anyway?" Marysia complains. "Nobody ever answers phone calls, nobody makes decisions. . . . It might as well be socialism, except it makes you more nervous: One day you think you're going to be rich and famous, next day you can't afford health insurance . . ."

"Speaking of rich and famous, did you hear about Wanda?" Jurek says in an amused voice. "Some producer flew her out to Hollywood and told her she's perfect for this role of a Russian aristocrat, if you can imagine our Wanda playing that. So of course, she got a whole new wardrobe, to make the right impression in Hollywood, you know Wanda, and she told Tadzio good-bye, that's it for them, he wouldn't fit in in Hollywood. Then she turns up in the producer's office, and he says, 'Oh, I'm so sorry, I should have called you, but I just started on another project, maybe next year, you're very talented, it was good to see you.' In the meantime, Tadzio is no fool, and he has moved in with Zosia, who was dying to have him, and Wanda's wardrobe isn't exactly right for the Lower East Side."

"Paranoia," Felek comments with glee.

"Well, you can't count on anything before you've got it signed on the dotted line," I explain.

"Dotted line?" somebody asks.

"Well, anyway, I wish to all of you that we should become rich and famous," Jurek says from the depths of his heart, and raises his glass. "Everything else will follow."

"Listen, let's go do Dodo's," somebody suggests. Dodo's is the latest exclusive discotheque in the downtown area.

"Oh, no, it's two o'clock, I've drunk half a liter of vodka, I don't want to go to any Dodo's," I protest.

"Oh, come on, just for a while, what the hell, what are you alive for if not to go do Dodo's?"

"Ah yes, good point," I say, and immediately everyone is up and ready to move on to the next thing. At Dodo's an individual with upper arms much thicker than his head tells us there's no room inside. "Listen, these are very distinguished visitors from Eastern Europe," I say, having clearly switched into the Polish mood. "Tomorrow they're having an audience with Mayor Koch. Do you want them to tell the mayor that you muscled them out of Dodo's?" But the Cerberus places his arms akimbo across his chest, and doesn't deign to answer.

"Prick," Stasiek says in Polish.

"Prick?" I say. "What's that?"

"So let's go to Lydia's," Joanna says in her sinuous voice.

"Well no, we can't, you know . . ." Stasiek says delicately, and

Joanna says, "Ah, right," since everyone knows that Lydia is now involved with X, who used to be her husband's friend, and this is a bad evening to visit. "Ah, yes, well then, then, maybe to Olek's? His party is going to go on all night," Marysia suggests.

"But that's all the way in the Bronx!" I protest. "I have to go to work tomorrow!"

"Poor Ewunia, she works so hard," Marysia says with pitying condescension. I know she thinks that I lose a bit of charm with every full day I put in at the office.

I get infected by this restlessness, playful but somehow different from the energy I felt among people talking about the latest political crisis in the Warsaw Literary Club. What are they looking for, my New York Poles? Maybe their restlessness comes precisely from trying to re-create that other excitement they left behind—the excitement of the long evenings when the coffeehouses filled with smoke and political intrigue, when everyone looked up discreetly because Y, who just wrote a compromising article in an official journal, walked in, and when heads turned just a smidgen because beautiful Z walked out publicly with famous writer R, even though her husband was expected to arrive any minute . . . Perhaps they're searching for the familiar heat of home.

And maybe, at the same time, they're looking for the America they imagined, while talking their long evenings away in those coffeehouses, as the essence of excitement itself, a mythological excitement. Perhaps they're still searching for the New York they knew only from the novels of Dos Passos and Truman Capote and funky movies featuring neon-garish streets and implausible chases along rainy sidewalks in the night—the New York that proves so elusive now that they're here.

But yet, variously disaffected or nostalgic or dislocated though they may be, my Polish friends hardly ever entertain the notion of going back. Somehow, it doesn't make sense, and though there are good political reasons why it doesn't, it seems to me a matter not only of politics but of size. It's hard to return to a smaller stage from a bigger one, especially if the smaller stage is nearly a box, a sort of Punch and Judy show. We may be to some extent puppets everywhere, but it's one of the features of a closed system that you always know who the puppeteer is, who's pulling the strings. The American stage is large enough, and indeterminate enough, to stand in for the world. In this performance space, almost anything can happen; and therefore, it affords us a more perfect illusion of being undetermined—an illusion almost impossible to exchange for the other one.

"Well, you know, let's just go home and finish that bottle of vodka," somebody suggests, and the car makes a U-turn with a screech. We walk up the dubious-smelling staircase trying not to wake the neighbors. "You know," Jurek says, as we walk in and behold the small, dingy kitchen with the debris of the evening beginning to melt and ooze over the table, "in Poland, when you came to somebody's apartment, and everything was cool and groovy, and just as it should be, you said, 'Ah, America!' " He extends his hands with comic eloquence.

"Ach, old man, don't worry," Felek says, clapping him on the shoulder. "Someday you'll get there, and then you'll see what it's like. Tall men in cowboy hats, producers throwing deals at your feet, a swimming pool in every penthouse, and a TV with remote control in every room. . . . I tell you, it's quite a country, America."

"Oh well, maybe I'll apply for a visa to go there, I hear they're easier to get these days," Jurek says and raises his glass.

Maria comes to clean my apartment once in a while, and usually, before she gets to work, we chat over a cup of coffee, which she makes extra strong. Maria came from Brazil a few years ago, with her daughter, Tony, who is smart and talented and who has hopes of becoming a dancer. In the meantime, all sorts of terrible things, New York–style terrible, have befallen them. For a while, they had so little money that they didn't eat enough, and Tony fainted in her ballet class several times. They were evicted from the apartment in Queens, and their place in the Bronx was robbed. "Maria," I ask her over one of our coffees, "do you think of going back, to Brazil?"

"Ooohh, no," she says as if the question astonished her, shaking her head several times for emphasis. "Things no good in my country. Salary—ice." She makes a cutting gesture with her hand, and then, seeing the incomprehension on my face, remembers another word. "Freeze. People so poor. Government no good. I no go back there, nooo."

I see, I say, and we stare at each other wide eyed, as if gazing at a stark truth that you can't embellish with too much commentary. I see.

"Maria, don't you want to marry?" I ask her another time. "Wouldn't it be easier? Maybe you could find somebody to help you."

She giggles with unexpected merriment, then looks serious. "I like mens," she says. "I had mens. But they don't help you. You find good mens?"

"Nah, not really," I tell her jokingly.

"Maybe for green card, I marry," Maria adds. "Now I have green card . . ."

"So you're just going to keep working hard?" I ask.

"Maybe I get a good job, nice lady's house. Tony finish school. She take care of me." Maria's eyes go a little dreamy. "Maybe the newspaper write about her. She talented, Tony. She so beautiful. Joanne Woodward once see her dance, she says Tony is good, very good."

Tony is beautiful, part Indian in her features, and on her face is drawn a mixture of still childish delicacy and the sturdy good sense of somebody growing up with a strong sense of necessity. She has taken a part-time job in a real-estate office to pay for her share of the rent, and she goes there in the afternoons, after a long morning of ballet classes. She loves those classes, except she tells me that "some of the girls are crazy. They want to be so thin, they starve themselves. I don't want to starve myself."

After a while, it becomes evident that Tony won't become a star. She's told she isn't thin enough, and her talent didn't develop as they hoped when they first saw her. I identify with her intensely: how was her talent supposed to develop under these circumstances? I go to plead her case with the director of her ballet school, but I'm told she hasn't lived up to her promise, and besides, she isn't thin enough. Tony takes stock of her new situation and decides to work in the real-estate office full-time. Then Maria decides to bring her grown son here, with his children.

"Why?" I ask, "why? What will he do here? Where will he live?"

"Ah, lady," Maria tells me with a touch of impatience, "this is better. Here, if you work hard, you get a few things. In my country, people no eat. They have no hot water. Here, he has a shower. After he works hard, he keep clean."

I mentally compare the slums I saw in Rio, the hillside *favelas* with their cardboard shacks and sewage seeping down in runnels, and Maria's Bronx apartment. Ah yes, it's better. As simple as that: better. This is what emigration, on a mass scale, has always been about. I'll never complain, I promise myself, and keep the promise for a week or so; where do the pangs of a bifurcated identity figure on this scale?

Maria's son arrives; he's a quiet young man with an engineering degree and obvious reserves of patience, which he'll certainly need. He might well get a decent job eventually and make it possible for Tony to go to college. Something might happen. The story isn't over, it isn't foreclosed, and that's the point: there's a tiny chink into the future that might be wedged open.

"You used to be able to emigrate to America," a Polish friend, who has been here several years, quips. "Now where do you emigrate to?" For her, the world is too small to sustain the fabulous America of people's dreams; there is no America any longer, no place the mind can turn to for fantastic hope. But for Maria, who nurtures no fantastic hopes, it's still America you emigrate to—this all-too-real America.

When my parents, or their Polish friends, use the word "psychological," it's to suggest something weird, verging on crazy. "It's something psychological," they say about a woman who's afraid to come out of her room, or a man who's celibate for too long. Normal human beings are assumed to have understandable feelings and motivations. People love, hate, and grieve; they get jealous when they are betrayed, angry when they're attacked, insulted when their pride is punctured. Emotions can get complicated—my mother understands quite well the injustices of human relations, and how people get resentful of those who are too generous to them, or persecute those who least deserve it—but feelings have a logic, no matter how irrational, that can be followed, intuited, understood. Outside those normal paths and knots of the human heart lies the murky pit of the psychological.

"Freud was the guy wrote that book about dreams, right?" an urbane, well-educated Polish writer asks me.

"This is the twentieth century, you can't be a modern person and pretend to be innocent of psychoanalytic knowledge," an American friend says.

"That's just one version of modernity," I say defensively. "Don't you think that what happened in Eastern Europe during this century is a part of the modern experience? Do you think that self-knowledge began in the year nineteen hundred?"

"Why do they go to psychiatrists all the time?" my Polish friends inquire, since I've become a kind of guide to the native morals and manners. "Is it because they don't talk to their friends? Or are they so well off they don't know what they want anymore?" No, that's not it, I say uncertainly, it's not only self-indulgence. See, there's a particular form of suffering that thrives in this land, even though it's as invisible as ozone, and it hits people in seemingly untroubled circumstances. But what is it, my Polish friends want to know, what's bothering them? What's bugging that movie executive who flies all over the world in his own airplane? Or that pretty woman with a nice husband and a university teaching job she likes?

Well . . . I say, it's hard to explain. It's a problem of identity. Many of my American friends feel they don't have enough of it. They often feel worthless, or they don't know how they feel. Identity is the number-one national problem here. There seems to be a shortage of it in the land, a dearth of selfhood amidst other plenty—maybe because there are so many individual egos trying to outdo each other and enlarge themselves. Everyone has to grab as much ego-substance as possible, and grab it away from everyone else, and they aren't sure it belongs to them in the first place. . . . Or maybe it's because everyone is always on the move and undergoing enormous changes, so they lose track of who they've been and have to keep tabs on who they're becoming all the time. . . . Oh, it's so complicated, but this is a complicated country, big and complicated . . .

"Aha, well, yes, maybe there's something to that, they certainly seem nervous a lot of the time," my Polish friends say, but I see that I might as well be talking Chinese. "Identity," for my Polish friends, is not a category of daily thought, not an entity etched in their minds in high relief. My American friends watch the vicissitudes of their identity carefully: now it's firm, now it's dissolving, now it's going through flux and change . . . They see themselves as pilgrims of internal progress, heroes and heroines in a psychic drama. If they're unhappy, they tend to blame it on themselves, on how they haven't fine-tuned their identity well enough, haven't exorcised anger or acknowledged it sufficiently, have exerted too little, or too much control. Their efforts to improve this fragile treasure of which they are in charge are strenuous and constant. For my Polish friends, an identity, or a character, is something one simply has. If they take to drink, or become unhappy, or get depressed, they look for reasons in their circumstances: it's because a lover left them, or censorship stopped their book, or the situation in Poland is hopeless, or life is hard. . . . The drama of daily life exists in the world, in small and extraordinary events, and introspection is a process of dwelling on what one has experienced, rather than a means of systematic analysis or self-reform.

My Polish friends cover the human territory by observation and gossip. They carefully note each other's raised eyebrows and curled lips, and who invited whom to dinner and when, and who said what to whom with what nuance of intonation. From this constant stitching of detail, they create a thick tapestry, a pointillistic picture of human behavior.

"Last night, he decided to put on a really grand show," Marysia tells me, describing a marital tiff. "He got dressed very carefully, spoke to me very politely, but of course wouldn't tell me where he was going, and then tried to shut the door behind himself very resolutely. But the door made a funny squeak, and he had to tug at it several times. . . . well, I've *told* him he should repair it. He came back several hours later trying to act very dignified, but somehow, that squeaking door spoiled everything. . . . It was quite funny, but really, I'm getting so fed up, surely, you understand me . . ."

"Surely, you understand me," or, "Well, you know how it is . . ." my Polish friends say frequently: conversational gestures that assume a common understanding and no need for explanation, and that can also convey a world of insinuation—surely, you understand what I mean . . .

My American friend recounting a marital disagreement parses it into entirely different categories and conversational devices. She might tell me about the anxiety her husband transfers from his work to his intimate relationships, or how uncertain he is of his desires and therefore defensive in his dealings with people, or how she needs to learn to hold herself within the borders of her identity so that she doesn't get submerged into his. . . . She assumes that everything needs to be explained, from the ground up, to herself and to others.

When my Polish friends listen to these analytic musings, they think they're being told nothing. To them, this is not self-revelation but the speech of specters, of smoke. In the most elaborate explanations, they miss the sound of the fundamental fact: "I love him," or "I wish he'd go away," or "The worst thing is that I've stopped being jealous anymore." To my American friends, the Polish mode of frankness—the telling fact, the bit of gossip—is a form of withholding. They don't feel they're getting the true story from these anecdotes; they miss the sound of a confession, the intention to tell everything.

A culture talks most about what most bothers it: the Poles talk compulsively about the Russians and the most minute shifts of political strategy. Americans worry about who they are. Each conversation breeds its excesses of overinterpretation and stupidity, and its compensatory wisdom. Each, of course, is delicious comedy to the other—the comedy from which so much expatriate writing is made.

The pervasiveness of identity-talk is the kind of second-stage question that émigrés—those who have the leisure and the curiosity to attend to such matters—confront, after the initial culture shock and culture thrill wear off, after one gets used to the strangeness and the excitement of new buildings and clothes and music and ethnic diversity and the extremes of wealth and poverty and the foibles of democratic elections and the difficulties of getting a job. After the immigrant's dendrites stop standing on end from the vividness of first impressions, comes this other, more elusive strangeness—the strangeness of glimpsing internal landscapes that are arranged in different formations as well.

"What's this thing Americans have about their mothers?" my Polish friends ask. "Why do they talk about their mothers all the time?"

Indeed, my American friends talk about their mothers a lot. The oppressive mother, or the distant mother, or the overloving mother, is an accepted conversational trope, like the weather or the stock market or the latest Mideast crisis. My American friends pay their mothers the indirect tribute of incessant and highly subtle scrutiny. They measure the exact weight the mother exercises upon their psyche, and they practice careful equilibriating acts between letting the mother too much in and keeping her too much out. In their accounts, the mother comes out both extremely close and remote, as if she were both a vampiric incubus and a puzzling stranger.

For my Polish friends, this is grist for cross-cultural satire. Only Americans can make so much fuss about something so . . . well, normal. A mother, for heaven's sake, is a mother. In Poland itself, you usually live with her until you get married, or sometimes until much later. After you move out, she comes over to help out in the kitchen or with the kids. Sometimes she even comes to America for a while and does some of the shopping and cooking. Things sometimes get uncomfortable in a small kitchen, and the mother and daughter, or son, quarrel. But basically, the mother is as familiar as the slippers in which she shuffles around the apartment, and getting along with her is not a matter for lengthy discussion. The air around her isn't charged with gothic menace.

To my American friends, it's the Polish mother who's the figure of sentimental and humorous folklore. Probably she doesn't exist at all. The American mother has to be deconstructed in order to be known. "See," I try to explain to my Polish friends, and to myself as well, "they grew up in big separate houses here, usually with nobody but the mother around. I think the mother exercised too much pressure by being such a heavy center of gravity, and in the meantime, she wasn't so certain of herself, and so she generated uncertainty. . . . Then the daughter, or the son, moves far away, before they can develop an adult knowledge of the mother, and pretty soon, they find that they're members of different generations, different species." The American mother exists both too close and too far for comfort; it's hard to see her in the middle distance in which people acquire firm outlines and three dimensions and an ordinary size.

As I translate back and forth, I get more defensive on behalf of my Polish friends, because I know that it's not only their views but their legitimacy I have to establish. A cultural dialogue moves between certain polarities: X and anti-X. The good mother gives way to the bad mother and then to the good mother again. Nobody involved in this exchange wants to hear that the mother shouldn't be a problem in the first place, and that what really matters is censorship. An oppositional voice—a voice that responds to a statement with a counterstatement and says no, you're wrong, it's not the mother but the daughter who's at fault—is part of the shared conversation. But a minority voice—a voice that introduces terms outside the tensions of a particular dialogue, terms that come from elsewhere—is usually heard only as an irritating mosquito buzz on the periphery, an intrusion that the participants in the main conversation want to silence quickly and with a minimum of rudeness, so they can get on with the real subject.

Or perhaps I am defensive on behalf of the minority voice in myself. For as time goes on, my own relations with my mother become . . . well, more psychological. She becomes the mother-in-my-head, a figment of my psyche and imagination with which I struggle mightily and in a vacuum. But then, she lives so far away; I don't have her concrete presence to wrangle with or to get angry at. In such commonplace dramas, we might come to some modus vivendi, an ordinary understanding of each other as two people struggling in the world. As it is, the drama has become psychodrama; in battling her, I battle ghosts, and those have the tendency to become both bigger and more insubstantial than life. It takes longer to catch them, stare them in the face, divest them of their charge and their mystique.

The distances, in America, are still the salient thing. The large facts of geographic distances and the smaller facts of the distances between apartments and offices and houses inform the most intimate distances between us. In the distended and foreshortened perspectives of the American spaces, others tend to become puzzling Others—and so do our own selves, which grow in strangeness and uncertainty in direct proportion to the opaqueness of those around us. There are so many strangers, in America. How can we take for granted that, surely, we understand each other? How can we infer meaning from a gleam in somebody's eye? Perhaps the homogenizing language of psychology is a way of coping with a bewilderment of heterogeneity. It's a language that provides universalizing explanations for strangers whose circumstances are unknown to us, a language fit for a still-young culture that has not yet accreted the layers of familiarity and of ripened habit from which the speech of colloquial intimacy and of common observation grows.

When I first decide to go to a shrink, I tell my mother not to worry, it only means that I've arrived; I've made it as a proper member of the American middle class.

"Aha, I see, so that's what it means to be successful here," she says acerbically.

"It comes with the territory," I answer tartly, though I share at least half of her skepticism. What's this weird ritual of full confession I've signed up for? What sort of thing is it to do for a sensible person, and an immigrant to boot, this burrowing in infantile memories and minutiae of entirely trivial events? Perhaps I've arrived too quickly for my own good. In the normal course of events, as a zero-generation immigrant, I should be worrying about establishing a solid material footing in the world; in the usual sequence, it would fall to my children, or even grandchildren, to contemplate the refined sufferings requiring such rarefied remedies.

"I've contracted this American disease, and now I have to get the American cure," I tell my shrink accusingly.

"And what's the disease?" he asks politely.

"Anomie, loneliness, emotional repression, and excessive self-consciousness, the latter of which is encouraged by your profession," I say. "Just pick up any fiction written nowadays and you'll see."

"Can you tell me what's been going on in the last few days?" he asks in a neutral tone.

"You don't believe that culture shock can be real shock," I say for the umpteenth time. "You don't believe that its trauma can be as real as seeing your father naked when you're three months old. You don't believe in the power of events."

"It all depends how you react to them, doesn't it?" he says. "And that is a question of temperament."

"If a person from a tribal village in Kenya found himself in a big city and became confused and disoriented, would you recommend psychological treatment for him?" I ask, taking another tack.

"In certain cases," my shrink replies.

"Then I think you'd be wrong," I say, but I'm no longer sure. I've become caught between stories, between the kinds of story we tell ourselves about ourselves. In one story, circumstance plays the part of fate, in the other, character. In one, I've been poised against my surroundings at an embattled tilt because I was thrown into an alien world. In the other, the world was alien because I was prepared to make it so, and all events registered on me as dye making patterns in the grain of already woven fabric.

Between the two stories and two vocabularies, there's a vast alteration in the diagram of the psyche and the relationship to inner life. When I say to myself, "I'm anxious," I draw on different faculties than when I say, "I'm afraid." "I'm anxious because I have problems with separation," I tell myself very rationally when a boyfriend leaves for a long trip, and in that quick movement of self-analysis and explanation the trajectory of feeling is rerouted. I no longer follow it from impulse to expression; now that I understand what the problem is, I won't cry at the airport. By this ploy, I mute the force of the original fear; I gain some control.

Once, when my mother was very miserable, I told her, full of my newly acquired American wisdom, that she should try to control her feelings. "What do you mean?" she asked, as if this was an idea proffered by a member of a computer species. "How can I do that? They are my feelings."

My mother cannot imagine tampering with her feelings, which are the most authentic part of her, which are her. She suffers her emotions as if they were forces of nature, winds and storms and volcanic eruptions. She is racked by the movements of passion—*passio,* whose meaning is suffering. Her vulnerability is so undefended that it is a road to a kind of strength. My mother has the knowledge of the powerless. No life is exempt from struggles of the will, even—or perhaps especially—with those closest to you. But my mother has never vied for any public power. Removed from the arena of the will, she has had the clarity to observe the ways of the will, the power struggles of others. She is finely attuned to affectations and pretense; she can be a merciless parodist of false tones, of people's attempts to give themselves superiority and make more of themselves than they are.

As for me, I've become a more self-controlled person over the years—more "English," as my mother told me years ago. I don't allow myself to be blown about this way and that helplessly; I've learned how to use the mechanisms of my will, how to look for symptom and root cause before sadness or happiness overwhelm me. I've gained some control, and control is something I need more than my mother did. I have more of a public life, in which it's important to appear strong. I live in an individualistic society, in which people blend less easily with each other, in which "That's your problem" is a phrase of daily combat and self-defense.

In the project of gaining control, I've been aided by the vocabulary of self-analysis, and by the prevailing assumption that it's good to be in charge. "I've got to get some control," my friends say when something troubles them or goes wrong. It is shameful to admit that sometimes things can go very wrong; it's shameful to confess that sometimes we have no control.

My mother stays close to herself, as she stays close to home. She pays a price for her lack of self-alienation—the price of extremity, of being in extremis, of suffering. She can only be herself; she can't help that either. She doesn't see herself as a personage; she's not someone who tells herself her own biography.

I've learned, along with my generation of American women, how to travel further; how to gain some detachment and nurture a sense of self-worth. But I wonder what price I pay for this greater distance from myself. The French, in the eighteenth century, classified ambition—a new phenomenon in the topography of behavior and emotion—as an illness, and, in a less literal sense, my mother does too. "This ambition is a sickness," she says to me often, after listening to some saga of work and stress. "Where are you hurrying to?"

Ambition, achievement, and self-confidence are the pieties I've picked up from the environment, and if I don't always work hard, I compensate by a sort of anxiety, an inner simulation of running hard. My friends and I tell each other heroic stories of how much we've accomplished, how we manage to get to the health club between high-powered conferences, how much energy we have, and how effectively we expend it. Like everyone I know, I'm in a hurry all the time. What are we running to, indeed? Or, as my father would say, "For what is the purpose?"

Good question. Clearly, the purpose is not only accomplishment, for even after I gather a modicum of it, the need to keep in seemingly forward motion doesn't become assuaged. Perhaps this is some internal correlative of the lure of the frontier, a psychological version, abstract and quite contentless, of moving on. Of course, the pleasures of sheer movement are considerable, and sometimes, as I go through my busy days, I'm exhilarated by the sheer momentum of it, as of riding a motorcycle, riding a wave.

But while I'm moving on, and moving away, I have a fantasy of being more like the lilies of the valley, a fantasy of quietness. Sometimes, the fantasy is nothing more than a memory trace of a country road, along which I move, flurrying the tall weeds through my fingers, and thinking about nothing much—that in-between time, in which the soul refuels and regenerates. But we have so little time of that kind. We've become underdeveloped on the receptive side, I tell my friends. We're efficient even in telling our stories, over a quick restaurant dinner, though we don't always have the extra leisure for the surprise of empathy, which takes place in slow time and is hard to catch between cocktails and taxicabs.

If all neurosis is a form of repression, then surely, the denial of suffering, and of helplessness, is also a form of neurosis. Surely, all our attempts to escape sorrow twist themselves into the specific, acrid pain of self-suppression. And if that is so, then a culture that insists on cheerfulness and staying in control is a culture that—in one of those ironies that prevails in the unruly realm of the inner life—propagates its own kind of pain.

Perhaps perversely, I sometimes wish for that older kind of suffering—the capacity and the time for a patient listening to the winds of love and hate that can blow you like a reed, for that long descent into yourself in which you touch bottom and recognize the poor, two-forked creature that we all are.

For me, therapy is partly translation therapy, the talking cure a second-language cure. My going to a shrink is, among other things, a rite of initiation: initiation into the language of the subculture within which I happen to live, into a way of explaining myself to myself. But gradually, it becomes a project of translating backward.

The way to jump over my Great Divide is to crawl backward over it in English. It's only when I retell my whole story, back to the beginning, and from the beginning onward, in one language, that I can reconcile the voices within me with each other; it is only then that the person who judges the voices and tells the stories begins to emerge.

The tiny gap that opened when my sister and I were given new names can never be fully closed up; I can't have one name again. My sister has returned to her Polish name—Alina. It takes a while for me to switch back to it; Alina, in English, is a different word than it is in Polish: it has the stamp of the unusual, its syllables don't fall as easily on an English speaker's tongue. In order to transport a single word without distortion, one would have to transport the entire language around it. My sister no longer has one, authentic name, the name that is inseparable from her single essence.

When I talk to myself now, I talk in English. English is the language in which I've become an adult, in which I've seen my favorite movies and read my favorite novels, and sung along with Janis Joplin records. In Polish, whole provinces of adult experience are missing. I don't know Polish words for "microchips," or "pathetic fallacy," or *The Importance of Being Earnest.* If I tried talking to myself in my native tongue, it would be a stumbling conversation indeed, interlaced with English expressions.

So at those moments when I am alone, walking, or letting my thoughts meander before falling asleep, the internal dialogue proceeds in English. I no longer triangulate to Polish as to an authentic criterion, no longer refer back to it as to a point of origin. Still, underneath the relatively distinct monologue, there's an even more interior buzz, as of countless words compressed into an electric blur moving along a telephone wire. Occasionally, Polish words emerge unbidden from the buzz. They are usually words from the primary palette of feeling: "I'm so happy," a voice says with bell-like clarity, or "Why does he want to harm her?" The Polish phrases have roundness and a surprising certainty, as if they were announcing the simple truth.

Occasionally, the hum makes minute oscillations. "I'm learning a lot about intimacy in this relationship," I tell myself sternly, and a barely discernible presence whispers, pianissimo, I love him, that's all. . . . "The reason he's so territorial is because he's inse- cure," I think of a difficult colleague, and an imp of the perverse says, "Well, simply, he's a bastard. . . ." But I'm less likely to say the latter to my American Friends, and therefore the phrase has a weaker life. In order to translate a language, or a text, without changing its meaning, one would have to transport its audience as well.

No, there's no returning to the point of origin, no regaining of childhood unity. Experience creates style, and style, in turn, creates a new woman. Polish is no longer the one, true language against which others live their secondary life. Polish insights cannot be regained in their purity; there's something I know in English too. The wholeness of childhood truths is intermingled with the divisiveness of adult doubt. When I speak Polish now, it is infil- trated, permeated, and inflected by the English in my head. Each language modifies the other, crossbreeds with it, fertilizes it. Each language makes the other relative. Like everybody, I am the sum of my languages—the language of my family and childhood, and education and friendship, and love, and the larger, changing world—though perhaps I tend to be more aware than most of the fractures between them, and of the building blocks. The fissures sometimes cause me pain, but in a way, they're how I know that I'm alive. Suffering and conflict are the best proof that there's some- thing like a psyche, a soul; or else, what is it that suffers? Why would we need to suffer when fed and warm and out of the rain, were it not for that other entity within us making its odd, unreasonable, never fulfillable demands?

But in my translation therapy, I keep going back and forth over the rifts, not to heal them but to see that I—one person, first-person singular—have been on both sides. Patiently, I use English as a conduit to go back and down; all the way down to childhood, almost to the beginning. When I learn to say those smallest, first things in the language that has served for detachment and irony and abstraction, I begin to see where the languages I've spoken have their correspondences—how I can move between them without being split by the difference.

The gap cannot be fully closed, but I begin to trust English to speak my childhood self as well, to say what has so long been hidden, to touch the tenderest spots. Perhaps any language, if pursued far enough, leads to exactly the same place. And so, while therapy offers me instruments and the vocabulary of self-control, it also becomes, in the long run, a route back to that loss which for me is the model of all loss, and to that proper sadness of which children are never really afraid; in English, I wind my way back to my old, Polish melancholy. When I meet it, I reenter myself, fold myself again in my own skin. I'm cured of the space sickness of transcendence. It is possible that when we travel deep enough, we always encounter an element of sadness, for full awareness of ourselves always includes the knowledge of our own ephemerality and the passage of time. But it is only in that knowledge—not its denial—that things gain their true dimensions, and we begin to feel the simplicity of being alive. It is only that knowledge that is large enough to cradle a tenderness for everything that is always to be lost—a tenderness for each of our moments, for others and for the world.

The gap has also become a chink, a window through which I can observe the diversity of the world. The apertures of perception have widened because they were once pried apart. Just as the number "2" implies all other numbers, so a bivalent consciousness is necessarily a multivalent consciousness.

Multivalence is no more than the condition of a contemporary awareness, and no more than the contemporary world demands. The weight of the world used to be vertical: it used to come from the past, or from the hierarchy of heaven and earth and hell; now it's horizontal, made up of the endless multiplicity of events going on at once and pressing at each moment on our minds and our living rooms. Dislocation is the norm rather than the aberration in our time, but even in the unlikely event that we spend an entire lifetime in one place, the fabulous diverseness with which we live reminds us constantly that we are no longer the norm or the center, that there is no one geographic center pulling the world together and glowing with the allure of the real thing; there are, instead, scattered nodules competing for our attention. New York, Warsaw, Tehran, Tokyo, Kabul—they all make claims on our imaginations, all remind us that in a decentered world we are always simultaneously in the center and on the periphery, that every competing center makes us marginal.

It may be only in my daily consciousness of this that the residue of my sudden expulsion remains. All immigrants and exiles know the peculiar restlessness of an imagination that can never again have faith in its own absoluteness. "Only exiles are truly irreligious," a contemporary philosopher has said. Because I have learned the relativity of cultural meanings on my skin, I can never take any one set of meanings as final. I doubt that I'll ever become an ideologue of any stripe; I doubt that I'll become an avid acolyte of any school of thought. I know that I've been written in a variety of languages; I know to what extent I'm a script. In my public, group life, I'll probably always find myself in the chinks between cultures and subcultures, between the scenarios of political beliefs and aesthetic credos. It's not the worst place to live; it gives you an Archimedean leverage from which to see the world.

I'm writing a story in my journal, and I'm searching for a true voice. I make my way through layers of acquired voices, silly voices, sententious voices, voices that are too cool and too overheated. Then they all quiet down, and I reach what I'm searching for: silence. I hold still to steady myself in it. This is the white blank center, the level ground that was there before Babel was built, that is always there before the Babel of our multiple selves is constructed. From this white plenitude, a voice begins to emerge: it's an even voice, and it's capable of saying things straight, without exaggeration or triviality. As the story progresses, the voice grows and diverges into different tonalities and timbres; sometimes, spontaneously, the force of feeling or of thought compresses language into metaphor, or an image, in which words and consciousness are magically fused. But the voice always returns to its point of departure, to ground zero.

This is the point to which I have tried to triangulate, this private place, this unassimilable part of myself. We all need to find this place in order to know that we exist not only within culture but also outside it. We need to triangulate to something—the past, the future, our own untamed perceptions, another place—if we're not to be subsumed by the temporal and temporary ideas of our time, if we're not to become creatures of ephemeral fashion. Perhaps finding such a point of calibration is particularly difficult now, when our collective air is oversaturated with trivial and important and contradictory and mutually canceling messages. And yet, I could not have found this true axis, could not have made my way through the maze, if I had not assimilated and mastered the voices of my time and place—the only language through which we can learn to think and speak. The silence that comes out of inarticulateness is the inchoate and desperate silence of chaos. The silence that comes after words is the fullness from which the truth of our perceptions can crystallize. It's only after I've taken in disparate bits of cultural matter, after I've accepted its seductions and its snares, that I can make my way through the medium of language to distill my own meanings; and it's only coming from the ground up that I can hit the tenor of my own sensibility, hit home.

"Hello, silly little Polish person," Miriam says, greeting me at the Boston airport.

"Good grief, it's good to see you," I say.

"Is the article done so we can play tomorrow?"

"Almost, almost," I say. "How's the mood?"

"Oh, the mood," she says. "The mood has its moods."

"How has Tom been this week?" I ask, as we get into her car.

"Quite well behaved," she says briskly, and we smile. "Except for an unfortunately regressive episode yesterday . . . Well, I'll tell you tomorrow. I've scheduled two hours of uninterrupted conversation after breakfast."

"Great," I say, and walk into her house, and into "my" room, where I've stayed over the years.

"You wouldn't guess who called me this week," I say as I hang up my clothes. "Ricky."

"No," Miriam says. "Where was he calling from?"

"Well, you wouldn't guess that either. London. Can you see Ricky in London? Except he seems to be doing very well. He's in some high-tech optics business, and he's managed to be married and divorced twice since we last saw him, and now he's married again and terribly in love. I guess that means he's doing well, right?"

"Good God, who knows what it means?" Miriam says. "It's certainly getting harder to keep up with one's friends. I wonder if we're going to meet this new individual he's married to."

We meander like this for a while; we know that tomorrow we'll go into various items in greater depth, that we'll register the most minute developments in our lives and circle around them until they yield some insight, or at least a few satisfactory remarks. We've carried on this conversation for a long time now, through our respective affairs, marriages, divorces, work crises, the composition of short stories, political disagreements, and indecisions about our fall wardrobes.

We've known each other for nearly twenty years, as occasionally we're wont to remind each other. This simple fact continues to astonish us partly because we're of a generation that was supposed to stay forever young, and a friendship that long demonstrates indisputably that we too are subject to the passage of time; it continues to amaze us because, after all, Miriam is from St. Louis, and I from Cracow, and our friendship sometimes seems as fortuitous and unlikely as that comical and incongruous distance suggests. For me, there is an additional jolt: so I've been here this long.

Well, yes. I've been here this long. I have a whole American past, extended enough to produce its own repetitions and recurrences: on the radio, songs that I'd first heard as wild, grunting sounds now have the mellow quaintness of something that summons one's youth; boyfriends resurface to replay former relationships at speeded-up tempo; I go back to Houston, where I hadn't been in years, and where I walk around the Rice campus with a double sense of surprise and recognition. These repetitions give my American life heft and substance, the weight of reality. Those who don't understand the past may be condemned to repeat it, but those who never repeat it are condemned not to understand it. The one-night stand, or the motel in which we stop on the periphery of a town we don't know, the job at which we once spent five months, and which doesn't fit on our curriculum vitae—such passing, isolated events can give us the brief excitement of stepping outside the fabric of ordinary meaning; but they also leave behind the gloominess of evanescence, the flat aftertaste of meaninglessness.

As long as the world around me has been new each time, it has not become my world; I lived with my teeth clenched against the next assault of the unfamiliar. But now, the year has assumed an understandable sequence within which I play the variations of a professional New York life. The social world in which I move has comprehensible elements and dimensions. I am no longer mystified by the rules and rituals of friendship and of love. It is only within such frames and patterns that any one moment is intelligible, that stimulus transforms itself into experience and movement into purpose. And it is only within an intelligible human context that a face can become dear, a person known. Pattern is the soil of significance; and it is surely one of the hazards of emigration, and exile, and extreme mobility, that one is uprooted from that soil.

Over the years, I have learned to read the play of wit and feeling and intelligence on Miriam's face, which at first seemed to me flat and impassive. I've learned to trust the subtlety of her judgments, and I can distinguish the quarter tones of happiness and unhappiness within the intonations of her urbane, civilized talk. I know when she's dissimulating, for her own or my benefit, and through this knowledge I can also detect her truths. I can triangulate from her concealments and confessions to what she feels. To some extent, I've assimilated the tenor of her mind and the accents of her speech, and sometimes, I recognize the phrases I've used in her conversation. It's difficult to tell the truth to another person. The self is a complicated mechanism, and to speak it forth honestly requires not only sincerity but the agility to catch insight on the wing and the artistry to give it accurate words. It also requires a listener who can catch our nuances as they fly by. Spoken truth shrivels when it falls on a tin ear. But Miriam and I have been each other's highly attentive listeners. We've woven intricate designs for each other, and have subjected them to close mutual investigation. To a large extent, we're the keepers of each other's stories, and the shape of these stories has unfolded in part from our interwoven accounts. Human beings don't only search for meanings, they are themselves units of meaning; but we can mean something only within the fabric of larger significations. Miriam is one of the people through whom I've gained a meaning here. Starting so far apart, we have, through painstaking back and forth, forged a language in common. We keep describing the flow of experience to each other with the impetus to truth, and thus we keep creating new maps and tapestries of a shared reality.

The sense of the future returns like a benediction, to balance the earlier annunciation of loss. It returns in the simplest of ways: in an image of a crooked Paris street, where I'll go on my vacation, or in a peaceful picture of myself, at my desk, writing. Quiet, modest images light up the forward trajectory, and these flickers that suppose a pleasurable extension in time feel very much like hope.

Psychological pleasure or unpleasure is, I think, channeled in time, as physical pain or satisfaction runs along the conduits of our nerves. When time compresses and shortens, it strangles pleasure; when it diffuses itself into aimlessness, the self thins out into affectless torpor. Pleasure exists in middle time, in time that is neither too accelerated or too slowed down.

For quite a while I've woken up tensed, coiled against the next disaster, right up against the wall of a possible end. But now, a succession of tomorrows begins to exfoliate like a faith.

It seems a tremendous, Pascalian gamble, this leap into the future, into the moving stream. It means, after all, that I give up on trying to stop time, trying to keep that ship from moving away from the Baltic shore, and that I begin to greet whatever awaits me willingly. When I image, imagine, those shimmers of nonexistent possibility suspended on a thread of purely mental light, time expands and creates a breathing space in which sensations can be savored, as I once savored the churning butter or the minor triad. If images, as some philosophers theorize, congeal out of the matrix of language, then perhaps I've had to wait to have enough linguistic concentrate for hope to arise. Or perhaps I've had to gather enough knowledge of my new world to trust it, and enough affection for it to breathe life into it, to image it forth. But once time uncoils and regains its forward dimension, the present moment becomes a fulcrum on which I can stand more lightly, balanced between the past and the future, balanced in time.

"Azalea, hyacinth, forsythia, delphinium," Miriam says, pointing at the flowers with a mock-didactic gesture. "I'm going to make you feel at home in the New World." I look at the flowers; some of them I've never seen before; some names I've read but haven't put together with the flowers themselves. This is the kind of thing that comes latest in my strange building of the language from the roof down. "Azalea," I repeat. "Forsythia, delphinium." The names are beautiful, and they fit the flowers perfectly. They are the flowers, these particular flowers in this Cambridge garden. For now, there are no Platonic azaleas, no Polish hyacinths against which these are compared. I breathe in the fresh spring air. Right now, this is the place where I'm alive. How could there be any other place? Be here now, I think to myself in the faintly ironic tones in which the phrase is uttered by the likes of me. Then the phrase dissolves. The brilliant colors are refracted by the sun. The small space of the garden expands into the dimensions of peace. Time pulses through my blood like a river. The language of this is sufficient. I am here now.